I0836402

THE COURAGE WE LACK

VOICES OF RESILIENT CHILDHOOD

THE COURAGE WE LACK

Milagros de Jesús de Féliz

Santiago, Dominican Republic
2026

THE COURAGE WE LACK
Voices of Resilient Childhood

First Edition: May 2026
ISBN: 978-1-939256-26-3
Independently published.

Originally published in Spanish as *El coraje que nos falta: Voces de la niñez que resiste.*

This is a work of nonfiction. The accounts in this book are based on the author's experience and on interviews with the children and young adults whose stories are told here. Some names have been changed to protect their privacy.

EDITORIAL COORDINATION
Ana Margarita Féliz de Jesús
INITIAL TRANSLATION
Dr. Walter J. Maldonado, with Idalis Chapellin and Melanie Tejada
Florida International University (FIU)
TRANSLATION REVISION AND EDITING
Ana Margarita Féliz de Jesús and Rosario Veras
PROJECT MANAGEMENT
Ericarol Carlo
BOOK DESIGN AND LAYOUT
Ángel Gabriel Abad
COVER ART
Original watercolor by Viggo Evers
COVER DESIGN
Bryan Perozo

For inquiries, contact the author at milagrosfeliz@gmail.com.

To the working children and adolescents
who taught me, in the streets, what dignity is.

With Special Attention

To the agencies that make up the National System for the Protection of the Fundamental Rights of Children and Adolescents of the Dominican Republic, and to all institutions charged with ensuring the full exercise of those rights:

These life stories bear witness to both the support that arrived in time and the support that, for various reasons, fell short. Through them, we see the progress already made and the challenges that remain. The urgency is unmistakable: we must strengthen the strategies that link every actor in this work, so that our responses become more effective, more coherent, and more enduring.

This book is a call to reflection and shared action. It reminds us that protecting the rights of children is not only a legal and institutional duty but an ethical imperative, one that calls upon our humanity and our professionalism, every single day.

These pages close with a clear and urgent message: we must build alliances that are solid, accountable, and lasting. Such alliances guarantee every child and adolescent the support, protection, and opportunities they need to live in safety, justice, and dignity.

We must recognize that, beyond legal frameworks and isolated interventions, what is needed is a shift in perspective: a new way of seeing children and adolescents as full rights-holders, not as passive recipients of policy.

Only with that change in vision can we approach them with empathy, listen with humility, and act with resolve. And only then will we build a country where childhood is a living, sustained priority, never a promise deferred.

Honor and Gratitude

To Dr. Bruno Rosario Candelier, Director of the Academia Dominicana de la Lengua, for honoring this work with his foreword and championing its reach.

To my husband, children, and granddaughters Elena, Beatriz, and Inaya, in the hope that they will never grow indifferent to this reality.

To Rosa Ruiz, a steadfast companion from the beginning of this project.

To Professor Rafael Emilio Yunén, for his wise guidance.

To the educational team at Acción Callejera Fundación Educativa, for their devotion and the testimonies they shared, which gave life to these pages.

To Dr. Walter J. Maldonado, Associate Director of Academic Advising Technology at Florida International University (FIU), who led the English translation of this work alongside Idalis Chapellin and Melanie Tejada.

To all those who helped gather and shape these testimonies.

Foreword

> *For Rafaela Joaquín de Lowden,*
> *a devoted cultivator of meaning.*

Milagros de Jesús de Féliz is a new voice in the narrative tradition of Santiago de los Caballeros. She is an author who takes up the word to bear witness to her social vision of reality, reflecting on the troubling manifestations of the conditions affecting the impoverished sectors of her community. Through this work, she seeks to foster social awareness among the more privileged sectors of our population.

In this, her second book, *The Courage We Lack*, Milagros de Jesús de Féliz offers a portrait of the social landscape of Santiago that has inspired the reflections underlying each passage, event, and character that captured her attention and gave rise to her writing. The factual details, illustrative anecdotes, and life journeys of her protagonists establish her as a chronicler of the inner life of this city of the Cibao region. By virtue of the authenticity of her events, the truthfulness of her subjects, and the force of the situations she portrays, she earns the stature of a sociographer.

Throughout the narratives in *The Courage We Lack*, the author — having immersed herself in working-class neighborhoods and shared in the lives of their inhabitants — draws directly from lived social reality. She recounts true episodes known firsthand and conveys testimonies from men and women who shared with her the course of their lives. Milagros de Jesús de Féliz possesses a deeply rooted social vocation, marked by a genuine identification with the challenges of communities pushed to the margins, with the hardships endured by impoverished sectors, and with the painful fate of so many fellow citizens cast aside.

What the author feels and has endured reflects a genuine social sensitivity shaped by a Christian spirit — one that has guided her concerns and her sustained commitment for more than a quarter of a century, advocating for the fundamental rights of working children and adolescents in the streets of Santiago.

The Courage We Lack, a testimonial narrative of sociological and anthropological character, is neither fiction nor history in the strict sense, but rather a lived account of what unfolds in the peripheral neighborhoods of the city of Santiago.

To write a work of this nature, the author had to live alongside diverse sectors of these communities — men and women from street environments, familiar street figures often associated with what is colloquially known as *tigueraje*, the world of street-smart hustling and informal toughness. Yet within these lived narratives, we encounter deeply moving passages marked by sincere compassion, spontaneous emotional connection, and a profound moral, emotional, and spiritual identification with the painful circumstances of vulnerable youth.

This is, indeed, the expression of a true vocation of service in Milagros de Jesús de Féliz — one that has led her to produce this revealing work, distinguished by the following qualities:

It reflects intellectual, moral, aesthetic, and spiritual depth that enables her to bear witness, through writing, to her sociocultural experiences.

It demonstrates a careful and disciplined use of language to express, with clarity and truthfulness, her perceptions and evaluations of social and cultural reality.

It conveys, with full intellectual and emotional identification, what her sensibility perceives and what her conscience intuits in the light of lived experience.

Anyone who reads these narratives with attention, rooted as they are in the sociocultural reality of Santiago de los Caballeros, will recognize that the events — presented with objectivity and authenticity — have been lived in diverse settings and involve a wide range of individuals from the most impoverished sectors of society.

Her powerful work is not a fictional narrative but rather a series of portraits — scenes of everyday life and lived testimony shaped into a sociographic account. The author does not invent or embellish; she neither adds nor adorns what has been told to her by those who have endured suffering and injustice. She bears witness to what she has come to know: real events, lived experiences, and circumstances shared by humble men and women who entrusted her with their stories.

For this reason, one may identify five intellectual qualities in this sociocultural portrait of impoverished Santiago de los Caballeros:

A command of vivid language, including the use of local speech and folk sayings, essential to conveying social and cultural reality as it is.

A deliberate use of sociographic narrative, grounded in truth and free from invention, drawing the reader into identification with those whose stories are told.

A deep knowledge of the reality that informs her work, gained through direct engagement with communities and meaningful connection with her subjects.

An intellectual, moral, aesthetic, and spiritual seriousness that seeks to reveal a painful reality often invisible to the middle and upper classes.

A sincere and empathetic identification with the needs of the dispossessed, echoing what Garcilaso de la Vega described as a "grieving sensibility."

This sociographic work offers eloquent testimony to the conditions of marginalized communities and popular environments in Santiago — a reality that calls us to both reflection and action.

Finally, in this book the reader encounters the testimony of an author who brings her creative talent and places her conscience, her sensitivity, and her voice in service of a human cause. Her work belongs within the intellectual and literary tradition of Santiago de los Caballeros — a city of rich cultural history that has inspired many writers to bear witness to its social and human reality.

In sum, this book is what flows from the heart of a woman deeply moved by the suffering of others. Her testimony — an echo of the Christian love that animates her conscience and spirituality — moves us and invites our recognition as a genuine manifestation of compassionate language and committed, exemplary action, faithfully reflecting the life and work of Milagros de Jesús de Féliz.

Bruno Rosario Candelier
Director, Academia Dominicana de la Lengua
President, Ateneo Insular del Interiorismo
Moca, Dominican Republic
March 23, 2024

A Word from the Author

If this book has reached your hands, I am deeply grateful for your willingness to open its pages. These words are meant to offer shelter and a sense of unity to the stories gathered here — stories of working children who have lived, and many of whom still live, in situations of grave social risk on the streets of the Dominican Republic. Each testimony is told with the respect and the dignity owed to a population whose courage moves us and calls us into question.

The stories are grouped by theme to make them easier to follow. Each one opens with a brief summary, prepared with care by a small team of readers who drew out the key moments to guide your reading.

This book gathers twenty-six years of honorary and volunteer service devoted to defending the fundamental rights of children. Some of the accounts come from experiences shared in vulnerable communities of Santiago, where I have witnessed firsthand the many sides of difficult and complex realities.

After five years of conversations and reunions with young adults I first met when they were children, this work is a tribute to their capacity to reveal the essence of their own lives. These are stories set in a world that may seem distant but lives among us — in our central streets, in our neighborhoods, at our traffic-light corners — woven into the urban landscape and, too often, made invisible.

To speak of children caught in a suffocating tangle of hardship is not to cross into some other universe; it is to be drawn into a deeper reflection, one that changes how we see and returns us to a shared humanity.

These stories are not mine. They were entrusted to me, and as I listened, I understood the urgency of holding them safe in words and of building a legacy that makes both their wounds and their strength visible: a living testament to the courage they have in abundance, and that so many of us lack.

This task moves me forward. To turn away from it would mean letting the struggles of those already gone dissolve into forgetting, the worst of all graves. And it would deny those who have endured the chance to carry the light of what they have achieved to others who need a reason to keep going.

The Courage We Lack is an urgent call to awaken conscience and to move the will to act. It asks us to understand a reality that has been kept out of sight, and to take responsibility for it. If, on closing these pages, the way we see vulnerable children has shifted, then this work will have served its purpose: to plant humanity where pain remains part of the landscape, and indifference the rule.

With gratitude and hope,
Milagros de Jesús de Féliz

Voices Accompanying These Stories

This book does not walk alone. Each account is preceded by the perceptive gaze of those who agreed to accompany these pages with generosity and awareness. To name them is to recognize that defending the rights of children is also a shared commitment.

Reflections by

Aida María Fernández • Altagracia Salazar
Aura Celeste Fernández • Carmen Rita Cordero
Carolina Enriqueta Pérez • César Román • Daniela Cruz Gil
Eduardo Sánchez • Edward Butler • Excélsido Féliz Mustafá
Freddy Ginebra • Gilda María Díaz • Giselle Sánchez Almánzar
Grisbel Medina • Hamlet Otáñez • Irenarco Ardila Estupiñán
José Luis Taveras • José Manuel Antuñano
Lina García de Blasco • Luis Felipe Rodríguez
Manuel Pablo Maza Miquel, S.J. • Manuel Ulises Bonnelly
María Consuelo Yunén • María Luisa Asilis
María V. Menicucci • Maridalia Hernández
Mario Serrano Marte • Marión Pagés
Mercedes Carmen Capellán • Mildred Dolores Mata
Patricia Solano • Pedro Ángel • Raúl Martínez Trémols
Reynolds Pérez Stefan • Rosa María Cuesta • Rosa Ruiz
Sally Rodríguez • Susi Pola • Thelma Amparo Kunhardt Javier
Vicky Pappaterra de Read • Xiomara García • Yesmín Haddad
Yudelka Pérez de Haddad

CONTENTS

WHERE THE STREET BEGINS

Every story has a starting point.

When a child understands, without anyone needing to explain it, that they must take charge of their own life too soon, something inside breaks.

From that moment on, life demands constant attention, learned distrust, and everyday courage. Everything turns to calculation, vigilance, and endurance.

In that instant, the gaze changes, the skin hardens.

El Peje[1]

Milagros de Jesús de Féliz tells us the life of her friend el Peje, and through it she leads us toward a way of seeing reality rooted in boundless fraternity and unbreakable hope. She gives us a story that must not be forgotten, one that continues to call us to commitment. El Peje also brings before us so many others who teach us lessons in resilience, love, and the struggle for life.
Mario Serrano Marte

In the late 1980s, Santiago was struck by a wave of migration from rural communities. Families settled in different outlying neighborhoods on the city's southern edge, mostly along the slopes of ravines and on occupied land. El Hoyo de Elías, La Yagüita de Pastor, Fracatán, Rafey, and El Hoyo de Puchula were among the most populated areas.

Entire families arrived in search of better luck, and in that effort, many boys — and some girls as well — went out into the streets to earn their own sustenance, and often their families' too.

A battalion of boys made their lives in the streets, wearing themselves down at different points across the city, in full view

1 Previously published in the anthology *Susurros del viento* (Buenos Aires: Editorial Rubín, 2025).

of drivers and passersby, working all day long. This population was — and still is — part of the landscape, yet invisible to a society whose collective imagination still believes that hard work dignifies them and teaches them to become well-behaved adults. It is a burden as heavy as it is unjust.

They spent long hours begging at traffic lights, selling fruit and small goods in the city center, becoming victims of sexual exploitation, or working in mechanic shops. They also sprayed herbicides on large plantations and fields, a dangerous job that, at such a young age, damaged their health and took many lives each year.

The boys did heavy construction work, labor so dangerous that some lost fingers and other parts of their fragile bodies. I remember the case of a valuable, hardworking boy who was left sterile after carrying loads far beyond what his body could bear; the weight injured his testicles and made it impossible for him to have children.

The girls, on the other hand, were not seen in the streets because they were inside our homes. They were child domestic workers in other people's houses, denied an education and exploited from their earliest years.

Out of that seven-meat social stew came a boy of about eight, arriving in the city alone. He had dropped out of school, had no family ties, and carried in his soul a hole larger than the ones visible in his clothes. He was the second of nine siblings, and I met him when the sun was walking the same path as his steps.

This beautiful little creature, with his luminous eyes, sunbrowned skin, and slight body, had migrated from a rural area of Puerto Plata, a city in the north of the country. He boasted of his astonishing gift for swimming. Because of the daring displays he made in the waters of the Yaque River, they gave him the nickname *el Peje* — the Fish.

El Peje was violent and there was no playing games with him. I remember him with his shirt sleeves always rolled up, ready to take on any fight. He threw kicks without warning and never explained the reasons that had driven him into the streets. He had made his way from Puerto Plata to Santiago alone, on sheer determination.

That restless boy moved through life the way he moved through water. Before long, he began working at the Hospedaje Yaque, a place that trains children in the hardest forms of labor and tightens their backs until life itself is wrung dry. There, he carried sacks in the early hours of the morning, unloading trucks filled with produce and provisions that usually came from Constanza and other farming regions.

Because the street is free, you can choose many things, including sleeping without asking permission, wherever your heart leads you. In his dreamer's stubbornness, *el Peje* chose to spend his nights in one of those old European-style houses in the city center, with an open gallery: an imaginary palace very close to his work, one that protected him from the weather.

There, more than sleeping, he nodded off, because the best hours for rest were spent working hard at a job that broke his tender back.

The owners of the house did not like the idea of *el Peje* sleeping at the front of their property, and on several occasions they warned him not to lie down there or use the gallery. *El Peje* insisted, until one night one of the owners — a cowardly beast with the devil in his head — stabbed him three times in the belly. He was barely ten years old.

Wounded and bleeding, *el Peje* managed to make it out to the roadway, and two drunken men with good hearts took him to the city's children's hospital. There were no cell phones then, but somehow, in the middle of the night, he called me to tell me what had happened.

"I'm dying, ma'am… come," he told me, in terrible condition.

My husband and I went to the hospital that same night, and we called a surgeon friend to lead the operation that, by a miracle, saved his life. Within a couple of weeks, he had been discharged. But where does a child who lives in the streets go, and who cares for him? God was with him, and a family took him in for two months while he recovered. That time, he promised he would reconnect with school and set himself to dignifying his life.

Time did not stand still, and *el Peje* finished high school while working at the same time. He trained in several areas through different Infotep courses in his native Puerto Plata. I lost sight of this fish with a heart of gold, eyes like a full moon, and burning coals in his chest.

Years passed — perhaps more than a decade — without my knowing anything of *el Peje*. One day, I was driving down a street in the city center when, suddenly, an AMET traffic officer ordered me to stop, and I obeyed.

"Ma'am, you have a fine for talking on the phone while driving," the officer informed me.

"I was not talking on my cell phone," I answered firmly.

"Are you Milagros de Féliz?" he asked, without having seen my credentials.

"How do you know my name if I haven't given you my documents?" I demanded, now uncomfortable.

Then, with the same eyes of that mischievous, beloved child, he said:

"I'm *el Peje*, that boy who lived in the streets, the one you cared for when I was wounded in the middle of the night."

I looked at him and reduced his lanky figure to miniature, and memory returned that child to me — a memory that sailed through my veins and bewildered me as it loosened, in a matter of seconds, all those feelings that had folded themselves into my soul. Moved, I got out of the car, and joined in a tight embrace, we listened to the beating of our hearts. Speechless, we were wrapped in the joy of finding each other again after so many years.

Without thinking, we remained standing in the middle of the sidewalk on that busy street while people looked at us in astonishment. I saw him tall and elegant in his olive-green uniform, serving society. He, with tears in his eyes, seemed to relive in silence that difficult moment that had marked his life.

El Peje, that restless and courageous boy, now a grown man, spoke to me of his family with pride, expressing with certainty his responsibility to raise his own well. Impeccably dressed in authority, with a wide-brimmed hat fastened beneath his chin and love in his eyes, he told me he was the father of two beautiful boys. He felt blessed by the family God had given him.

I saw him standing there, properly uniformed, his head held high.

That boy who had been stabbed in someone else's gallery now protects the streets that watched him grow.

He has a family.

He has a name.

He has a story.

And he carries it with honor.

Where the Dream Rests, Hope Is Born[2]

Sometimes, certain mirrors let us find ourselves again. In this story, the author shows how Manuel refused to dwell on the dusk of a heartbreaking past. Instead, he saw the radiance of a boy whose unshakable faith built the future he had dreamed of and made it real.
Gilda María Díaz

Not long ago I had breakfast at home with a remarkable young man I had met in one of those worlds life sometimes hands you. He had lived and worked in the streets since he was a boy, and with extraordinary strength of spirit he had decided to defy whatever stood in his way and hold fast to his dreams.

He slept in the parking lot of a commercial building, or at a friend's house, or in the hidden corners of the Monumento a los Héroes. His favorite refuge was the Hospedaje Yaque, where they let him use a wheelbarrow lined with plantain leaves for a mattress and pieces of cardboard for a pillow while he waited out the small hours of the night. There he would doze for an hour or two until the trucks rolled in loaded with provisions and vegetables, and he unloaded them before daybreak.

2 Previously published in *Cambia el mundo con un lápiz y un papel*, the commemorative volume for the 40th Anniversary of Fundación CODESPA (Madrid, 2025).

Our conversations had wrung my soul more than once. Over bread and cheese, this young man with a heart of polished steel took a sip of juice, his face dry and unsmiling, and began to tell me his story.

"When I was very small, my parents decided to separate. With no explanation given, I carried my father's sadness on my fragile shoulders, and together we arrived in Santiago with a backpack full of failure and frustration. It was too high a price and too heavy a load for a four-year-old. My father found work selling ice cream at a nearby school. He'd leave before the sun was up and come back at dusk, furious and exhausted, with little money in his pocket. I'm still grateful for the thick noodle soup he used to leave waiting for me — the soup that kept me company all day long.

"I lived through times of deep anguish, caught between the wish to stay by his side and the terror that gripped me whenever he came home, because he would beat me hard, and for no reason. His presence became a need I despised. I reminded him of his frustration over my mother's leaving, and of the ruin of what had once been our humble home. I felt like the debtor on an obligation I had never taken on — a debt I was too young to understand. Loneliness, mistreatment, the beatings and the insults pushed me out into the streets to shine shoes around the neighborhood.

"It was a hard decision, because I was very shy and I sensed that something unpleasant was waiting for me out there. On rainy days, when I couldn't earn what I needed, the beating from my father came twice as bad. So, full of fear, I decided to start shining shoes downtown and stop going home altogether. That's how I began to sleep wherever the night happened to find me.

"That first night was very hard. It was seven o'clock and I had nowhere to sleep. Every place I looked seemed unsafe, dangerous. I begged God to help me, and I came across an evangelical church with its doors open and a service in progress. I went in and knelt down, asking God in blind faith to help me and to protect me. Every time I have prayed that prayer, from then to this day, I feel that God is with me — and that the church is still sheltering me.

"I kept walking, and whenever I sat down somewhere in the park to rest, people looked at me with contempt because of my smelly clothes and disheveled appearance. They had no idea my soul was in pieces and my heart had a hole in it. My only luggage was a plastic bag I clutched in my hands, holding everything I owned. My whole estate fit inside it.

"That same night I made friends with Lino, who already had experience living in the streets, and together we slept in the yard of an abandoned house on Calle Cambronal, very close to the Hermanos Patiño Bridge. We laid a long piece of cardboard under the eaves, on top of the concrete that ran around the edge of the property. We lay there with our hands behind our heads, our elbows out, feeling the hardness of the ground beneath us. Looking up at a sky with very few stars, I prayed for a long time, asking God to keep me safe.

"For a moment I cried, and my friend heard me. He suddenly sat up, his face stern, and there in the dark he laid down for me the first laws of surviving in the streets:

> "You have to be tough. Crying solves nothing. You have to show people you're a lion, even when you're scared, because if you don't, they'll use you for a chopping block. So you can't be soft. The hope of living is never lost, and above everything else, you have to defend your own life tooth and nail. And one more thing — I promise I'll always look out for you."

"That one sermon was enough to settle my fears. I calmed down, and in his face I understood that God had sent me this friend as the angel who would give me the protection I had been begging for in my clumsy prayers. Calmer now, I fell asleep and didn't wake until morning.

"It was still dark when I got up, and I noticed that the cockroaches had also slept close by. That was how I began to face life and its hardships — something already familiar to me. I looked around. With a sense of freedom, I felt like the owner of that yard. It had been a long time since I'd gone a night without a beating, and I felt that, in itself, was a gain.

"When Lino got up, he showed me a rusty pipe sticking out of the remains of a granite washtub abandoned in the alley beside the house. There was a tap on it that still ran with water, and I brushed my teeth with my fingers, washed my face, and wet down my hair. I was ready to face the new day. Then Lino took me to the Hospedaje Yaque, and on the way he explained the other laws that ruled that place:

> "At the Hospedaje you've got to be sharp. There are guys way bigger than us, real brutes, and if you show weakness they'll take the money you've earned right out of your hand. If you have to fight, throw the first punch and throw it hard. There's plenty of work you can do here. On the corner there's a place that sells plucked chickens — you can help pluck them, but watch out for the boiling water in the kettle. The shops need boys to haul merchandise from the trucks into their storerooms, which are always in the back of the building.
>
> "A lot of well-to-do ladies come here to buy fruits and vegetables. Some are stingy and some give good tips. For that work, you've got to keep two sacks in your hands at all times to carry

whatever they buy, and don't forget to treat them with respect and call them ma'am — they like that.

"With time you make friends with the stall owners and start bringing them customers. In return, they give you oranges, guavas, ripe bananas, things you can eat. And starting around two in the morning, the trucks begin coming in from Constanza, loaded with vegetables. The drivers pay you to unload them carefully. If a truck sits a whole day without being unloaded, they'll also pay you to spray the cabbages so they stay good. When you unload the vegetables, set aside the ones that are damaged or split, but don't even think of throwing them out — you can sell them later, cheaper than the perfect ones. It's important to save up for a wheelbarrow, because that helps you carry without ruining your back. There's a lot of business you can do here — you just have to keep your eyes open and stay sharp."

Recalling all of Lino's advice, Manuel went on with his testimony.

"I listened carefully to those business ideas. They were strange to me, but I was curious about every one of them. I'd sit on a corner watching everything move, trying to decide which line of work to choose. They were all long, brutal days. The ground was slippery, covered with a thick crust that was always damp — a mix of mud and refuse. The whole place gave off a rot that didn't match the hygiene a market should have. I had nowhere to wash myself, and that was a problem, because I'd end up reeking of cabbage and rotten eggplant. I couldn't even stand my own smell.

"I remember moving from one place to another was an ordeal because I smelled so bad. I had nowhere to clean up, and *concho* drivers — and society itself — don't really understand that someone who lives in the streets has no way to keep clean, unless you go down to the Yaque del Norte, which most of the time was filthier than you were.

"In the middle of all that, I was always talking with God, and He sent me Doris, a psychologist who invited me to come to her evangelical church. After many prayers and many sacrifices, God set me free there. I leaned on the Lord's Prayer, and forgiveness became my best therapy. I also took shelter in the educational programs at Acción Callejera, where they didn't just enroll me back in school but guided me with steady follow-up and care.

"Because of my situation, my neighborhood school expelled me more than once. The rules required us to come in dressed properly, immaculately. They scolded me often for falling asleep in class and not turning in my homework on time. On top of that, I was supposed to be a well-behaved boy. Their demands were impossible for me to meet, given the way I was living, and each time they expelled me, the educators from the Foundation reminded them of my right to an education. Because of those just demands, the school would take me back — reluctantly, but it would take me back.

"Through all those readmissions and negotiations with the teachers, I came to understand that I had a right to an education and that I had to defend that right above everything else. That's how I finished high school, and despite all those setbacks, I now hold a doctorate from the university of life.

"Along the way, I came to see that many teachers don't have the tools they need to work with children living in vulnerable conditions. I wasn't a bad student, but I couldn't concentrate enough, because I was barely catching a few hours of sleep at the Hospedaje. With no real rest at night, on top of the effort it took to do the work that kept me alive, I usually nodded off in class.

And since I lived in the streets, it was hard to show up in a clean, ironed uniform the way the school demanded.

"I was born a dreamer, and I wanted out of that kind of life. The sorrows are hard to sum up, but I went through plenty. Each stage stirs up its own memories, and now, with time on my side, I tell them so other ears might understand what an unprotected child — a child who lives in the streets — has to bear.

"I studied, I shined shoes, I sold flowers around the Monumento a los Héroes, and I unloaded trucks at the Hospedaje Yaque. I sold phone chargers, and later phones and cell phones.

"One day I worked up the nerve to rent a small place near Parque Duarte to sell chargers, phones, cell phones, cases, batteries, memory cards, and so on. I'd laugh to myself just looking at the sign.

"Then I rented a space in a downtown shopping plaza. I opened a branch inside an upscale supermarket, and after that another one beside a busy, well-known store in the city's historic center. I opened another branch on Avenida Presidente Antonio Guzmán, and recently I opened yet another on Avenida Yapur Dumit in Santiago. All of them supply *colmados* — through a wide team of salespeople — with phone cables, universal headphones, and other accessories.

"As a loving gift to my father, I set him up in a small business of his own, and I'm always there alongside him. We share a barbershop, where we also sell face masks and bottled water to our customers. Seeing him at work, and being able to keep us close, has been a blessing from God. Every day I thank Him for my father's life, because he brought me into the world. I feel that life has gathered the two of us up in its arms long enough for us to love each other as what we are: a father who gave me everything he had in his heart, and a son who honors him and respects him exactly as he is.

"Along the way, I met a remarkable woman God had been keeping for me — a friend introduced us in Santo Domingo. I fell in love with her at first sight, and we've now spent thirteen years building a home together, with God at the center of it. We have two sons, Isaac and Sebastián, two gifts from God who put the finishing touch on my life.

"This is a short story of a long life," my guest remarks.

Before he left, he confided a wish he had been carrying in his heart:

"I want to give something back to my country, and I have political aspirations. I love dreams, and I make them real, because I feel that God protects me and inspires me," this fine young man added.

As he said goodbye, Manuel rose with a calm, certain smile — the kind worn only by those who have walked through the storm and come out stronger on the other side. This young man is no ordinary entrepreneur; he is a man who has turned pain into strength, loneliness into companionship, and adversity into a bottomless wellspring of inspiration.

I sat there with the coffee cup still warm between my hands. Manuel's words kept echoing in my mind, an echo that refused to fade. His story reminded me that, even when the road is strewn with stones, every stumble can become a stepping stone toward something greater.

As the morning unfolded and sunlight reached every corner of the house, I felt my spirit replenished by a renewed faith in humanity. Manuel had not only conquered his own fears; he had now made it his work to sow hope in others, offering them the hand he himself had once needed. In that moment I understood that his mission went far beyond business. His true legacy was the light he cast over everyone his story touched.

As if placing a final seal on the moment, Manuel restated his readiness to serve:

"I want to invite people to take a chance and to keep fighting on, over and above whatever stands in their way. I'll help them! I'm **Manuel Celular**, and my number is open to anyone who believes in God and wants to start a business of their own. Wherever you see one of my branches, I'm there to serve you," this remarkable young man said in closing. He smiled one last time and told me firmly: "Life isn't easy, but it's always worth fighting for the dreams that God plants in our hearts."

His words, full of humility and resolve, hung in the air, leaving a wake of hope behind them. Manuel walked away, his figure carrying the steady strength of someone who has learned, time and again, how to get back up.

In the end, I sat in silence, thanking God for having allowed me to know this human being of such rare worth. I celebrated Manuel's life in my heart, and I knew that, from that day on, his example would be a constant source of inspiration for many — and for me as well.

Manuel told me of his triumphs, and also of his scars — the ones he carries with dignity and without bitterness. His life, woven of hard moments and brave decisions, has inspired me to see adversity in a new light: as a force that pushes us to grow, and to help others do the same.

The Way the Great Ones Do[3]

A tribute to Luigi — both nine and a thousand years old — for restoring hope to the streets around el Monumento and announcing the end of adult indifference. With this story, the author invites us to thank those who let themselves be moved by him, and who in moving were able to wrestle life into yielding. Bravo, Luigi, bravo!
Susi Pola

"There's a dead man here!" different voices cried out at once, in the same shocked tone.

"In a reality that felt like a dream, that was the cry that woke me one early morning. I was lying stretched out near the Monumento a los Héroes de la Restauración, in Santiago.

"Before sunrise, I would often hear the echo of footsteps from people on their morning routine, exercising around the iconic Monumento. They never quite managed to wake me — at nine years old, exhaustion always won out. But that time was different. A commotion of strangers had gathered, shouting almost in unison: *There's a dead man here!*

"It was a Sunday of my childhood, and I woke with a start. When I turned toward the voices, I saw a dead man lying just

3 Story previously published in the anthology *Ritmo en el asfalto* (Colombia: Editora Mítico, 2024).

a short distance from me. I kept touching my own body for reassurance, refusing to accept what I was seeing. The body looked so fresh, as though he were merely asleep. He was young, his belly swollen, his skin soaked with sweat — from a final struggle, perhaps, or from the effort death demands. His face, fixed in sheer terror, had taken on that sallow color the dead always carry. That image, so close to me that morning, still shakes me. It comes back to me often.

"I had finished work that day a little after three in the morning, once the usual crowd around the Monumento had scattered. I collapsed, spent, onto the soft green carpet of grass that the imposing marble structure seemed to have kept for me. My favorite spot to rest was where Calle Restauración came to an end, because it was the quietest. There was also a small mound that served as a pillow when I dozed off in those forgotten corners of God's earth.

"I worked the streets under my aunt's command. She knew every strategic spot for begging in the city. Our family portrait was distorted by relentless poverty and a thousand other calamities. It forced me to step into adulthood before I had finished being a child.

"I have three younger sisters. My older brother, Marcos, was eleven at the time. There were five of us in all. None of us went to school, and none of us had a birth certificate.

"In my family, working the streets was a tradition that ran back through generations. My aunt and my mother begged for money on street corners; we would also go out with my grandmother to ask for handouts around the neighborhood. For my cousins, panhandling was almost a sport. My father worked nights at a bakery.

"All of us worked the streets. The jobs were divided up: my sisters sold flowers, while the boys begged and sold hot tea. Others in our group took tourists who wanted carriage rides around the Monumento — the area where my family camped out.

"By day we hunted for food and for something to do, fending for ourselves. I always wanted to be the protective brother, but in that world it was hard to shield anyone from the dangers that constantly stalk children who live in the streets.

"On a good day we'd bring in as much as 500 pesos. We contributed to the household, but the cost was steep: exposure to sexual exploitation, every kind of abuse, serious health problems, malnutrition, and a life far from any classroom. I remember dreaming once that I had 20,000 pesos, and that with that money I would build a house for my family, buy them food, and get myself a bicycle. It was a dream that sweetened the small fantasies of my childhood," the young man went on, his hurt childhood still close to the surface.

As Luigi relives those years of so much struggle, a knot tightens in his throat. He takes a sip of water and falls silent for a moment before resuming the procession of nightmares, the long litany of his childhood. Bitter memories crowd his mind. We pause together, letting the worst of them pass through.

Then a happier memory comes back to him: the day he met the educators from Fundación Acción Callejera. Luigi tells me he had fallen asleep at the edge of a street that day when someone whose Spanish came out thick and halting woke him up.

"What are you doing there?" a young man asked. He looked like a foreigner.

"I sell tea and ask for money around here," I told the stranger.

"He was Joan Crosas, a Catalan volunteer with the Foundation, and he won me over the instant he sat down beside me on the curb as if we had been friends for years.

"After I unloaded a little of what was weighing on me, Joan promised he would come to my house the next day. That promise planted hope in my heart, and it remains the happiest memory I have, because that meeting changed the course of my life.

"Joan and I became confidants. I told him about my fears, about what was happening in my family, about how tired I was of living in the streets. He brought me right away into the Foundation's educational programs.

"I still haven't forgotten the welcome they gave me in that learning space, where I learned how to play and discovered the rights that, as a child, belonged to me. Joan also took my siblings and me to the Centro Comunitario. We ran freely through the open spaces, feeling untethered and so happy, no matter how harshly the midday sun bore down.

"Any ball was enough to amuse us, and at the slightest opening we would start to play with the bright joy that belongs to children. That place lifted the weight of daily life off my shoulders. There I understood that being a child wasn't only about working: I had the right to play, the right to a name on paper, the right to go to school. All of this was new to me, because what I had understood until then was that I had been born for one purpose only — to work and to protect my family."

For his part, Joan Crosas remembers Luigi as the boy who carried the morning in his eyes, empty hands, and, in his heart, all the moons still waiting for him. He tells us that the day after that first meeting, he went to visit Luigi at home, taking up the invitation this boy with the soul of warm bread had offered him.

"Luigi always believed I was the one who taught him so much about life, but that wasn't the case. He was the one who taught me courage, bravery, and steadiness, young as he was. I can still see his quick, squirrel-bright eyes and the determination with which he set out to change his family's fate.

"His house was a tiny wooden structure, just two rooms with a single large bed in each. I will never forget the way Luigi, slipping into the role of breadwinner, walked me through his home with care and pride. There, on the floor, a little girl was sleeping, her hair gathered into pigtails, a pair of rubber sandals resting beside her. Beyond the bedrooms there was a narrow space that doubled as living room, dining room, and kitchen. On a table off to the side stood an *anafe* holding a pot that gave off a scent of eucalyptus — most likely from the tea the boys sold in the streets.

"That's where our friendship was born," Joan continues, "and after many visits and many heart-to-heart conversations, we managed to convince the family to enroll all five children in school. The condition was that they stop working at night. Getting them to agree was a marathon battle, because it cut into the family income, but in the end we won them over.

"We obtained birth certificates for the children while they kept making their way through school. After the father lost his job, he had no way to cover household expenses, but they got by, working a few hours in the streets and studying at the same time. What I remember is that Luigi never blamed his father for failing to provide; on the contrary, he understood the bind his father was in.

"At school, the siblings began their primary grades, and their progress was unmistakable. The girls came along astonishingly well, and one of them stood out for her grades. For Marcos and Luigi the road was harder — neither of them had much taste for schoolwork.

"Luigi's life is a song of courage," Joan emphasizes, "an admirable example of grit.

"Their mother passed away, and the father took over caring for the children, but an aunt kept luring them out to work at night. Eventually, the siblings drifted away from their father," recalls this dedicated educator who stood by the boy through those hardest of stretches.

After dwelling on these memories and on Joan Crosas's remarkable devotion, I return to Luigi's account of what became of his siblings.

"Marcos and I went to live with that aunt of mine, and we kept working at the Monumento with her so we could go to school during the day. My three sisters stayed with my grandmother, but not long afterward she died of cancer, and the girls decided to work as domestic servants in private homes while keeping up with school.

"After that, we lost track of one another. My sisters worked in different parts of Santiago, and later they left the country. I don't have any contact with them, but I know one came back to live with my aunt. It seems all of us wanted out of that wretched life, and never to look back.

"I barely speak to Marcos these days — he moved to Santo Domingo. When my father died, we scattered. That's the sad truth of it. I think those broken bonds, on top of everything else I've been through, marked me so deeply that I refuse to have children, out of fear that the story might repeat itself.

“I wish we could all live together,” he said at last — the same brightness in his large eyes the color of polished gold, his face wrung dry by life.

With enormous effort, Luigi finished high school. He works at a well-known company and is now twenty-one years old. He believes in God, and because the nobility of his heart has remained intact, he helps any child he comes across in the streets, or offers a steady word of guidance to girls who set out down the same paths he once walked.

This young man is living testimony of quiet struggle and of hope born again. His road, traced through the hard streets of Santiago, is a mural of courage — painted in the colors of survival and tenderness, and of those small daily victories that, though invisible to the world, glow fiercely in his heart.

Today, Luigi remains the guardian of the dreams that once drove him to defy the impossible, and he has become a lighthouse for others who, like him, once felt invisible. His life was forged in adversity, and today it leaves an indelible mark on the sands of history — the way the great ones do.

I Came into This World for a Purpose

This is a story of resilience. Iván is one of those souls born with an innate greatness, capable of growing and shining despite adversity. He shows us the importance of strengthening ourselves and pressing forward, no matter the barriers in our way. The author invites us to look closely at the reality so many children live in, and stirs in us the urgency of standing by them without conditions.

Manuel Ulises Bonnelly Valverde

It seems that, at my age, long trips wear you down — all the more when you've made them in formal clothes, with work still piling up, and traffic that keeps you on edge. That was how I got home that Holy Monday.

Relieved to have arrived at last, I caught sight, from the carport, of the face of that boy who felt almost like my own — so dearly loved, and not seen in a long time. It was Iván, dropping in unannounced. His smile said it all, and his eyes carried me back to his childhood.

That skinny boy, his face always smiling, who used to shine shoes around the neighborhood with his cousin, had become a thirty-four-year-old man — handsome, with a well-trimmed beard, the same smile as ever, and now the father of two healthy daughters.

Iván loved Christmas. He had been my helper for putting up the little trees and the seasonal decorations until he turned into the household expert at hanging the lights. I remember how, as early as October, he would start hovering around the house asking when we were going to decorate for Christmas.

I also remember that my own children taught him to read, with books suited to his level, and that this was how he learned to read the newspapers we kept on the terrace. Joy lit up his face whenever he managed to read a whole sentence out of any printed thing that fell into his hands. He had a deep desire to learn to read and write properly.

He was very tall and very thin, which is why we gave him the nickname *el Flaco*. He was born in Tamboril, in January 1990, in a place he himself can no longer pinpoint, because his mother handed him over to be raised by a close relative. As a result, he never knew his mother, much less his father. It was only in adolescence that he began to take an interest in piecing together his mysterious origins.

With gestures that sometimes betrayed pain, and a few sighs of despair, he began to tell part of his story. As he shared his memories and put his past back together in words, I came to understand — and to take into myself — the stages of childhood that had shaped this good young man. Listening to his testimony, I can attest that he carries the blood of the brave.

"I have five siblings on my mother's side, each by a different father, and seven on my father's side, each by a different mother. From what I was told, my mother worked in a *zona franca*, and later in a beauty salon, but I didn't know her. I had never seen her face. I didn't even know her name — because before I was even a month old, she had handed me over to an uncle of mine.

"Then that uncle, on his own, passed me on to a family in a rural part of Tamboril when I was barely two years old. They were cruel people, and I don't remember a single moment of affection from them — only the abuse that marked me forever, in body and in spirit.

"I say this because that family was truly cruel to me. I still don't understand why they treated me the way they did. I had trouble with my bladder; I often wet myself. Now I think it was because of the terror I felt for the matron of the house.

"When it happened, the woman of the house would force me to kneel on a *guayo* — a metal grater — with a stone on my head, under the midday sun, as punishment. As I stayed in that position, crying from such undeserved torment, the rest of the family would say cruel things to me and mock me with words like, 'You'll stay there all day without eating!' And they made sure I did.

"When those memories come back to me, I think they were people possessed, abusive people. Once, kneeling there with my knees bleeding, I even came to doubt the existence of God.

"I have never forgotten one afternoon when they beat me so badly that, in a single swing, the buckle sank into my skull."

As proof, Iván leaned forward and showed me, in his hair, the scar from the wound that day. Then he went on with more detail.

"The blow from the buckle made me bleed heavily, and as the blood was already running down my ear, that first hit was followed by a punch near my eye. I thought I would go blind — I didn't get my sight back right away, and for a long stretch of time everything was darkness.

"After all that abuse, one final blow sent me flying through the air, and I came down on the ground almost unconscious from the force of it. Some good-Samaritan neighbors picked me up and tended the wound with aloe, and the bruises with salt and lime — a remedy I have no doubt was effective, though it hurt all the same. All of it happened because I had not carried enough water for them to bathe with. That family crossed every limit of cruelty with me, and beating me for any reason at all had become an everyday thing.

"In that house, on top of carrying water, I had to work the tobacco beds, sweep the yard, feed the animals, haul firewood, and wash the dishes, among other chores, no matter how heavy they were.

"But none of it was as crushing as the abuse I suffered at the hands of a member of that household when I was only six years old — something I still remember with sorrow. The abuser was an older man, and I was barely a child. He was a sick man who threatened me into silence. At first he would coax me into sitting on his lap, without my understanding what he wanted. Through abuse, he took my innocence, and he did it again every time I was left alone in the house. Unable to say a word, I spent my days crying, and he mocked me, calling me a crybaby because — as he put it — 'I cried over every little thing.' One day, in tears, I bolted back to my uncle's place once again.

"He took me in along with his own children. But, as my luck would have it, his wife wanted nothing to do with me in the house, and behind his back she would hit me on the head with iron ladles. On top of that, the money I earned shining shoes had to be handed over to her. She would only leave me enough to replace the cleaning liquid and polish, which I always thought was unfair.

"To get away from that woman's mistreatment and stay out of her path, I started going out with my uncle, repairing fans and washing machines. That way I felt safer. To fill the rest of my time, I enrolled in school — but the schedule got under my aunt's skin. As a result, she would only give me breakfast when my uncle was around. She never set anything aside for me, not for lunch and not for dinner.

"I didn't starve, because when I washed the dishes, I would scrape the leftovers meant for Popeye, the family dog, into a bowl. I'd quietly eat part of his food without the matron noticing. That's how I survived.

"But God doesn't fail anyone, and so I came to meet Sergio, a man who worked at a *pollera* — a chicken shop — nearby. He said I reminded him of his own son, and he gave me the food I was denied at home. He took me to his house on weekends, and I even shared the Christmas holidays with his family. Sadly, Sergio died of a heart attack, and his loss was a heavy blow to me.

"That was a terrible stretch, because my uncle died as well.

"I was ten years old then. I was told my biological mother was coming to her brother's wake. I was anxious to meet her — I saw in that meeting the chance of going away with her. I knew very well that my aunt by marriage did not want me in the house.

"In that air of mourning, heavy with grief over my uncle's death, as I went around offering coffee and small cookies on a tray to the people at the wake, a neighbor pointed out a woman dressed in half-mourning — tall, with a fine figure, her clothes fitted close to her body, her face still holding a certain grace. She was my biological mother. She caught the neighbor's gesture before I did. She looked at me and gave me a shy smile, and said, 'Hello, Iván — you've grown so much.'

"I looked at her without blinking. I wanted to hug her. My mind was boiling over with a thousand questions: Why had she given me away when I was only days old, and never asked after me again? What kind of mother was she? What had I done to make her abandon me?

"She invited me to sit on her lap, but I refused — my heart wouldn't let me. I felt mistrust, because that was the very thing the man who had abused me used to ask of me. So I stood there motionless, staring at her for a long time, the tray still in my hands.

"Seeing me there in front of her, unable to move or to speak, she turned to talk with someone beside her, as if I weren't there. A few minutes later, as a kind of courtesy, she said to me, coolly, 'I have to go. Take care of yourself.'

"She rose from her chair with a strange calm. She walked out, and once on the sidewalk across the street, she opened a black umbrella. The umbrella kept me from seeing the rest of her from behind. Wanting to call out to her, I followed her with my eyes until she turned the next corner — and I would not hear of her again for another ten years.

"After my uncle's wake, before the nine days of mourning were over, I had to leave the house. I went to live with another uncle who had a son my age. We went to school together and shined shoes in Licey al Medio and the surrounding communities. Because of the difference between our builds, people called us *el Flaco y el Gordo* — nicknames that stuck for years."

It was at that point in his life that I first met Iván and his cousin. They would come around our neighborhood to shine shoes, and the neighbors received them with real warmth, because their faces revealed not only their poverty but also a plain lack of affection. The neighbors helped them with school, and for our own children they became playmates. When I think back on Iván in those years, I see him as one of those defenseless children who, paradoxically, must learn to fend for themselves from a very young age.

I remember Iván used to talk a great deal about wanting to meet his biological father. At last, his grandmother told him that his father drove a car at a well-known taxi stand. Iván then went on radio programs to say he was searching for his father, and on one of them they let him put out a public appeal. One day he went to the taxi stand, and they told him where "the most-wanted man" lived.

At sixteen, he found his father. Once he had the address, he made his way there as quickly as he could. A woman opened the door, and the moment she saw him she said simply, "You are Josué's son."

That day he spent time with his father, his stepmother, and his three brothers. They received him warmly, and he even felt, for once, like he belonged to a family. Under what he believed was a safe roof, Iván stayed in school and went to work at a well-known medical center, in charge of collecting the parking fees. From that job he managed to put aside a fair amount of money, since he didn't have to pay for room and board. Everything was going more or less well, until Iván confided in his father about his savings. Without wasting any time, Josué asked to borrow the entire amount, and within a week he had left for the United States with the whole family. Iván was out on the street once again.

By now well used to climbing over cruel obstacles, he rented a room and kept on working at a nearby supermarket without giving up his studies. His tasks kept him for hours in the cold storage room, which damaged his lungs, and he had to quit.

With that courage of the brave so much his own, and putting his entrepreneurial side to use, he started doing yard work.

Working as a gardener brought him modest success. It was then that he received a call from his mother. She had terminal cancer, and she was asking him for help.

The nobility of this young man knew no limits, and he went to care for his mother until she died. He used that time to forgive her, to understand her, and to thank her for having brought him into the world. A few days after she was gone, his other siblings threw him out into the street, fearful that Iván might lay claim to some inheritance, or carry off a few boards from the small house she had left behind. May God keep her in the light.

"This time I went out to the street very sad, because I felt that something of me had gone with her, and I knew that mother of mine was the only thing I had. Even though my time at her side was short, I had grown to love her. I came to understand the life she had lived, the hardships of her own childhood, and the disappointments that had battered her.

"In the middle of all that sadness and abandonment, I had no choice but to put my life back together. So I rented another room and found work as a security guard at a company. With what I had saved, I set up a video arcade in Barrio Lindo, near where I was living. It was there that I met the mother of my two daughters, and we got married.

"Today I am a security supervisor at a well-known security company. During the day I make donuts to deliver to *pulperías*, *colmados*, and schools. I work to support my daughters, and to inspire them by my own example.

"I think I was born for some purpose," declares this champion against adversity — an expert at getting back on his feet after every fall, brushing off the dust, and walking on with his head held high, a discipline that belongs to brave souls.

Listening to him, I am moved by the optimism with which he faces life's challenges. I admire his capacity to forgive, the way he meets adversity, and the light that comes into his eyes when he speaks of the joy of having two daughters. They are what keeps the hope of living more alive in him than ever.

I said goodbye to Iván with a knot in my throat, and also with the gladness of having known this young man — one who never let the weeds of resentment or discouragement take root in his heart, and who chose, with admirable resolve, the path of rising above, absolutely convinced that he had come into the world for a purpose.

The Street Has a School of Its Own

To stand up to ignominy is never easy, because the risks you run are many. And yet Adelso did just that, even from where he stood — a child who worked in the streets. Milagros de Jesús de Féliz tells us his story, and we feel Adelso growing before our eyes. He moves us! What strength in his words, and in his gestures of dignity!

Irenarco Ardila Estupiñán

The morning broke into celebration, because it was *Día de la Patria* — Independence Day. The streets were planted with billboards bearing the frozen smiles of the candidates from the recent elections, while many houses proudly hung the tricolor flag from their façades, a tradition that strengthens the patriotic spirit.

I went on without stopping, passing the place where Las Tres Cruces gives its soul over to Calle Beller, on my way to the heart of the city. The morning was humid, and the country was getting ready to listen to President Luis Abinader's annual accountability address. I was happy to be heading off to meet Adelso again — that shy boy I had stopped seeing back when he was already an adolescent with an open face, large hands, and a gift for the flute, which he played with masterful enthusiasm.

Time does not stand still, and Adelso is now thirty-seven years old. He is a father, still hardworking, a born entrepreneur.

Our joy at meeting again was plain, and the prospect of hearing the stages of his life filled me with anticipation.

Adelso was born on *Día de la Raza* — October 12 — in San Víctor, Moca, in 1986. He grew up among fourteen siblings of various ages, in a home marked by precarious circumstances. When he was six, his family moved to Santiago and settled in Rafey, a densely populated neighborhood where people fight, with great effort, to climb out of poverty.

On top of so many other hardships, the area also suffered the flooding caused by Hurricane Georges. That time, the water swept away many houses, the home of this good-natured, hard-working young man among them. The government at the time took those affected to the pavilions of La Barranquita, and there the families placed their lives in God's hands until, many months later, they were relocated to a safer area.

"Dad worked in the warehouses of a well-known company, and Mom made *habichuelas con dulce* to sell at the Hospedaje Yaque. But despite the effort of both of them, our income kept falling short, and the boys had to go out and shine shoes to help feed the family.

"When I was seven, I put together a shoeshine box with everything I needed, and my brother *Buche* and I started working around the neighborhood. On average we earned 180 pesos a day, and that was what we brought home. Because I wanted to earn more, a friend invited me to Parque Duarte, in the historic center of the city. There was more foot traffic there, and a real chance of earning more so I could help my family more. Dad had to give permission for that move, but he refused to authorize it. So one day I went without his say-so. That time I brought 400 pesos home. Dad caught on to where I'd been, and I had to tell him the truth.

"I bring this up because many people think that children who work in the streets have no one looking out for them, that the parents are irresponsible, or that you're a *tíguere* — a hustler, a streetwise troublemaker — and that isn't always how it is. Need, the absence of guaranteed rights, and the relentless lash of poverty push you out into the street to find a way to survive. I come from a dignified, hardworking family that hoped for a better future, but our circumstances were suffocating us, and we needed to improve them. In that situation, the only choice left was to go out and work with dignity, without doing what was wrong."

When Adelso speaks of his dignity, the light in his eyes takes on a particular hue. With that same feeling, he tells me how he decided to shine shoes in Parque Duarte, the epicenter of working children, with no idea what was waiting for him there.

"At seven years old I had never seen a park before, and I was thrilled to sit down in that great plaza, full of people, with a railed bandstand that looked like a gallery for the wealthy. There were shops all around, tons of cars all honking at once, and so many tame pigeons near my feet.

"With childhood's innocence, I faced many troubles, because working there and learning the routine was no easy task. The park has its own laws, and the dangers lie in wait even from the bandstand that welcomes you in. Violence lives on its benches, fights are an everyday thing, and drugs are forever after you. But what marked me the most was being stalked by pedophiles — well-off men who would make big-money offers to children in order to act out their sexual fantasies. It's a more common problem than people imagine," Adelso says, speaking from what he has lived through firsthand.

"I remember once a man approached me about shining around twelve pairs of shoes at his house. When I got there, I noticed the house was empty, almost unfurnished, with only a small table and two chairs. In one of the rooms, in poor sanitary condition, stood a large bed with very worn sheets. That gave me a bad feeling, and I put myself on guard.

"While I was shining the shoes, the man began to undress and to make himself 'comfortable.' I kept working, though a cold sweat was running down my back. Trying to put me at ease, he asked whether I wanted juice or water. I told him water, and when he stepped out to a *colmado* nearby to buy some, I felt as though my heart was about to burst out of my chest. In a burst of panic, I tore down the street and ran across the Hermanos Patiño Bridge at top speed, afraid that the abuser would catch up with me. I left everything behind, and empty-handed, I ran with all the breath I had.

"The next day, the abuser came to the park and asked me what had happened. That was when I let him have it. Even so, I would see him hanging around the park often, making shameless propositions to my friends. Society doesn't recognize pedophiles, but we who worked the streets could spot them at a glance.

"Another day a group of us boys were down at the river. We didn't have much clothing to cover ourselves, and the pedophiles knew it, so in the blink of an eye they would show up to peep at us. But the educators from Acción Callejera already knew about it, and they would pull us all out of the river to keep us from falling into their claws. That is how far the educators of the Foundation went to look out for us.

"Another day, also in the park, a pedophile came up to me and offered me 2,000 pesos for a pint of blood. It was another way of luring boys in to use them for that curse that corrupts childhood. I didn't accept, but I know friends who did, for the money, and it ruined their lives forever.

"The street is very dangerous for children. There was a time when I tried washing windshields near the park to bring in more money, but I had an experience in which I now know God was with me. One morning I started in on the windshields and tossed my sponge onto a driver's car. The driver looked at me, drew a gun, aimed it at my head, and ordered me to pick up the sponge — and I did. That was the first and last time I ever did that work, as dangerous as it was wounding.

"Those of us who lived through Parque Duarte learn to see danger from a distance, to defend ourselves, not to give in under pressure, to practice solidarity with each other, to fight against injustice, and to look out for ourselves without bodyguards. Fights were a daily thing, and you had to face them so you wouldn't end up the *sambá* of the plaza — the one everyone picks on. The street has a school of its own!"

Adelso keeps remembering, and he tells us that not long after he started working in Parque Duarte, a friend invited him to breakfast at Acción Callejera. He tells the story with excitement, as the best day of his life.

"I'd never felt such joy as I did the day my brother *Buche* and I arrived at that Foundation. I was wary, and from childhood I had a nose for whether a place was good for me or not. But from the moment I walked in, I felt welcomed. I had never seen so many games I could play with, no questions asked. They showed me the skills room, the music room, the sports room, the meals and hygiene room — and I was smitten when I came upon the creativity room.

"I was hungry, and that day they served me a hearty breakfast: two rolls, three slices of salami, and a tall cup of hot chocolate, all for just 3 pesos. Now I understand that the meals the Foundation served us were just the hook to draw us in and educate us.

There I learned to play and to enjoy myself. And in those years I made some friends who became like brothers to me. Sadly, many have died tragically — because the street takes lives.

"I remember *el Chino*, *el Sureño*, Juan *Oreja*, Robinson, Alberto, and others. Kelyn, Álvaro, *Cuquín*, *el Maco*, and *Caco de Martillo* are gone. Some grew tired of life; the others died in fights and accidents of one kind or another. They were all good boys.

"With nearly all of my needs covered by the Foundation, I poured love into its lessons, and the team of educators returned that affection in learning of every kind. I fell in love with the flute, and I felt I had a gift for it. I still have that flute, and through it I keep those moments of glory close.

"With time I kept growing, and in those rooms I also learned to read and write. That brought immense joy to my heart.

"Once I could read and write, I started school at eleven, with the guidance and follow-up of Acción Callejera. I remember my first day of class as marvelous. I started in second grade, and before a month had gone by they moved me up to third. I stayed focused on moving forward, so much so that within three months I was already in fourth grade. Later I went on to fifth. The thing is, I have a head for numbers.

"I went to school and kept attending the Foundation. I remember how I loved rainy days, because I didn't have to work in the streets and I could spend the whole day in that place, which to me was sacred. I felt so fulfilled that shining shoes no longer interested me, and I delighted in going to the educational programs. When I was there, I felt protected, listened to, and guided by the educators.

"That's why I want to give my eternal thanks to Jochy Taveras, *el Aguilita*; to Carlos Gómez; to Bentodina Jiménez; to Yohanny

Rodríguez; to Cinthya Lora; to Raydiris Cruz; to Carmelo Mateo; and to that whole team consecrated to educating us. From them I received the best tools, and I have put them into practice all my life. I also harvested wonderful friendships there with the groups of volunteers who came up from Florida. Among them I remember René, Eric, Camille, and Cristina."

To talk with Adelso is to bring the past into the present. His eyes light up when he tells me he has seven children, counting the five from his second wife. To all of them he passes along the values that life has placed within his reach. He told me, with pride, that not one of them, thank God, has had to work in the streets, and that together they make a family of fighters.

Near the end of our conversation, he ran his hands over his head and stretched in the chair where he was sitting. With the taste of certain childhood memories returning to him, and with a casual gesture, he opened his left hand and began counting on his fingers the jobs that make up the résumé of his life.

"I have done every honest job a working child can do. I was a shoeshine from the age of six. I also worked as a volunteer at Acción Callejera, passing through every area as a collaborator. I worked at a private school, keeping watch over the students and handling the logistics of receiving and dismissing them. As a *canillita* — a newspaper boy — I sold *Hoy* and *El Nacional* on the busiest corners of the city.

"These days I work at a foundry, with twenty-five unbroken years on the job. On top of that, I sell exercise weights and supply them to gyms and to people who look after their health. I also have a small café, run by my wife. But the most important thing is that I have a family. I look after my mother's health, I keep working with joy, and I thank God every day for the life it fell to me to face. Acción Callejera was everything in my life. I would describe it as my guide and my teacher."

In spite of everything, Adelso's hope has stayed intact. His words gather a collection of realities and certainties that he now shares freely. Perhaps what each of us does with his own story is, in the end, the true measure of dignity and resilience.

I bow my head with reverence before the courage of these boys who, even with their lives exposed to immense risk, walk forward with their heads held high. In their steps lives a silent lesson in courage and in faith. And as I listen to them, I understand that the homeland does not dawn only in the flags that wave in the streets, but also in the hearts of those who, like Adelso, get up every day to keep moving forward.

Child of Destiny, Godson of Dread

Milagros de Jesús de Féliz tells us that Jose came to know uncertainty before he ever knew young love. He came to know separation from his family as well, and the corruption of immigration agents. Without surrender, he carries it still — in every sun that scorches the blooming gardens of hard work, and in prayers cast toward the far side of the river. This is Jose's story.

Pedro Ángel

"*Kouri, kouri, kouri!*" several children shouted as they played in the yard at six in the morning, scattering in panic at the sight of agents from the Dominican Republic's Directorate of Immigration.

"*Kounye a, kouri!*" is the warning cry the children use to alert their families to flee in time, away from that cluster of rented rooms and shacks where so many families of Haitian descent live.

Like a startled herd of goats, young and old alike bolt in every direction, hiding among the cassava plants of a nearby *conuco* — a small farm plot — until *la camiona*, as they call the truck that hauls people away, has gone.

These raids have their own rules. If the agents catch one of the children, the father turns back to protect his own — and that is how they take them in pairs and load them into the dreaded truck. If you have money and you offer those same agents a couple of thousand pesos, they put on the theater of carrying you off and then drop you somewhere along the road. If the shacks are locked, the agents blow off the padlocks and door bolts to force their way in, on the pretext of saving the homeland. And if they get inside and find no one there, they take whatever cash they can, along with anything else that catches their eye — cell phones being among the most coveted.

That is exactly what happened to Jose last week. After these raids, the soldiers walk out of the operation wearing heroic faces for having "protected" a homeland they carry tattooed only on their uniforms — and, with great satisfaction, in their pockets as well.

This is Jose's day-to-day — a young man, a child of destiny and a godson of courage. *La camiona* has hauled him off to Haiti eighteen times. Nine times he has made his way back through the mountains, and just as many times he has come back hidden in vehicles.

I have known Jose-André since he was a child wandering those hard roads of God. In 2004, he was barely four years old when he became a victim of child trafficking. He was brought from Haiti so that his innocence could be borrowed and put to work, made to beg at traffic lights in sun and rain, at the mercy of God and whatever stranger might pass. The trade was run by a well-known "auntie" who made a business of it, and who lived north of Navarrete.

For several years, they dressed Jose in poverty and turned him into a tool for begging — sometimes others asked for alms in his name; other times, they forced him to do it himself. He spent long hours at traffic lights and on busy avenues, with the face of orphanhood, languid eyes, a belly drawn tight, barefoot, almost naked, and hungry. That was his training in the "art" of begging.

But at eight years old, he managed to break free from the network that had kept him, along with so many other children, in conditions of begging.

It was on those corners of abuse and exploitation, after he had cried every tear he carried in his heart, that I met this young man — who today is grown and a father. To find him a man now is to glimpse a parallel world, full of rough patches, lived experience, and journeys that have only sharpened in him the will to live.

Like someone with the urgent need to lay out something of utmost importance, he went on, telling everything he could remember, without any order in time.

"Carrying a sense of abandonment that still eats at my soul, I changed my line of work. I came to Santiago and turned to shining shoes, sweeping other people's yards, selling flowers and phone chargers. I also washed cars, set up chairs at businesses, and now and then picked up the trash that customers left at the *chimichurri* stands ringing the Monumento a los Héroes de la Restauración.

"At night, sleep, sadness, and exhaustion would catch up with me wherever I happened to be, but I usually ended up sleeping in a big empty lot at the corner of Calle del Sol and Avenida Francia — a downtown palace under the open sky that God lent to all of us who had no roof and no one to look after us."

As we spoke, Jose remembered those years as the worst that can happen to a child. He confided that he no longer remembered his family, that he didn't even know the date of his own birth — among other thorns that still pricked his feelings.

He says that one day he met his older brother, who had also crossed the border and was working the streets. In a long embrace, they shared all those years of loneliness. He swears it was the best day of his life: he felt accompanied, and although both of them had drifted aimlessly through life, in the end they had found each other. Then his long-lost brother began to tell him stories about their relatives. He felt so happy he didn't want to leave his side.

With a brightness in his eyes, like someone glad to have come through many trials, he goes on to say that some time later, his brother took him home to Haiti to meet the family he could no longer remember. He was shaken to see the extreme poverty that still battered his own people in that country where his roots are buried.

"I stood in the middle of that strange house I was visiting for the first time. It smelled of kitchen seasonings, surrounded by its few pieces of furniture and its many sorrows. But to see Mama serve me food at the table, run her hands over my head again and again, look me in the eye and look me in the eye some more, and hang my clothes on the wooden pole — that was every bit of love I had longed for since I was a child. I would walk again and again through the rooms of that little shack, and its corners bloomed inside my heart. I had a hot breakfast every day, and I went with Papa on his trips to the *conuco*."

Jose was born in Lenbe, west of Cap-Haïtien — a very poor rural area where people live off the land, with no basic services of any kind. There is no electricity, and water has to be fetched from more than two kilometers away. To make matters worse, violence runs through the whole region in ways that defy imagination.

This young man is Catholic, though he comes from a family that practices Vodou — a religious tradition that venerates animals such as the serpent, and whose rituals include sacrifices to its deities. His family firmly believes that, through this practice, one can harm others, gaining the power to make them sick through witchcraft. It is beliefs of this kind that lead his community to respect the devotees of Vodou.

"In my family, people start attending the festivities in honor of Vodou from a very young age. But I have never believed in those mysteries."

Jose explains that these festivities are gatherings something like a birthday celebration here. According to those who attend, they please the spirits, who manifest in gratitude in keeping with what is offered. There is plenty of cake; the drums are played; there is dancing the whole time. Toasts are made with *clerén* or *triculí*, and there is plenty of food to share. Cows, goats, and other animals are sacrificed as offerings to the spirits at these well-attended celebrations. In Lenbe, the sponsorship for these gatherings generally comes from remittances sent by relatives living abroad.

"Right now, Mama works in agriculture, because Papa died from a curse that was put on him. The sorcerers wrote his death sentence on a large *pringamosa* leaf, in red and blue ink. On top of the leaf they placed the penny of death. Papa took the curse into his hands 'trusting in God,' but before he could get home, he collapsed with a fever. When my brother went to find a healer to save him, the man cheated him — took his cash and didn't do a thing for him, because Papa died that very morning.

"We are nine siblings — two girls and seven boys. I am the youngest. Of the boys, six of us fled poverty for the Dominican Republic. All of us work honestly to support our families. Three of them work at the slaughterhouse of a poultry plant, another at a lumberyard, and the oldest at a cabinetmaker's shop. I do landscape design — I'm a landscaper. The two girls are housewives and live in Lenbe; one has eleven children, the other has fourteen and is currently pregnant. In the twenty-four years I have been in this country, I have crossed through the mountains nine times without papers, and that is no easy task.

"When I would leave Lenbe to get to the Dominican Republic, I had to take a *tap-tap* up to Cap-Haïtien, and once I reached Juana Méndez, to the north, I would cross the Massacre River. Then I would cross through the mountains at night — and lately, by day as well. There are many guards along the way, and they know what we're up to. The soldiers order you to take off your clothes so they can search you thoroughly, and then they leave you a hundred pesos or so, like a tip for the abuse. From experience, I can tell you: if you want to make it into the country in one piece, you have to bring money for them. When you give them money, they'll even point you to the safest path, where there aren't any agents. Then you pick up the pace to make up time before nightfall.

"On top of the guards, there are plenty of dangerous *tígueres* out there — not soldiers, but Haitian criminals who'll often kill you whether you have money or not. Their trade is killing people. You have to defend yourself from those heartless thugs, because they kill for the pleasure of it.

"From Juana Méndez to the border there is a lot of walking. There have been times when I have spent up to three days on foot, and if you don't know the trail and lose your way, you can easily end up back in Haiti. So the wise thing is to pay a *poté* — a guide — because it is a dangerous route, full of brush and very dark at night. On those near-blind treks it is common to come upon human bones, people who died out in the middle of nowhere. You have to cross many rivers and go down and back up steep ravines. And when you want to rest, the mosquitoes and the vermin make sure you don't. It is, without a doubt, an exhausting journey.

"After a while, on the horizon of the road, you start to see lights in the distance, and closer in, the country folk working in fields of tobacco or tomato. That tells you that you are close to the country you set out for. Once on this side, some stay and work in the Línea Noroeste for some months, and if they get the chance, they come on to Santiago. It all depends on the work you can find.

"Crossing the border in a vehicle is another ordeal — quieter, but every bit as dangerous. The first thing you have to do is contact a person who'll help you cross. That person charges 12,000 or 13,000 pesos, and has plenty of contacts among the border military and at the inspection points. The key is to line up the person who will receive you on the other side.

"The last time, I came back in a small car with twelve people — thirteen counting me. In the back seat, three rows of three people, stacked one on top of the other; three more in the front seat, plus the driver. You can imagine how cramped it was, but if you complain, they put you off the road. Because the vehicle is overloaded, every time it hits a pothole or a dip you feel it in your stomach — but you can't say a word.

"That's how more than three hundred Haitians enter this country every day, give or take. And if there are soldiers who don't go along with the chain of corruption, you can hide for two or three nights in some strategic spot where they can't find you. The situation gets worse on a weekend. In that case, the guards tip the driver off about where the police are, so the car can take another route. And that is how we go — passing from one checkpoint to another along these roads of God, sown with illegality, with a fierce need to survive, and with a very cruel poverty."

Jose has taken refuge in work since childhood. After a stretch of various jobs, and to avoid trouble with Immigration, he labored in tomato fields in Solo Gordo, in the Línea Noroeste, near Barrio Lindo — a very remote place. Later he was clearing weeds from plantain and banana plantations on another farm in the same area. He also worked at farm jobs in Pueblo Nuevo, a zone that lies just before you reach Mao. Hoping for a change of luck, he spent a good while in Monte Plata, in Bayaguana, cutting and stripping wooden poles to be used as electrical posts. But the work was very demanding, and he decided to go back to Santiago.

Once in the Ciudad Corazón — a place he knew, where he could dust off old longings — he worked at a bus-painting shop, and also as a night watchman at the slaughterhouse of a farm. During the pandemic, he changed trades again and started cleaning yards. To improve his income, he took a training course in Punta Cana as a landscape designer. He has been in this trade for eight years.

"My passport is expired, and I have done everything I could to renew it, but Haiti is in shambles. I submitted all the paperwork to obtain residency in this country, but its issuance has been suspended too. And even though I have the receipt of my application, which proves my intent, the people at Immigration don't recognize it.

"My situation is very hard, because I have two children in Haiti, and it is my duty to provide for them. It shames me to live without papers. My chest twists every time I have to pay off the corrupt ones who stop me. It hurts me to bear witness to the destruction of Haiti, and to live with the uncertainty that my family could be killed at any moment. It is a constant worry, and it costs me my sleep.

"I work tirelessly, more than ten hours a day, to support my own, but my savings vanish in any one of those raids that come at dawn. They take not only what you've earned, but the hope of seeing any of your plans through.

"Last time, they took all four of us. We rode in *la camiona* under arrest, and my heart was crushed all the way through the journey, seeing my wife nursing our youngest, with nothing but one bottle of water for our five-year-old daughter. Thank God they bore the trip better than I did, because for me, fear has worn itself out by now. They stayed behind in Lenbe, in my wife's care, in the middle of poverty, without school and on a precarious diet. But they sleep in peace, without the dread of the night watch.

"I am sure the Lord protects them, and that is enough for me to begin each day with hope. I am a Christian, and I believe in a just God. I am very grateful to this country, which has been a source of income for my family, but I know that one of two things awaits me: a life apart, with my children far away, or a return with no way back. Either one I will accept with humility, if it pleases *Papá Bon Dieu* — Father Good God."

When he finished telling this Way of the Cross without altar or rest, I thought of Luke 7:50:

"Your faith has saved you.

Go in peace."

ASPHALT ON FIRE

In these seven stories, childhood burns early — like green wood under the harshest sun. These are lives marked by forced labor, the dangers of the street, and forms of violence so normalized that the world barely manages to notice them.

And yet, these boys, girls, and adolescents endure, clinging to life like someone shielding a spark in the heart of the blaze. Some — not all — turned that fire into strength enough to keep going, to open a path of their own

The Little Girl Who Helps[1]

Poverty marked Tulia's fate — the girl who helps, or the maid, as people say nowadays. Tulia was "lent out" as a child: a mortgage paid with her life, dissolved into days and nights wedded to the weariness of paying tribute to the family that thought it owned her. Tulia is the girl of yesterday and the girl of today, handed over "for her own betterment," condemned to a debt of gratitude that can never be repaid. Here, the author paints an early form of slavery that culture disguises as custom.
Grisbel Medina R.

She was born on June 12, many years ago. With time I came to learn that the date coincides with the International Day Against Child Labor — a symbol that would etch itself into her life. No one warned her that her name would come to belong to those silent statistics of girls working as domestic laborers in other people's homes — a scourge that persists like a long, unbroken shadow across many parts of the world.

Behind what passes for "normal" work, culturally accepted and rarely questioned, there are today 160 million girls and boys laboring under conditions that work against their development. The International Labour Organization and UNICEF say it with-

1 Story previously published in the anthology *Cuento ilustrado* (Chile: Factor Literario, 2025).

out ambiguity: one in every ten children in the world works, and the number keeps rising.

We have these figures within reach, and yet we tend to perceive them as distant, as though they always happened somewhere else — when in truth they happen here among us as well.

I once knew a woman who worked in other people's homes for seven decades, without respite. She began as a child, at the very age when dreams take shape, and died at eighty-three, still performing the same domestic work she had been given on her first day.

Her name was Tulia.

From a young age, in everyone's eyes, she was a tireless worker — in a society that still insists on believing that this kind of labor "dignifies" the children who perform it.

And so, at thirteen, she was "handed over" to a family in the countryside of La Vega. Tulia was a slender *mulata*, with a shy smile and hands still those of a child — long-boned, with a neck at once strong and delicate, and a graceful waist. In her figure there was a mixture of early strength and quiet sweetness that revealed itself in her gaze. Her character was firm, and yet she was deeply loving and tender.

As has happened to so many girls, even in this century it remains common for girls like her to be entrusted, without any disguise, to relatives or employers "to be raised" — an expression that often conceals exploitation and abandonment. It is presented as an opportunity, as a way of "helping a poor family's child get ahead," under the promise of an education, moral guidance, and protection.

But the reality tends to be otherwise.

In that passage, nearly all her rights dissolve. In their place, a narrative of gratitude is imposed — directed toward the family that takes the child in and promises to treat her "as a daughter." In Tulia's case, those promises never came to anything. Poverty pushed her out early, and her fate would always be the same: endless workdays at the stoves, until firewood and sweat slowly dried away her smile.

The family that "took her in" was a young couple — Catholic, Apostolic, and Roman — well-off and highly respected in the community. On the day she arrived, the lady of the house, her *patrona*, told her with a kindness that allowed no reply that she would be in charge of the household chores, and that they would care for her as if she were part of the family.

Trusting and very young, Tulia would begin her days before dawn. She always kept a reverent distance from those "compassionate" owners. As the days went on, she discovered that the estate employed a sizeable number of farmhands who had to be fed: a breakfast of *víveres*, an abundant midday meal, and supper for the entire household. All of it fell under her charge.

In time, she also took on the raising of the lady's thirteen children. She loved them and cared for them as her own, with a devotion so complete that she never had room left to fall in love. Tulia rarely left the bounds of the estate. Her only outings were to Sunday Mass, after the visiting townspeople had gone.

Sundays were holidays for the grandchildren and days of unrelenting work for Tulia. The grown-up children of the house would come for the day with their families, grandchildren, cousins, and godchildren. I remember that one of the daughters had nine boys who could "raise the roof." That little baseball team, joining the rest, was enough to make you think of calling on Herod.

To be fair, the children respected her. Tulia was gentle, but when she fixed them with eyes of ice and raised her index finger to order that the yard be swept or the trash gathered up, all of them obeyed without a peep. A single look from her was enough to contain so much pent-up energy at once.

Meanwhile, the family waited in comfort while she cooked the finest meals over a wood fire — an art she had mastered with grace, though at a tremendous physical cost.

Coffee, too, was roasted on the *fogón*. Tulia would devote whole afternoons to it. She would bathe beforehand, the way someone prepares for an important undertaking. Only she knew the exact moment to lift the *paila* off the heat. Then she would grind the beans in a tall *pilón*, carved to the height of her elbows. Pounding the coffee with both hands was, for her, a precise choreography — until it was reduced to powder; and if anything didn't quite convince her, she would roast it again. She could read its aroma, its body, and its acidity like the most refined taster.

Now I understand why that coffee was so special. It carried the imprint of all her effort, her intuition, and her dignity. No wonder they said Tulia was a woman of mettle.

But years do not pass in vain. She grew old before the stoves; the fire wounded her sight and broke down her strength, and her eyes turned gray, as if the flame of the fogón had left its ash behind in them. Swollen veins came up in her hands, and her fingers, twisted by arthritis, looked like roots clinging to time. Exhaustion hollowed out her body, and her breasts as well. Even so, she kept on with her duties, while she offered a smile that was already only the shadow of itself, almost a grimace of fatigue.

"Never contradict Tulia or treat her with disrespect," the patrona would warn her children.

After more than sixty years of service, they built her a small blue house with pink trim, surrounded by *catalanas*, *yínyeres*, *celias*, and *coralillos*. The little house still stands across from the cistern, near the cocoa-drying racks. At night, Tulia would sit outside to listen to the programs on Radio Guarachita, on an old transistor radio — and maybe that, many times, was her only window onto the world.

Toward the end of her days, the arthritis worsened, and her sight nearly faded out altogether. Her smile disappeared, but she never stopped praying the rosary in silence, over and over. By then, in bed, her left forearm would tremble out of control, and she would try to subdue it with her other hand — like someone refusing to surrender command of her own body.

She died at the Ninth Hour, after the Angelus, with a scapular in her hands and a rosary resting on her chest. I think now that perhaps it was her way of holding on to a cross she had carried all her life.

I still don't know whether she truly lived or merely survived — so that the rest of us might come to understand that sons and daughters are not to be given away or handed over, that poverty does not justify emotional exile, and that even in the midst of want, love is essential to every human being.

This story still tends to repeat itself, and it is one of the main reasons girls hardly appear at the traffic lights. They are invisible because they are inside other people's homes — yes, often inside our own — like Tulia, watching the world pass by from someone else's kitchen.

Tulia left this world among stoves and pots, spending her life pleasing others at the cost of her own health. She was invisible, but she was also eternal.

While the orange trees blossom and we look the other way, thousands of girls wither in silence — and that is the wound we have yet to close.

Tulia's story did not end with her death. It repeats itself every time childhood is handed over, as if it could pass from one home to another without something essential breaking inside.

In the Dark

In this story, the author presents the life of Manuel — a boy whose existence, already marked by precariousness, becomes still harder after an attack that wounds him deeply. Along the way, his desire to rise resurfaces, and he discovers the gaze that grants his life its true worth.
Rosa Ruiz

I met Manuel when he was scarcely more than a child, along those mysterious paths only God knows how to trace. He had a serene beauty, full of the freshness that belongs to childhood. His lively eyes caught the morning sun, and his face still held the untouched innocence of his age.

He wandered the corners of Hoyo de Elías, in La Yagüita de Pastor of Santiago, where everyone in the neighborhood knew him and looked after him as one of their own — a grace Manuel still gives thanks for today.

Now, seeing him again after so much time, I had already heard something of what had happened to him; but what struck me was that he still carried a luminous outlook on life: brave, willing, and with a smile that shyly kept him company still.

He had been a student at a community homework center — a space that still supports vulnerable children in El Fracatán, in Santiago, a ravine settlement next to La Lotería, from which it takes its name. Manuel studied in the mornings, and in the afternoons he earned his living through whatever work would secure him a plate of food. As he told me, he remembered the happiness he felt bathing in the river — his one chance to wash and change his clothes.

This young man grew up in the streets under a relentless sun, amid the smell of gasoline at the traffic lights and torrential rains, surviving on the charity of passersby, with loneliness weighing heavy on his shoulders. Many nights he slept wherever night caught up with him — or, as he himself puts it, "wherever the labor pains caught me."

Orphaned for as long as he can remember, he says he never knew his parents. One day, a woman from the community told him that his mother was from San José de las Matas and his father from Puerto Plata, but no one could shed any further light on their whereabouts. On that subject, he told me he had been through so much hardship and rejection that he had no wish — neither then nor now — to find them.

Manuel knew abandonment from a very tender age. His surroundings offered no real chance to study or to enjoy the kind of childhood other children had. Even so, he made the most of every moment, learning whatever little he could find within reach, always with a hopeful spirit.

His world was the burning asphalt of the busiest streets. There he lived alongside people of every kind, on the corners where he asked for a few coins to eat. In those corners of fate, he made a few friends who protected him from the worst dangers; but even they could not spare him the everyday blows his tender age did not deserve. He sold whatever he could at the traffic lights: gum, flowers, bottled water, phone chargers, cookies, even popsicles.

He also washed the windshields of the cars passing through, fighting to survive.

In the early hours of the morning, Manuel worked at the Hospedaje Yaque, unloading trucks packed with fruits and vegetables. He became an expert at plucking chickens at a shop near the market. He helped housewives with their shopping and, every now and then, sold vegetables from a wheelbarrow in the heart of Santiago. He was quick on his feet and respectful — qualities that led many small-business owners to hire him to clean their shops or to fill their orders efficiently.

More than ten years had gone by since I last saw Manuel. We met again last month, at a chance gathering, where he asked me to write his story and to publish it. He needed to give voice to his feelings, and to make sure his tragedy would not be repeated — that those who turn to cowardly means to harm others would be punished with the full weight of the law. Until then I had not known that part of his life, and I had not understood the urgency behind his request. We sat down to talk, and it was in that moment that he revealed the events that had marked his life. The emotions that played across his face moved me deeply.

Manuel let his story out without stopping, his eyes fixed on the floor. He told me that, despite living in the streets and being an orphan, everything had been going as he had hoped. By the age of twelve he was already paying for a small room he shared with a friend — but everything changed when he turned fourteen.

He confided that, on a somber late afternoon, while he was in the fifth grade, a man known for his cruelty attacked him without any apparent reason. With a bottle of *ácido del diablo* in his hand, he hurled that infernal liquid at Manuel's face; it splashed across his shoulders as well, causing immediate, devastating pain. In an instant, Manuel's life changed forever. The afternoon seemed to halt, and the sun took its leave in sorrow, as if it sensed that this act would tear the thread of this striving young fighter's dreams.

Ácido del diablo is a lethal mixture of corrosive acids — sulfuric, hydrochloric, and muriatic — and paint strippers, to which the attacker added molasses so that it would cling to the skin all the more fiercely. Manuel's face, once full of innocence, was left completely disfigured. He has gone through twelve surgeries to ease the pain, to restore the tissue, and to try to fill in the deep scars that left their marks on skin and soul alike. He lost the sight in his left eye, and he cannot fully close his right.

"I would run out of verbs to conjugate the pain of those days, ma'am; it was horrible," Manuel told me, plainly still marked by that callous act.

Another painful aspect for Manuel is that the attacker never served the sentence imposed on him: an influential politician arranged for his release.

Manuel spent months in the hospital with little support, and when he began to recover, he took refuge in a small room offered to him by a generous family. For a long time he did not leave that space, fearful of others' eyes, sunk in a deep sadness, carrying a self-esteem wounded to the death. His physical pain gradually gave way, but the emotional pain, by his own account, stayed intact.

"I have asked God's forgiveness, because in my loneliness many bad thoughts crossed my mind — among them, the thought of doing away with myself," this young man said, regretful for having harbored such thoughts.

"With time, and praying every day, something inside me began to change. I started looking for work, but every time I showed up, some excuse would come up not to hire me. I was more than certain it was because of the disfigurement of my face. That was when I decided that, even if my face was no longer pleasing to the world, my mind had to free itself of that burden. And that process of liberation was harder than any surgery.

"But God walks with those of us who are most in need, and with those of us who never give up. One day, near the Monumento a los Héroes, I met don Ignacio — a sensitive, generous man who listened to me with empathy. He owned a veterinary supply distributor, and he hired me to work for his company. There I came to know the world of fertilizers, along with other agricultural supplies.

"I shipped out the merchandise, and I slept in the warehouse itself, working as the night watchman. I carried out both jobs with the responsibility expected of me, and that way I earned don Ignacio's trust, and his family's as well. It means a great deal to me that they still invite me to their family gatherings at Christmas, and to their children's birthdays.

"Through the affection of that family, I came to understand that sometimes people don't realize the meaning of small gestures. I used to feel self-conscious about my face; even so, they would include me in their photographs, and that meant the world to me. I thought that if they could accept me as I am, then it was my duty to accept myself just as I am. Their acceptance taught me to accept my own life as well."

I followed his account closely. He told me he had begun studying again, and that he used the hours of solitude to read any book, magazine, even any newspaper that came into his hands. Reading became his window onto the world, while he kept on with his duties as the night watchman. He felt that every page he read of *The Little Prince* coaxed him toward freedom. That book changed the way he saw life. He told me that, since it was short and good, he read it four times.

Years later, he finished high school, and at the graduation ceremony he gave the speech on behalf of his classmates. Hearing the applause, he felt, for the first time, truly blessed. That night, after the ceremony was over, he gathered the courage to confess his love to Clara, a classmate. He felt there was something in her that gave him the courage to open his heart again. With Clara he did not fear being judged for his appearance; to her, Manuel was a safe presence.

Their bond blossomed, and they moved together into a small house in the mountains of Jarabacoa. There they devoted themselves to growing flowers at a nursery very close to the house where Clara's family lived. Surrounded by pines, they made a home where Manuel finally felt safe.

"Clara did not see my scars — only the love lodged in my heart," Manuel told me with utter certainty, as the shy smile that has always set him apart returned to his face.

In time they married, and for him, his marriage was a true liberation. He maintains that Clara's voice — soft and steady — keeps him company in his daily tasks and in his thoughts. He continues to be drawn to reading, and he ventures ever deeper into the study of agriculture, with respect for the gifts of the natural world. Together they have created a very humble space where the scars dissolve through the power of noble feeling and the willingness to keep growing.

Manuel knows that the memory of that tragic day, when *ácido del diablo* was thrown at him, will never disappear completely; but he no longer fears its echo, and God has shown him the way forward. With time he has made peace with his appearance, and at Clara's side he has found the joy of being accepted and loved just as he is — though he admits the process has not been easy.

When I sensed that we had finished, I rose from my chair to say goodbye. But he took me by the hand and gently invited me to sit down again. And then he confided that Clara, his wife, has been blind from birth, and that everything she does, she does by feel. I understood then that marrying a woman who knows the truth of his heart, even though she cannot see his face, had allowed him to make peace with his own reflection.

At that moment, several questions about Clara came to me. But he gave me no room to probe further. He reminded me that he had already shared all his sorrows — but that one joy still remained to be told: they have a ten-month-old son, on the verge of taking his first steps.

"Luis Manuel is our joy; his presence fills us with happiness," he said, smiling.

I understood that this child had come to bring light into their home. I congratulated him, feeling in my heart that such joy had come at the right moment, and was deeply deserved. I understood then that his life is a testimony of endurance and transformation, and I saw clearly that the scars had stopped defining him — because love had given him back his joy.

A Different Heart

The author tells the story of Joel, a boy who faced the hardness of life with courage and chose a different path. A testimony of resilience, faith, and a greatness born of pain. To listen to him is to understand that yes, it is possible — when one follows the heart. Thank you, Joel, for being light, for being inspiration, for being a gift even to those who do not know you.
Xiomara García

By a fortunate turn of events, I came to know Joel — a remarkable boy who, on an ordinary day, knocked at my door and offered his services as a shoeshiner. I remember it as if it were today: the brightness of his large eyes, the dimple that appeared when he smiled, and the way he could persuade you to take him on, revealing, at a glance, the strength of his character.

I feel deeply fortunate to have known him in those first chapters of his life. At the time, he was a boy of about seven, perhaps even younger — a chubby little thing whom everyone called *el Gordo*, a nickname that has stayed with him among those who know him. What stood out in him was an innate wisdom, an unshakable faith, and a tireless willingness to work.

As a quiet gift life has given me, I have watched him grow up, work hard, face many setbacks with hope, marry, and now become a father. It is a privilege I hold close.

Joel's life has been a pendulum of feelings, emotions, and events that have shaped him. His courage and resolve were tested by trials no child his age should ever have had to bear.

This story holds images that not only portray his family in full but draw him into the events themselves, where he took on a role beyond his years to carry the burden destiny had placed on him.

Joel is the eldest of three boys, the cherished brother of two sisters. His father worked as a motorcycle taxi driver; his mother spent her days cleaning other people's homes. With those modest earnings, they raised their family with dignity, even amid crushing hardship, in Hoya del Caimito, in Santiago.

"The housework was divided among us while our parents were out working. My older sister, at just seven, was already caring for the younger ones. She cooked for all of us and got us ready for school. Even though poverty pressed hard on us, each of us carried out our duties to the letter," Joel recalls, the weight of memory carried in his words.

"The best meal was white rice with eggs. Many times we had only sugar water with a squeeze of lime; other times, nothing at all," he says, sighing with a quiet longing.

He goes on:

"When you need so many things, all kinds of dark thoughts cross your mind, and they plant deep insecurities. I used to think my parents were going to die, or fall ill. I would ask myself: if that happened, could I bear their absence?

"Sometimes I had to look after the younger ones. What worried me most was the time I came home from school, when there was usually nothing to give them to eat. I came to know need from a very young age, and it taught me how to walk across the embers life sometimes lays in your path. What my parents earned went to paying the rent for our little house and buying whatever food we could. It was a very hard situation — one we could only endure by the grace of God and by staying united as a family.

"Faced with so many difficulties, and without telling anyone, I put together a shoeshine box out of herring crates and went out into the street, determined to help support the household. I knew I was risking a stern scolding from my parents, who were always warning me about the dangers of the street. I would walk for hours and never feel tired, knowing I could contribute something, even a little, to the family's needs.

"I kept shining shoes in secret for a long time, until one day I spoke to my parents about it. I knew I wouldn't be spared a beating, but I managed to negotiate their permission to keep working — on the condition that I would not leave school," Joel told me, with a quiet pride.

It was through this work, in those days, that I came to know him. He went around with his cousin Joan. The two of them were a pair, ready to take on any work that might bring in a little money. Beyond shining shoes, they swept patios, took out the trash, helped out in people's houses, and even set up Christmas trees during the holidays. Their eyes spoke more than their mouths, and there was something in their bearing that revealed them for what they were: brave boys, carrying themselves like little men before their time.

"While my sisters went to school and looked toward their future, one of my brothers started working at City Hall. The youngest of us has epilepsy, and we had to manage his seizures at home. At my age, that was a lot to handle with my mother gone all day.

"Even so, things were going along, more or less, until I began to notice that my father's friends had a certain look about them — something connected to drug use. I was too young to see further than that, but something in me knew it wasn't right. I also saw that my father had more money in his hands and was carrying a gun — an expensive thing that, to me, seemed completely unnecessary.

"It wasn't long before my father was imprisoned for selling and using drugs. That morning, with the day's first heat already settling in, the police carried out a sudden raid on our house that woke us all. My siblings were beside themselves. My mother stood with her hands on her head. The neighbors watched the commotion. Everything was turned upside down in the search, and it ended with my father being taken away for a crime as shameful as it was punishable.

"My world collapsed. I had to hold myself together, being the eldest of the boys, but inside I felt undone. Until that day, my father had been a towering figure in my life, and to discover he had been mixed up in the underworld struck me at my core. Shame overtook me. I felt hopeless. I wanted to run away from the house, to disappear from myself.

"That moment drew a line through my life. It shattered my image of someone I had loved and admired so deeply — my father. Even now, it is hard for me to give shape to those memories. But the blow had to be faced, and we faced it.

"After that painful event, life grew harder for my mother. She had to look after us on even less, in a job that took up all her time. She would bring food to the prison for my father, though it had to be left at the guard house and she wasn't allowed to see him. Standing there with her, at my young age, so many questions pressed in on me: Why couldn't he come home with me? Why had he never said he was dealing drugs? What had become of that wise, upright father who didn't want me out working in the streets? All those questions crowded into my head at once.

"One day, on my way home, I got into a public car packed with people. The driver had the radio blasting, and I heard a piece of news that shook me. The inmates had erupted into fighting at Rafey, the very prison where my father was being held. The report was devastating. They said the men were fighting with knives, and that someone had been killed. I was terrified. I thought of turning back to be near my father, but I would have been left without the fare to get home, and I knew I wouldn't be allowed to see him in any case. The whole thing was a living nightmare for me.

"I would set aside part of what I earned shining shoes to help him, because in prison everything has a price: drinking water, cigarettes, a mattress to sleep on, even water to bathe with. Thank God, the time he served made him reflect on the danger of drugs — but that experience marked us forever.

"When you have a relative imprisoned for drugs, you never know how their associates may react. That's why I was always wary, alert to every detail at home. I was also afraid the police might come back for another raid, and that kept me on edge, as if it were my job to protect my family.

"On top of that, we carried the weight of a community that saw us as dangerous, simply because we were the children of a man already branded a drug trafficker. I remember the wounding mockery, the way the people in the neighborhood pointed at us. The sum of all those feelings became a heavy load on my back.

The helplessness that tormented me began to wear down my sense of self.

"Beyond the grace of God, my grandmother was my great source of strength. She was a woman of deep Christian faith, someone I had always admired. I would tell her my fears, my needs, the hard turns I was going through — moments she would use to teach me the essential values of life. She always assured me she would be with me, that I was not alone, and that lifted some of the weight from my heart. I remember her as a hardworking, honest woman. For many years, she made her living selling clothes on the street.

"By good fortune, we found a house very near hers. After much hard work she had managed to grow a well-tended garden in her yard, and she kept chickens and pigs as well, so there was always food enough for everyone — something that eased a need as urgent as hunger. In her embrace, I felt sheltered from every storm.

"Carrying all those mingled sorrows, I went on with my studies at Las Palmas Zeneyda Blanco School. My grades were very low because I couldn't concentrate, and I had no spirit to do my homework. As best I could, I made it to the third year of high school, which let me take technical and vocational courses.

"I think parents don't always realize the trauma their bad behavior can cause. In my case, what I have always rejected is more than the illegal drug trade and the dirty money it brings — it is the harm those substances do in other people's lives, often young people, even children, as I was at the time.

"All those tangled feelings about a father who had been everything to me filled those early years with bitterness and unease.

"The truth is, I was a working child out of necessity from the age of seven, and I took on whatever job I could, always avoiding anything that wasn't right. After I got my ID, I worked in three free-trade-zone companies in Santiago. Later I worked as a machine operator at a well-known tobacco company, and at another cigar factory in Tamboril, where I was in charge of raw materials. I also worked at City Hall as a 'utility' worker. In that job I taught myself to drive trucks, doing laps in the office parking lot. I went on to become my father's assistant — by then he had turned his life around and worked as a driver for that institution for several years.

"I always had dreams. One of them was to travel to the United States, and it seems God heard me. By a turn of grace, and through social media, I met Candie — a beautiful woman of elegant bearing and noble heart, who lives in the United States. We began a serious relationship, and I got to know her children online.

"The day I met her in person, I was captivated — by her beauty, but also by her kindness and her thoughtfulness. I had found my soulmate. I told her clearly who I was and what my intentions were. I introduced her to my family, and we spent time together for a good while until we decided to marry. We had Celeste — a daughter who smiles when the afternoon asks for her, whose eyes bring light into my heart. Her arrival strengthened our family here in Los Angeles, California, where we now live.

"When I arrived in the United States, I'll admit the feeling of statelessness hit me hard. It is something difficult to explain to anyone who hasn't lived it. It is a strange sensation — you feel yourself swaying in a void with your eyes wide open. But finding refuge in the arms of the woman I love made me feel blessed and fortunate, even after everything I had been through. Now I see it all as transformative — those experiences have made me stronger, and even freer," this young man concludes.

And so, all along the way, while others saw only the stigma he carried, the mark of his vulnerability, he acknowledged the wound but kept for himself the freedom to see it as a reason to become a better person and to clothe his heart in wisdom. What tormented his life for so long was enough to plant warnings within him — signs that still guide him today, helping him steer clear of the obstacles he has learned never to stumble over again.

What Joel has overcome, with such tenacity and courage, gives us hope. Perhaps without knowing it, Joel offers us a kind of manual, a humane perspective on how to face the swings and turns of life. In a way new even to him, he built — stone by stone, brick by brick — fortresses of dreams. And at a very young age, he chose paths that would lighten the heavy burden he had carried for so long.

The Pulse of the Streets

Through Andrés's story, Milagros de Jesús de Féliz illuminates a reality that unsettles us: the lives of those who grow up among traffic lights and the hardships that come too soon, in a world where our humanity is put to the test. Like so many others, Andrés meets life unsheltered by society, yet sustains it with faith, gratitude, and hope. It is a testimony that moves us and forces us to look more deeply.
José M. Antuñano

Early that morning, determined to be among the first in line, I went to the government offices to renew my passport. The day was just waking, and the plaza was filling with hurried footsteps. Among so many faces I caught sight of Andrés — whom I had known as a child, and who now stood before me a slender young man with a modern haircut and a steady gaze. We greeted each other with joy in our eyes, both of us glad for the chance to meet again after so many years.

He has eleven siblings, but as the eldest he had never felt like just another child among them. In a way, he had been the father to them all — a responsibility that drove him into the streets to work from very early on. Andrés used to sell avocados, oranges, and candy at a school in Hato del Yaque, the neighborhood where he grew up. He also sold whatever goods or seasonal fruit he could find along the city's busiest streets and avenues. I remember Andrés always telling us he wanted to be a teacher when he grew up.

Andrés has spent most of his life being reborn in hope, carrying in his noble heart a past heavy with hardship. His tireless cry for a more equal world has never gone quiet, and he is still set on bringing into the present what long ago went missing from his life.

"Ma'am, where have you been! It's so good to see you!" he said, with the same smile he had as a child. "I've been wanting to ask you something for a while. Are you friends with President Abinader? Could you tell him about the conditions we live in here at the traffic lights?"

"Andrés, you don't go easy on me — that question goes straight to the heart," I answered, a little evasively, leaving him room to say what was pressing on his wounded heart.

Wanting to show me what life is like at the traffic lights, he invited me to walk with him to the corner and share a freshly peeled orange — one of the kind he had been selling for so many years. I accepted, glad and at ease, and went with him to the intersection of those same three lights that, in their own way, had stolen his childhood.

As we walked, the traffic was heavy. The cars crawled along the overpass and the avenue, and the drivers' impatience showed in every maneuver, keeping time with the changing colors of the traffic light where Andrés had grown up.

Now under the full weight of the sun, we paused on one of the sidewalks at the intersection, and with the knowing slyness of someone shaped by the street, he said:

"If you want to know whether a country is poor, go and see what happens at its traffic lights. Around here, all you have to do is go by the Monumento a los Héroes at night and stop at any corner where there's a light. Those places will tell you exactly how poor we are — right then, right there, no surveys needed."

The red light brought the cars to a stop, and at once a swarm of makeshift vendors poured into the lanes with their wares. Their faces carried the rush of the day and the weight of life. Andrés explained that behind each of them was a different story, but every story came down to the same urgency: to survive, and to bring bread home to their families.

He described how the business of renting people with disabilities works — how they are placed at corners "to stir pity" and beg. Then, pointing with firm certainty, he said:

"You see that man pretending to be blind, with the child who begs on his behalf? He's not blind at all — he's a hustler who lives off begging, using kids as guides, and people believe him. And that little girl with the pigtails sitting on the curb selling cookies... look over at her mother on the corner. She's the one who sends her out there."

"We work seven days a week, weaving between the cars, under the sun, the rain, and the wind, in the middle of all this hopelessness," he told me, his skin weathered by the soot of the asphalt.

As I listened, I watched the corner fill with urgency. Oranges in buckets, pumpkin sold in chunks, guavas in mesh bags. A boy with Spanish limes in one hand and flowers in the other. On the median, a young woman held bottles of water and a silence that said more than what she was selling. A little farther on, an older man offered cashews strung together, and just beside him, another young man laid out phone accessories on a makeshift stand.

"See that, ma'am? This is where poverty lives. When I tell you the donkey is gray, it's because I've got the hairs right here in my hands!"

I tried to listen without interrupting. I gave myself over to watching that world so different from my own — a reality that wounds all of humanity.

"Thank you, ma'am. That's what I wanted to show you. And remember — if you ever do speak to the president, tell him to step out at a traffic light, so he can see for himself how we live here."

Andrés disappeared into the traffic, oranges in his hands and his dignity intact.

The light turned green. I crossed. He stayed.

I'm Alive out of Sheer Stubbornness

The author takes us by the hand of Daniel and leads us into the inferno of his early years, and one cannot tell which wounds more deeply in his story — the merciless violence he endured, or the admirable human quality of Daniel himself, expressed in his unwavering love for life, for his wife, for his children, and for the memory of departed friends whom he invokes as if they were saints in a heaven of his own.
Fr. Manuel Pablo Maza Miquel, S.J.

Daniel was barely seven, and wise beyond his years, when I first met him darting through the streets. He was a restless boy, with sparks in his eyes and hope asleep in his feet. Today, with the same smile that still carries the scent of his longings, he is thirty-six. By now he has been married for twenty-four years, is the father of five children, and the grandfather of two beautiful granddaughters.

If there is one thing I genuinely enjoy, it is sitting down with these boys and seeing them now as the men and women they have become. This time, Daniel and I reserved a table just for the two of us. There, between stories and memories, we raised our glasses to friendship and toasted the affection that came in time, choosing as our main course the gratitude that binds us.

Today, Daniel is a devoted father and a tireless worker who loves his children and honors the woman who has been his only companion in life. He is the fifth of ten siblings, born to four different fathers.

Even before he turned seven, his days were already spent in the streets, mostly around Parque Duarte and at the traffic light on Avenida Estrella Sadhalá. He remembers his friends from those days with nostalgia. The same asphalt swallowed most of them in the end. He told me their stories in detail — Rona *el Búcaro*, Papito, Juan Carlos, Orlando, Rafelito *Chichigua*, *el Chino*, *Bembe*, *Cuquín*, Kelin, and Magdalena. He also brought others back to mind: Alberto, Robinson, Chago *el Lince*, Toba *el Albino*, Samuel, Iván, *Buche*, Pablito, Óscar, Rafael, *el Colorao*, *Chiquito*, *el Capi*, and many more. Almost all of them came to tragic ends.

He learned to read and write through the educational programs at Acción Callejera, and he never attended any other school; what he had learned there, he believed, was enough to make his way in life. About school, he remembers always being in a hurry. In those years, he understood that spending a morning in class was both a waste of time and a luxury he couldn't afford.

"If I stayed in school for class, I had nothing to eat. Sitting there, I wasn't earning money to bring home. So first I survived, and only then did I think about school," he told me — a boy with courage in his blood and urgency in his decisions.

None of his siblings can read or write, he said, because school was never a priority in their household. His mother had never been to school herself, and his father had no interest in whether his children studied, and no real concern for them at all.

"I'm alive because I started a family when I was twelve, and I had my first child at thirteen," Daniel said, smiling the same smile he has carried since boyhood. "When I first found out, I thought it was a curse. But having a child so young is what made me work — honestly, hard, every single day — to lift my family up. I didn't want any of my children ever to need the street the way I did. Today I have my own home, and I work hard to be the kind of father I never had. I only saw mine once. He came to the house drunk and beat me without my ever knowing why. Thank God, I never saw him again. It was a bitter moment from my childhood that still echoes in my memory sometimes... But you don't give bad things any room in your head.

"My two oldest sons are married now, and both are responsible men. I have one in his second year of high school, and the one after him just graduated and wants to keep studying. The youngest is two — a child we hadn't been expecting. Because he came so long after the others, plenty of people advised us that the best thing was for my wife to end the pregnancy.

"I'll confess, ma'am — we even bought the bottle, the one that makes a woman lose the baby. But when I held that thing in my hands, I didn't see a bottle anymore. I saw the weapon I was about to use to kill my son. Right then, I decided he would be born.

"'I can't be the murderer of my own child,' I thought, and I threw the bottle into the brush. I felt that he wanted to live, and that he deserved to. People use all kinds of pretty words and find every excuse for killing children in the womb, but it is a crime. Today he is the joy of our home; there is so much light in his eyes. To take another life is cowardice, all the more so when that life is innocent. As a gift from God, Javier was born healthy, and we welcomed him with the same love with which we conceived him," he said, visibly happy with the decision he had made.

When he speaks of his family, his words seem to light up from within — full of gratitude to God for his children, for what he has been able to build, and for the good fortune that has followed him.

"I've been through a lot in the streets, ma'am, but thank God I've kept my hands clean. These days I have two jobs: I'm up at dawn parking cars at a well-known supermarket, and I also manage a group of rose vendors.

"I learned to arrange flowers from *el Capi*. He and I trained together at a flower shop and became experts at making rose arrangements. But diabetes cost him a leg, and after that he sank into a deep depression. His mind unraveled, and he stopped wanting to live. One Monday he didn't show up to work, and we found him dead in his room.

"The street swallows boys whole. My brother Pablito — we found him dead on the empty lot where the old Cine Doble used to stand. He'd just had gallbladder surgery, and a short while later, high on drugs, he was picked up by the police. He must have talked back, and they gave him a beating that ruined whatever was left of his health. Maybe, knowing he was going to die, he just let himself go out there in that empty lot. By the time we found him, the smell had already set in.

"*El Colorao* never grew up, no matter how much we tried to set him straight. He tried to break into a house twice. The second time, they killed him. Óscar — they took him down in the capital. He probably died fighting the same bad luck that had hounded him all his life. His life had always been hell, one long mess from start to finish.

"They doused Iván with diesel and burned him alive. And Samuel — my best friend — his own family never accepted him. He hanged himself in front of his oldest son.

"Elías... do you remember him, ma'am? We called him *el Tuerto*. He was good people. He was missing an eye he'd lost in a fight, because he was always quick to start one. He was living at a construction site with a Haitian man, and the bastard hacked him to death with a machete while he slept. Then he crossed the border, and no one ever heard from him again. Only three of us went to the funeral: Raúl, Orlando, and me.

"They took poor *Buche* down too, and he turned up dead. We only knew it was him by the tattoo on his ankle. Magdalena died of AIDS and left four children behind. Before she died, she asked us to look after them, and we placed them in a children's home, where they're being well cared for.

"They lured Richard out and killed him, then threw his body off the dry bridge on Yapur Dumit. Berto met just as cruel an end. For years he stole under orders from the police, until one day, in the precinct itself, fed up with being beaten, he confessed that he was doing it for the very officers who kept arresting him. That confession cost him his life. Afterward, the story they spread was that he had died in a shootout. Ma'am, that was a lie. I knew Berto well — he never even carried a knife. He was an old drifter, incapable of facing anyone down. He never listened to advice, and in the end the police themselves did him in. *Bembe* was good people, even with his reputation for snatching purses from women. At that, he was like a magician. He lost an arm in the same business he never gave up, and the police 'put a 29 on him.'

"When I think about all of them, I tell myself: I'm still alive out of sheer stubbornness.

"And the hardest part of all this is that, when you spend so much time cut off from your family, no one even misses you when they kill you, or when something happens to you. Months go by without seeing your own people. By the time they hear anything about you, you're already dead, or something big has happened — and most of the time, you face it on your own. The loneliness, the rejection — it drives some boys to the point where they don't want to live anymore. You have to be brave for this, ma'am... it isn't easy. You've got to be made of something solid.

"That's why I did everything I could to get out of the street and build my own little place in Hato del Yaque, where I come home to my family every day. For most people, that might just be routine. For me, having my own little place is a blessing."

When we said goodbye, we had run out of time. There were more moments to revisit, more boys to remember, more stories to gather — of those who had fought to survive in that battle that wears them down and consumes them.

Grateful to have found each other, we embraced with the strength of those who have survived. In the midst of so many absences, Daniel is still alive.

In his smile, there was room for all the ones who were gone.

And that is enough.

Let Us Change the Way We See

While he sold his body, Lucero tried to keep his heart safe beneath six letters for which the Real Academia de la Lengua Española lists eleven meanings. At the same time, Richard was building an identity we still struggle to accept. The author invites us to understand that to practice tolerance is to look inward with the gentleness those scissors never had, and with a collective love in league with goodness.
Daniela Cruz Gil

While the world marked the International Day for Tolerance, Santiago witnessed a scene out of Dante. A young man who lived in the streets was lynched without mercy. His death, as merciless as his life, became the smothered cry of those who have never been allowed to belong. On a day dedicated to respect for difference, Lucero became the victim of the very thing the world had spent that day claiming to defend.

Tolerance is respect for the beliefs, cultures, and opinions of others. And yet, in our society, words heavy with exclusion still circulate — xenophobia, discrimination, homophobia, and so many other forms of rejection that keep filling the headlines. We forget that every human being is, by definition, different. Prejudices forged in religion, culture, or gender keep us from valuing anything that does not fit our mold.

That is why I write about the brief and endlessly long life of this young man — a life marked by poverty and by a society that never guaranteed him even the basic rights of a dignified life.

He was born, lived, and died in the streets of La Yagüita de Pastor, in Santiago — a community where I worked for many years on behalf of children. Lucero was a restless, slight, good-natured boy with caramel-colored curls and lively eyes. A shy sweetness lived in his gestures, and when he spoke, certain feminine mannerisms came through, drawing merciless mockery from the other children, from neighbors, even from his own family.

His life was as sad as his death.

"He was a student in *Amigo de los Niños y las Niñas* — Friend of Boys and Girls — a program for children still too young for formal school," his teacher, Raquel, recalls with sorrow.

She and the other teachers knew how fragile his home life was, and they tried to help him. But the lack of love, the poverty, and the humiliations weighed more than any gesture of care. In his immediate family, prostitution was a means of survival, and his father never tried to stop it. Lucero suffered abuse and learned, far too young, to sell sex for money. He was singled out, discriminated against, and in the end, all of it drove him into the street.

The park became his home, and abandoned houses his shelter. There he slept, played, and faced the elements alongside others who lived the same fate. Carrying his wounds, he survived by selling flowers, begging, handing out flyers, sweeping yards, and running errands. He smiled, even in misery, as an act of resistance.

Though he grew up surrounded by violence, he was never violent. His heart was noble. Even in his last moments, as he lay dying from the scissor wounds, he forgave the man who had attacked him. Alone in the middle of a crowd, people filmed his agony to mock him on social media. Even so, Lucero spoke no words of hatred.

He lost his childhood, his innocence, his dignity — and even his name, because few knew he was called Richard Paulino. To everyone he was Lucero — a nickname he answered to with humility, even when others spoke it in mockery or contempt, as they so often did. When the news of his death spread, many exclaimed with relief: "Lucero's finally dead!" But his death left behind a bitter mirror — one that reflects the cruelty of a society that still has not learned to tolerate difference.

He bled to death on the pavement of indifference, in plain view of many, pleading, "Don't kill me!" No one came to help. He died with no mourner and no kin, forgiving those who beat him, while collective cruelty turned his agony into a digital spectacle.

Richard "Lucero" Paulino lived a life marked by exclusion and abandonment. But his story does not end with his death. It remains. It looks back at us from every act of exclusion, from every taunt dressed as custom, to remind us that true tolerance begins where indifference ends.

Where God Dwells

The author introduces us to Esmelda, who, in the midst of a hostile world, found her most sacred refuge in faith and work. Her story is an everyday miracle: a broken girl who, by God's strength, became a luminous and generous woman. She chose to be for other girls what no one had ever been for her. To read her is to find your way back to hope.
María Luisa Asilis

As I looked into her eyes — into the depths of an adulthood that had come too soon — I began speaking with her: a young woman already carrying the full weight of womanhood, with long hair, a graceful figure, and carefully kept hands. There was a story in her gaze that demanded to be told. She wanted to tell me how God had watched over her, and to bear witness to her faith for other girls who might feel just as alone and unprotected.

After we greeted each other and settled in, ready to share a cup of coffee that steamed like her own soul, my guest began to speak of her past, almost without pause and without detours. First she drew a deep breath. Then she gave thanks for the chance to empty her sorrows and, in the same breath, to reaffirm her gratitude to God for the gift of life. And so, with her eyes fixed on the floor, she began.

"As a child, many years ago, I went to the Acción Callejera programs. I never knew my father, and I never asked about him. I was raised by an aunt on my mother's side who ran what was really a brothel — a cabaret dressed up as a *colmado*, the small corner store, where they sold beer. In the back there were five rooms where couples, while they drank, arranged their encounters.

"In that same place, my mother went off with the men, and I grew up watching her tangle herself up with them in the shadows of that unforgettable red light that barely lit those small rooms. She lived right nearby — always exhausted, always irritable, with that persistent smell about her of hangover, rum, sweat, tobacco, and neglect. It was a heavy mixture, hard to erase from memory; above all, that pungent breath of hers, like burnt rope. The endless nights, along with the alcohol and drugs, ate away at her teeth, and I remember her face always worn down, marked by fatigue and lack of rest.

"My mother and my aunt lived in a foul mood and fought over anything. I grew up hearing curses and insults — what they hurled at each other and what filled the brawls that broke out in that so-called 'lively' place. In all of that, I don't remember a single tender gesture from either of them. Mom never held me with affection; as far as I can recall, she never carried me in her arms, and once I was older, she didn't look after me either.

"She was diabetic, and because she neglected her health, they cut off first a toe on her right foot, then the entire foot, and over time her leg up to the thigh. That misfortune, which slowly consumed her, she took out on me — and sometimes on my aunt as well.

"When I turned nine, my aunt's husband told me I was old enough to start working in the business. He told me I'd had enough school, but I wouldn't accept that, because school was my one chance, my one hope. It was the only way I could get away, even for a few hours, from the music that blasted at full volume from early in the morning, and I remember that the racket only died down well into the small hours of the night.

"I refused, and as revenge — on top of trying to assert his control over me — my uncle by marriage tried to abuse me sexually on several occasions, before I had even turned ten. The last time, he gripped my arms with such force that he broke one of my wrists, and I had to spend several months in a cast to recover.

"I ran away without looking back and went to my grandmother's house, hoping she would help me, without telling her what had happened. Now I think she probably sensed it.

"My grandmother couldn't take me in because of her own precarious situation, so I went out into the city to look for work, but I found nothing that brought in enough for me even to eat. Besides, I didn't want to leave school. The only places where I could earn a little money were Parque Duarte, the traffic-light corners, or the Monumento a los Héroes — three places far too dangerous for a girl my age. It was during that time that I came to know the Acción Callejera programs.

"At the Foundation they were good to me. Back then, Acción Callejera worked out of a building near an abandoned school, in the area around the Cathedral.

"One day, while I was sitting on a bench in the park, a man came up to me saying he was my uncle, but I read the lie in his eyes. Thankfully, I never saw him again. He had the look of a lottery vendor — he carried one of those wooden boards with bills and betting slips clipped to it for people to see. Like him, plenty of others propositioned me for sex in exchange for money. I was wary of every offer, even though I was in such need.

"One day, alone and exhausted, I went into Iglesia La Altagracia. I felt a great sense of relief and even managed to settle myself behind the church gate. I fell into a dead sleep right there and slept the whole night through, until early in the morning, when I was woken by a harmless vagrant who also slept somewhere nearby. I remember that moment like a nightmare.

"And so I spent some time looking for work until I found a live-in job down on Calle 16 de Agosto. They treated me well, but the lady of the house died, leaving only her son, whom I didn't trust. So I went out looking for work again and found a place in Los Pepines, at a beauty salon. There I began to find my footing. Even though all I earned was the tips clients gave me, they let me go to school in the afternoons and to Mass on Sundays.

"I have to say the owner was a good woman; she just had days when no one could stand her. That's why I left, to work at another salon in the same neighborhood. The owner there already knew my story. She helped me, and even gave me a place to stay.

"With that support, I made it to my second year of high school and trained at the Academia de Belleza Miss Key, where I specialized in hair care and qualified as a manicurist as well. Later, I found a better opportunity at another salon in Los Jardines, and since I was earning more, I could afford to rent a room of my own. You see all kinds of things in those boarding houses. Men can be shameless, and I noticed there was a sick one who liked to spy on me when I bathed. One night, before dawn, he broke the lock and tried to force his way into my room with bad intentions.

"I screamed with all my strength, and the neighbors came running to confront him. The next day, everyone looked at me as though I had done something wrong, and I felt deeply ashamed. Feeling singled out, I left for San Francisco de Macorís, to stay with a friend I had met at the academy. I helped her at her beauty salon, and together the two of us built the business up.

"That was when I met a good man, and we married just the two of us, with no one else there. God blessed me with two beautiful daughters whom I care for with devotion. I have a thriving beauty salon now with eighteen employees, all of whom I treat with dignity.

"I belong to the Legion of Mary, in the Catholic Church, and together with my husband and daughters we have grown in faith. I can tell you with certainty that God has not left me alone — that I came to know pain, and everything a girl feels when she is violated and left without protection."

Listening closely to Esmelda, I see how being an unprotected child means inhabiting a world where danger wears the face of family, where home itself can become a minefield, and childhood a ground you step on with fear. It is learning to defend yourself without weapons, to silence what torments you inside, and to run with a broken soul in search of a refuge that never quite arrives. That defenselessness trails after you like a shadow — surfacing in nightmares, in remembered scents, and in the silence of those who should have cared.

And yet this woman — the fragile girl I once knew — did not remain in the abyss. With grit, faith, and dignity, she wove her own destiny. And though no one held her up when she most needed it, she chose to hold others up, and that choice speaks to her goodness. At the same time, her journey reminds us of a painful truth: *no girl should ever have to be that brave just to survive.*

MURALS OF COLOR

In the streets, too, there are murals that delight us. For the children who wander them, happiness walks barefoot and arrives unannounced. It shows itself in a knowing glance, in a shared laugh, in the smallest gesture that reminds them they, too, have a right to joy.

And when someone stops to look at them with respect, to listen without judgment, murals of color are painted — illuminating their hearts and, along the way, our own

Pieces of Joy

In this story, the author brings us close to Juan Oreja's friend, the boy who played the flute — an instrument that, like him, had its openings. Through the flute's holes and the child's wounds came the music that gave them their "piece of joy." "Saved from the streets"... his beautiful destiny was etched into his very name. Would you like to know what it is?

María Consuelo Yunén

Giving in to our children's contagious excitement, we went out as a family to a well-known international pizza chain on a particularly busy night. Several families were waiting their turn — some seated, others standing — while restless children darted between the tables and the servers hurried past, doing their best to keep up with a packed house.

We were number eight, and just as we were about to leave, a kind young man encouraged us to stay. There was a special line, he explained, reserved for guests our age — a discreet but unmistakable reminder of the passing years.

A few minutes later we were shown to a table, where a simple floral arrangement had been placed at the center. Pleased, we placed our order.

Looking around, I noticed ours was the only table with flowers. We were almost certain there was something behind their insistence and the quiet privilege they had given us, though we couldn't imagine what. I even thought, with a touch of irony, that being old had its advantages.

A very polite waiter came over and asked for our name, so the order could be identified when the pizzas were ready. It seemed reasonable enough, and we gave it. We ordered our drinks, and not long after, a young man approached — smiling broadly, his manners impeccable. Instead of calling us up to collect the order, he brought the pizzas to the table himself, with a certain formality.

"Good evening, ma'am. I'm Moisés, the Cibao regional manager for this chain, and it's my pleasure to bring you your order."

I noticed that this handsome young man — every inch the elegant executive, with his impeccable white shirt and refined manners — looked me in the eye with a particular brightness, his smile open and clear.

"Oh, thank you so much!" I said, a little taken aback by such kindness.

He served us with care, arranged my children's plates, and turned back to me, a quiet joy shining in his eyes. Then he said:

"Ma'am, for many years, when I was a boy, I lived in the streets, and I knew you back then. I'm Moisés *el Gambao*, from the little school in Hoyo de Puchula, a friend of Juan *Oreja*."

Those words moved me deeply. I fell silent, lost in memory. Stirred, I recognized in him the child he had once been — so different from the dignified young man now standing before me. I worked hard not to stumble over my words. What came to mind first was that fragile, small, thin Moisés, while the man now speaking to me looked healthy and strong, his arms as solid as an athlete's, very tall, with the firm presence of a grown man. From that boy, two things remained untouched: his smile, every tooth flashing in the light, and his thick eyebrows.

It all happened so quickly, and in truth I can't remember ever feeling a deeper satisfaction. Still a little unsettled, I tried to summon more details about that boy who, standing before me now, was nothing short of a miracle. And then the image returned: that child with a shoeshine box strapped halfway up his leg, a cap pulled low over his ears, selling newspapers around Parque Duarte. He had a natural gift for persuasion, a touch of mischief about him. At the traffic lights he would draw passersby in by calling out tragic headlines for events that had never actually happened. I remembered, too, how much he loved to play the flute, and how he knew every note of the national anthem.

The pepperoni pizza faded into the background. All I could manage to say was how much he had grown. Seeing him now — a successful young man — I felt a flutter of butterflies in my chest. Emotion blurred my vision, and the urge to embrace him was impossible to resist, as though that single gesture might somehow bridge the barefoot child and the polished manager standing before me. I looked at him for a long moment, taking the full measure of this man of real stature who, against every prediction, had carved out a place for himself in a world that had so often tried to shut him out. Amazed, I thought of how the threads of life weave together until they place us before tangible miracles — miracles that grant us moments of fullness.

His presence alone was testimony enough to clothe the night in eternal gratitude.

A Carnival Danced Right[1]

The author surprises us with a Fairy Godmother who, with golden curls and blue eyes, arrived as if dropped from the sky — with a touch that turned straw into wheat, and the cars of Santiago into magical carriages filled with little princes, barefoot and longing to slip on their glass sneakers at the most unforgettable, life-changing street celebration of their lives.
Maridalia Hernández

The boys who worked the streets, used to the heat of the asphalt and the exhaust of passing cars, felt that February had brought them a small miracle. They were dreaming of a different kind of day — joyful, almost magical. In their imaginations they had become the owners of the carnival, dreaming of cardboard floats and brightly colored hats, certain that, at last, the world belonged to them.

It was a time much like the present — the world had moved into the second month of 2007. Santiago pulsed on every corner with boys putting in long days at the traffic lights. Among them were windshield washers, street vendors, shoeshiners, and girls who sold flowers — even, at times, their own bodies — for a

1 Originally published in the anthology *Cuentos y poesías* (Chile: Editorial Factor Literario, 2026).

few pesos. Most came from impoverished neighborhoods on the south side of the city and made their way into the urban center, where they took whatever work they could find: enough to survive, and enough to bring something home.

Tired of being rendered invisible, the boys felt an urgent need to take part in something public — an occasion where their presence could not be overlooked, where they could finally give a knowing wink to the very city that had been pretending not to see them.

To make it happen, they decided to enter the city's carnival — a popular celebration bursting with color, movement, and traditional characters that still parades through towns across the country during the month that marks our independence. Without preamble or debate, they agreed unanimously on what to call their *comparsa*: *Los Limpiabotas de Acción Callejera* — the Acción Callejera Shoeshiners.

With the instinct only the street can give, they chose Aida María Fernández to lead their unlikely comparsa. There could not have been a better choice. She had always stood with this group, and she brought with her a solid grounding in the arts. She was a free spirit, an artist by vocation, an explorer of every form of artistic expression since her earliest years.

Versed in many disciplines, Aida María was blonde, her eyes the soft green of hope, her gaze lit by a sense of justice, her heart wide enough for laughter, tenderness, and the whole carnival. Her hair, golden then, danced in the wind, while her soul — made of watercolor — gave itself without measure to the dreams of others, as if they were her own.

Her many-sided gifts made it possible to lead that small army of boys hungry for direction. Through that shared energy she drew out in them the skill they needed to dance with rhythm, discipline, and a touch of magic — without losing the joy that belongs to carnival.

When we met with Aida María to lay out the plan, we watched her eyes light up in the same colors as the festival. The spark of the dream caught at once, as if even the sequins had heard the agreement. Brimming with enthusiasm, she embraced the project, supported by a team of experienced educators who, for years, had been working alongside this remarkable group.

Like a fish in water, she began the rehearsals, imagining how that platoon of shoeshiners — brown and black ink staining their hopeful souls — would step into the parade.

A teacher whose heart was kneaded from bread and cinnamon, she slipped the rules into her pockets and let her imagination run free. And so she put together a magical, one-of-a-kind comparsa, with multicolored costumes that became creatures of fable and fantastical figures from some roadside tale.

Most of the boys in the parade were children who worked in the streets of Hato del Yaque — some part of a sports league, others who came into the city center on their own. All of them had been working since they were very young, on long schedules. Rehearsals had to be arranged around their hours, not ours.

Her memories still take flight whenever we return to that strange float: a replica of an enormous shoeshine box, built especially for the King of the Shoeshiners — His Imperial Majesty, Cucharimba!

This well-known and gifted magician accepted at once. Besides the heart of colored cardboard he wore on his chest, he had once, in his early years, been a shoeshiner himself.

Cucharimba played his part masterfully. He carried scepter and crown, and a royal cape adorned with a wide array of shining ornaments that flirted with the sun — as if, that afternoon, the sun itself had decided to crown him. At his side stood Her Highness, Princess Anabel I, a respected lawyer for the people, and Prince Alberto, a beloved little imp with eyes the color of the sun, who had been living in the streets since the age of three.

And then the magic happened.

They burst into the street like a miracle, dressed in dreams, their costumes embroidered with hope. On their chests they carried reclaimed dignity; in their eyes, the brightness of those who, at last, knew themselves to be seen.

They wore black cardboard hats, the crowns rising tall as towers of dream; garlands that still smelled of December; cheap fair-day shoes bought with street-earned coins; and paper ties that flapped like flags.

On their hands, white gloves bright as childhood; vests patched together from scraps of dignity; bracelets in impossible colors, made from the same cardboard that had once been thrown away.

Some carried the air of magicians; others wore the masks of warriors. Some were princes of neighborhoods without thrones; others, urban sprites with sunlit faces and voices made for refrains.

The crowd watched in awe — some with tenderness, all of them, at last, with their eyes open.

"Lechón cuajao, amarillo y colorao, brinca en la calle de lao a lao," they sang, while the city seemed to wake with every beat of an improvised drum.

"We won first prize in the Fantasy category!" Aida María said, her eyes shimmering like tulle.

They handed us twenty thousand pesos, which covered part of the costs. But the true gift was something else: the boys felt like the protagonists of a spectacle made with respect and pride. Surrounded by floats, whips, *vejigas*, and masks, they received the ovation of a crowd amazed by the miracle of their being there.

To celebrate, they threw a party — *de apaga y vámonos*, the kind that burns bright and unforgettable. From that celebration came new troupes, like *Ganaron las Águilas*, also recognized for its creativity, featuring *el Aguilita* — Jochy Taveras, who had come up through the educational programs of Acción Callejera.

Some time later, I sat down with Aida María to remember that adventure. We shared coffee at the home of Carolina Pérez — another fairy godmother to the boys. As she stirred sugar into her second cup, she seemed to be stirring memory along with it: those days when she rode happily atop the float, at the foot of the Monumento.

"With them, it's possible to dream," she would say. "We need to walk beside them. It is only right to honor the bravery and courage with which they meet each day."

Not long ago, Aida María left us. But somewhere inside February, when the carnival shakes the city again, her watercolor soul parades once more alongside the children of the traffic lights. In every improvised drum, in every ribbon that defies the wind, her deep conviction still beats: that joy, too, is an act of justice.

And that was her legacy.

The Bus of Life

A journey into the heart of the mountains, made to lavish care — to serve as a balm, a breath of fresh air, a touch of tenderness — on a group of working boys and girls. The author's loving voice gathers the scents and the beauty of that place and shapes them into a gesture of release and consolation for these vulnerable children.
Sally Rodríguez

It was five in the morning when the "bus of life" pulled up in the still-drowsy heart of Santiago's historic center. The day of the trip to the mountains had finally come — an educational outing organized for twenty-five working boys and teenagers. Many of them lived much of their lives in the streets; others endured the punishing work of child labor in mechanic shops, on construction sites, or washing windshields; and others still begged at the traffic lights.

Their days made no room for rest, for play, for joy. Their childhoods were spent surviving rather than dreaming. But that morning, as they climbed onto the bus, they discovered that a place had been set aside for them too — up in the mountains, a place that promised to give them back their smiles.

Dawn was barely stirring; the moon had already gone to her rest, and the stars lingered overhead, holding their breath as they watched the boys come hurrying toward Parque Duarte, full of excitement. Some came from the Hospedaje Yaque; others appeared from different corners of the city. They came in from every direction, carrying nothing but a plastic bag for luggage and a joy too big for their faces to hide.

It was summer, and the boys chosen for the trip had moved up to the next grade. Some had not, but they had done everything they could to stay in school, and that, too, was honored. Others had been recognized for their service or their conduct. For all those efforts, they had earned this trip as their reward.

The bus of life would carry us, for one weekend, to La Molino Blanco — a great country house under a four-sloped roof, ringed by a natural belt of rivers, neighbor to Loma Novillero in the very heart of Villa Altagracia.

In that magical place, we toasted with coconut water poured into cups carved from the coconut's own shell, simply for the joy of being there. Alongside it came oranges, juice pressed from lemons picked in the yard, wild avocados, sugarcane, and produce gathered right where we stood.

The team of educators at Acción Callejera spent months mapping out a program of activities for those three days. Right up to the moment of boarding, everything had its order. From the time the bus left Santiago until it reached La Molino Blanco, the ride itself became a space for reflection — on the importance of helping others, of giving thanks, of practicing empathy and nurturing friendship, among other lessons that wove learning into play.

The distance between the city and the country house unfolded through educational activities and games for that small army of boys who, day after day, left their hopes behind on the pavement. Arrival had its own rules, and the stay itself, carefully arranged, sought to tattoo onto each child an unforgettable experience of love.

The supplies were many and had to be carried on our shoulders, since the bus could not make it all the way to the house. The effort itself became a lesson in solidarity, an awareness of others' needs, deepening their sense of belonging to the group and their willingness to share in a different kind of weekend.

The hill was steep and long, but the certainty of joy waiting just ahead lightened the climb.

Sweaty and tired, we made our way through the cool rustle of the orange groves. Along the way we knocked down Spanish limes and lemons, and tore ripe bananas from their bunches. We slipped beneath the passion fruit vines, playing at "the curtains of the palace," and for a moment we were all children again. We dipped our feet in the streams, washed our faces, and shook off the dust of the road. And in quiet complicity with the boys, the wind — always the first to arrive — brought us the scent of oregano, like part of a welcome arranged just for us.

Far off, we could make out the roof of the house, set in the middle of a green carpet that had made peace with the pines and that, over the years, had become sister to the many varieties of male ferns standing guard around it. It was a place out of a dream, set in the very neighborhood where that loving God lives, watching over every child who lives and sleeps under the open sky.

Once at the house, some of the boys could hardly believe the place was meant for them — that there, no one was a shoeshiner or a windshield washer, that we were all equal: the boys, the assistants, the psychologists, the educators alike. We all shared the same charge: to set aside our usual roles and let ourselves be happy.

The first task was to unload everything: costumes, wigs, ties, food, tents, sleeping mats — anything that might let the imagination take flight. The point was to enjoy ourselves.

Once everything was in place, everyone joined in to cook the day's stew, though the celebration had long since begun in the natural pool, where cool currents ran between crotons and flame trees. A pool reserved just for them felt like too much luck, more than the boys could quite believe.

By midafternoon we would head out to forage for fruit. Sitting in circles, we ate our snacks and talked about life, while the boys and the older ones told their stories. Some of those stories made us laugh; others were so hard they called for an embrace. What mattered in that playful moment was the sharing, the enjoyment, and the chance to set down some of their grief — to leave it right there, in that place, lightening their shoulders.

Each day brought its own theme: self-care, resilience, how to handle the harmful temptations within reach, and ways to face the violence in the communities where they lived — along with whatever else surfaced as they wove together the stories of their lives, marked by hard labor before its time, by violence, and by many kinds of abuse.

Between stories and jokes, we made the most of the last light of the afternoon, until dinnertime came and each one performed his role to the letter.

Then night arrived. A clear sky and a clean moon settled over the treetops and washed the valley in silver, marking the start of a new joy. In that stillness, with the steady song of the cicadas and the night birds, our hearts held in a tender warmth and our souls full of gratitude, we would begin "the nights of theater."

Those performances were cultural spaces filled with joy, improvisation, applause — and with moments of deep reflection. Gifted young actors stepped bravely onto that imagined stage, beneath spotlights that existed only in our hearts and that yet all of us could see lighting up the gallery of the house.

Theater became an extraordinary channel for them to bring their stories to life and make sense of their daily reality. The themes worked through during the day came alive at night, before an attentive audience that learned alongside them.

Each educator stayed with a group, and each group worked on a theme: violence in the home, street fights, dropping out of school, conflicts between teachers and students, the right to an education, punctuality, street leadership and positive leadership, among others. With whatever they could pull from the trunk of odds and ends, and with whatever the land around them offered, they assembled costumes and characters, and chose a master of ceremonies — the perfect role for getting past stage fright — whose job it was to call up the applause and to introduce, with solemnity and imagined fanfare, the stars of the night.

Iván was the king, with a broomstick for a scepter and a crown cut from crate cardboard. *El Bolo* was the prince, in a red wig and banana leaves tied at his waist. Frank Junior, the king's son, was wrapped in a checkered tablecloth, his eyes shining like beacons. Rudy played the grumpy grandfather, his hair whitened with flour, a sheet falling all the way to his feet. That was how the dialogues came to life — drawn from their own experiences and delivered with a truth that needed no rehearsal.

I am still moved when I remember Pedrito playing a violent father, in a faded suit, a belt in his hand ready to strike. And the mother — beaten down by poverty, with nothing to feed her children — pushing them out into the street, while every morning she entrusted them to God.

Another striking scene showed how drugs were peddled out of the *colmado*, the small corner store on the block. Each performance opened a space for reflection and helped the psychologists understand the realities of these children's lives more deeply.

Every group worked with devotion, but the most intense were the ones that took on family violence and street fights — perhaps because those were the conflicts that most threatened their lives.

At the end, they reflected on what they had learned, and from those reflections came the themes for the next day. The audience applauded, the actors signed autographs, and, between laughter and silence, the boys found a place where they could empty out their stories.

And in the end, amid costumes and shared emotion and joy, a meaningful celebration would unfold — enamel mugs raised, full of steaming tea brewed from leaves picked in the yard, toasting the simple good fortune of being together.

When it was time for sleep, each one knew where he would lie down. His mat might be in a tent, on a balcony of the house, or — if he was lucky — on one of the big beds inside. The favorite spot was the second-floor balcony, where under the moon the mountains seemed to converse, offering the boys an unforgettable sight.

The next day brought hikes, board games, baths in the rivers, and walks down to the Zumbón, the swimming hole that always welcomed them. We also climbed up to camp at a summit that already felt like ours. There, seated on dry logs, we brewed the best coffee at dawn and gave thanks for so much green folded into so few days. We christened that sacred place "El Alto Palatinado," and amid that thick green canopy, for a moment, we felt like princes and princesses.

The activities went on as planned, but the most unforgettable of them all happened on the second night of that trip. The boys sat in a circle in the yard, with the team of educators. Each was given a sheet of paper and a pencil and was asked to draw, write, or speak about all the sorrows kept in his heart. They knew those stories would live only until that night — that, right there, the stories were to be handed over to the fire, watched as they burned, and forgotten forever. It was a pact.

One by one, the boys began to tell stories from their lives — stories in which mistreatment, humiliation, abuse, poverty, inequality, and injustice were the central characters. Beneath the timid light of a waning quarter moon, they wept with their whole bodies, anguish written across their faces, like people pulling something up from the very viscera of their conscience. When one of them could not go on, the others would close around him in an embrace and give him the strength to keep emptying his soul. We spent long hours in that hard group therapy — one that eased their hearts and wrung out mine.

The team of psychologists and educators took the lead, urging them to let go of all those burdens from the past. Meanwhile, other educators had kept three fires going for some time. Into one of them, the boys threw the papers where they had drawn or written their lives, with the promise that those wounding events would no longer trouble them. It was a way of exorcising the hard ordeal they had carried on their backs. In that fire, the flames burned red-hot with each sorrow given up, each story of suffering pulled from the deepest place in their hearts.

Over a second fire, hot chocolate made with water simmered with ginger. At a third, a bonfire fed with mountain wood, the boys roasted marshmallows skewered on long ribs cut from coconut fronds, to go with the warm chocolate that soothed their souls. With their spirits lighter and their tears dried by the heat, they took in the moment with less sorrow on their shoulders and a new hope to meet what waited for them.

And I, who am neither educator nor psychologist, gave myself over to being a student of these boys, in awe of the courage and the bravery with which they kept going. I learned so much from their stories that, without any fear of being wrong, I bear witness: every one of them is still my teacher in life.

On the third day, it was time to leave. We came down the hill with steady smiles and lighter loads on our backs. We had been given three days of grace, a gift from the boys themselves.

On the way down, the air was thick with the scent of oregano, though this time it smelled different to us. The rivers stepped aside as a courtesy. The sky bore witness to our happiness. And the branches of the pines applauded as they bade farewell to these boys who ask for nothing more than a little dignity and respect for their most basic rights.

Though the following Monday would send them back to the streets and to washing windshields at the traffic lights, they carried in their hearts the joy that La Molino Blanco had given them — that place which, by the light of the moon, took an oath to keep watch over their stories and to hold, like a sacred chest, the truth of their lives.

JUST AROUND THE CORNER

We keep walking together, and at every turn fragile lives appear before us — children exposed, far too early, to danger and abandonment. They move through the streets with instinct as their only defense and with a courage that astonishes, the very courage they have to spare and that so many of us lack.

Some voices are still holding on; others were lost in the trying. Each story leaves a mark that forces us to look squarely at an uncomfortable truth. No childhood should have to grow up alone and unprotected

Jochy, el Aguilita

The author tells us that Jochy's life has been a steep climb, but the road has revealed his resilience, his gift for adaptation, his extraordinary survival. The joy he radiates to the crowds rises from the same inner strength that carries him through every trial, casting his work ethic and his example onto everyone around him. And as in baseball, the game isn't over till it's over. Jochy still has several innings left to play.
Hamlet Otáñez

There are stories that read as if they were written in sweat and hope. Lives born on the corners of the barrios, where dreams tend to fall asleep early and only a few decide to wake them. One of those stories is Jochy's — the mascot of the Águilas Cibaeñas, a man who learned to fly with the wings life lent him, and to show that even from the deepest alley you can still see the sky.

Sitting down with Jochy is like opening a book written in his own hand, where every page bears the fruit of an educational program designed for the most vulnerable children and young people. Back in the eighties, Jochy was one of the program's pioneers, when it was being run in an alley by the Escuela Colombia, in the very heart of Santiago's historic center.

As an alum of Acción Callejera, Jochy embodies the noblest result of an educational initiative that transformed lives marked by inequality. To speak of him would take several volumes — his whole life is a lesson in coming through.

Talking with Jochy, no nickname strikes me as more fitting for this well-known, well-loved figure who, for more than twenty-five years, has been cheering on and charming the fans of the Águilas Cibaeñas.

He was born in 1967, "in the analog era," as he likes to say with a smile, into a family of four boys and two girls, raised under the firm and loving care of his grandmother doña Rosa, in the heart of barrio Pekín.

"To be born in a barrio in this country is an education in itself," he says, his tone reflective. "From there, you see everything, and you learn a great deal about life. You learn to value people's hunger to get ahead, and the laughter that rises right in the middle of want. On the corners, you learn to pick out the very sound of everyday life — the music from the *colmado*, the lament of poverty that is never absent, the advice of the doñas, the customs and rituals of the neighbors.

"From a young age, I was restless, full of energy, a dreamer. I did theater, I took part in youth groups at the Catholic Church, and I was already showing the makings of a community leader.

"I was a shoeshiner, a newsboy, and I worked at every honest trade that could help me get ahead. That's how I came to Acción Callejera, at the end of 1988.

"Barely twenty-one, without having finished primary school, with a child on the way, I arrived at Acción Callejera. I was caught up in everything that was happening day after day in the barrios, and I was looking for work, for some compass to steady me. It was a hard time. I felt the world coming down on me with the responsibility of supporting my wife and my unborn son — *a mano pelá*, as we say, with nothing in hand.

"That was how I found Acción Callejera, an organization with no roof and no walls. All it had was a few sturdy wooden stools — the kind shoeshiners use — and the dry trunk of a tree we'd picked up in the small plaza beside the Cathedral. That trunk stayed with us, and in its own way, it schooled us for life. Irenarco, the director, taught us that the trunk stood for each one of us: if we cared for it and dressed it with something, it stopped being a dry piece of wood and became a symbol of dignity. That was how we learned that, just like that trunk, we could build a new life out of something many people thought worthless — but that, in truth, held great value. 'Remember,' Ardila used to tell us, 'dignity is something you carry in your soul.' He was certain no one could ever take it from us.

"Irenarco Ardila was a teacher of life for me. With him, I learned how to learn.

"In that trunk, we planted little seedlings in recycled tin cans, each one with a name, a quality, and a purpose. Day by day, we gave life to that trunk, until we could see ourselves in it, inside and out. Through those ideas, we began to understand dignity, responsibility, and the chance to become lives that society could call worthy.

"In one of the cans we planted *recaíto* — Caribbean cilantro. In that little plant we discovered something useful: it gave off scent, color, and flavor. We put a sign on it that said 'Life has a scent' — and, if you tend to it, it smells of something good. In another we planted small tomatoes, and we labeled it 'Gratitude.' That one taught us to give thanks for life, for the sky we could see, for being able to walk, for the little tomato we once harvested, and above all, for being part of that new family of boys raised by the streets. And that's how it was. Even now, when I see the boys who made it through, we embrace each other like family.

"At Acción Callejera, the days were simple, but everything had its meaning.

"For breakfast we had bread with salami when things were going well, and bread with tomato sauce when money was tight. Everyone chipped in a peso, fifty cents, or whatever they could. When someone had nothing, he helped by sweeping the place, preparing breakfast, or washing the dishes. The point — the lesson — was that all of us have something to give. That taught us that, together, we could reach what we set out to do, that there was no need to beg in the street, and that we could build bridges of support, one for another.

"I remember, with great respect, doña Vilma Guzmán Taváres, who lived close to the park, on a street that has since been absorbed into the Cathedral grounds. Every afternoon she would open her living room to us and bring out the best fresh juices. In that generous living room, we would sit and listen to maestro Ardila and tell him what had happened to us the day before. The boys who slept in the streets would speak their feelings out loud. Irenarco took that solemn, very private moment to ask us how we could learn from what had happened to us the day or the night before. It was an exercise in dignity, in growth, in awakening to ourselves.

"In those talks, kinship and respect took root.

"Trust and support began to rise up between us — something that filled in what we lacked. All those activities built up our self-esteem and made us feel like princes chosen by God to enjoy life. It prepared us to face the dangers of the street with sharp wits, and to tell good from bad. Through different teaching tools, Irenarco gave us a kind of symbolic backpack — for holding up against hard times and learning to 'eat through' whatever life put in front of us. Seen from that angle, the world looks different — and that way of seeing helped me become the man I am today.

"All those lessons prepared me emotionally to step out onto a stadium in front of thousands of people, and when that happens, I see them all as accomplices in joy, as friends of my own.

"After everything I had learned with Irenarco, he gave me the chance to become an educator at Acción Callejera — an honor I'll be grateful for as long as I have life left in me. That position gave me the privilege of traveling, of training in Puerto Rico alongside boys living in the streets. I also trained in Bolivia in non-formal education, and did fieldwork at the youth services center there. That trip, I recall, was my first time setting foot in the United States.

"Once I was an educator, I finished high school, and later I trained for five years as a puppeteer at the Centro de la Cultura, with Acción Callejera's sponsorship, so I'd have more tools as a street educator. With training in those areas, I gave workshops in different parts of the country — both as a puppeteer and in non-formal education. I have very special memories with the young people from barrio Guachupita and from many other barrios in Santiago.

"With Irenarco, I learned the hermeneutics of the traffic lights, and together with other educators we mapped the city — corner by corner, every spot where the boys who worked the streets gathered. They taught me another rhythm of days, another way of seeing life.

"I trained as an electronics technician at Infotep, looking ahead to other paths in life. I also took courses at PUCMM on Dominican popular culture as it lives in the barrios, which became the foundation for my work with the young people.

"I came out with a master's degree without a diploma," he says, laughing, "but with a human education no university can give you."

He remembers, with gratitude, Sheila and Cecilia Gossetti — and above all his teacher Irenarco Ardila and Ardila's wife, Delia Gutiérrez de Ardila. She became a guide, a mother, a compass for his personal growth.

"Delia was a blessing. She was always there, with the right word and a look that lifted you up. From the Ardilas, I learned what it means to walk beside others with tenderness and steadiness."

From those years, he still carries many companions in memory: Juan *Oreja*, Rafael, Alvin, Adelso, Hermógenes, Juan *el Mujeriego*, *el Peje*, Robinson, Isidro, *el Ruso*, Gabriel, Orlando, Iván, Javier, Samuel — some are living, others the earth has taken, he says, but every one of them left a mark.

With all that experience behind him, Jochy felt the time had come to fly.

"I knew I had potential, but I didn't know where to point it. Until, twenty-five years ago, I was offered the role of mascot for the Águilas Cibaeñas. Moving my body, lifting the crowd, lighting up the fans — that all came naturally to me, because those are the very things the street demands.

"I had already learned all of that at Acción Callejera. I was trained in discipline, in respect, in love for the work. I enjoy this role. I feel welcomed by the public, and by my bosses. That energy, that affection — they feed my soul. Walking out in front of thousands of fans in a stadium puts me 'in my element,' and every time I feel the joy others take from what I do, I humbly give thanks to God."

Since then, he has traveled with the team to the Caribbean Series, carrying his joy and his commitment to every stadium, doing the job the way it should be done. He also takes on entertainment work for groups and events, with the same grace as *el Aguilita.*

Jochy has built a beautiful family portrait — four daughters and four sons. José Ramón and Herandy, both graduates of PUCMM with degrees in Physical Education, have made names for themselves in the field; Cynthia lives in the United States, Patricia in Canada, and Raunny works in the private sector. Yvianny, fourteen, is already a medalist in track and field, while Josmely and Josmel are still in primary school. Watching them grow, Jochy wanted to share with other children his love of sport and the values he had been raised on. That's how, in 1998, his baseball academy came to be — for children and teenagers who went to school in the morning and trained in the afternoon.

"The idea began with the support of Dr. Delia Gutiérrez de Ardila, who helped me build out the academy and hold to its educational spirit for almost thirty years. Many of its players went on to be honored in the United States. From the start, it filled up with boys; even the ballplayer Luis Polonia trusted us with his son's training — may God hold him in His glory. The families of Santiago entrusted me with their boys, and I cared for them with the same respect I had learned at Acción Callejera.

"But God always tests our faith, and just when everything was at its best, life set a hard trial in front of me.

"At the very top of my career, they found a tumor in my head. I thought it was the end of me. But God, the doctors, and my family gave me a second chance. I stuck my tongue out at death," Jochy says, with a smile that shines.

He came through it, though it left lingering effects on his memory, which has been returning to him little by little, like a miracle. Because of that, he had to close the academy, but he stayed in his role as *el Aguilita* — a role he has carried out with passion for more than a quarter century.

"I've spent twenty-five years in this costume, and many more in gratitude. Every time I step onto the field, I think of my grandmother Rosa, of my children, of Irenarco, of Delia... and I say back to myself what they taught me: life, even when it hurts, smells of something good."

Before closing this story, I sat down with José Ramón, the eldest of *el Aguilita*'s children, who, with a luminous smile, told me:

"My father is a fighter who rose from extreme poverty to become a respected figure in this country, with a work ethic worthy of admiration and a public that celebrates him at Estadio Cibao. He is, by far, one of the hardest-working people I have ever known, and no matter the circumstances, he keeps his head held high. He is my pride and my compass."

When our conversation ended, my soul smiled along with his. When the stadium falls silent and the lights go out, Jochy continues to shine as a symbol of resilience. His laughter, his dance, and his faith echo those early days when he learned that life, tended with tenderness, "smells of something good." Today, each time he lifts the wings of that yellow suit, he does more than animate a team — he reaffirms the stories of hundreds of boys who, like him, once chose not to give up.

What the Body Forgot to Tell[1]

The story Milagros de Jesús de Féliz tells us is not yet over for that girl who began selling flowers at a city traffic light and became one more victim of the cruelties and inequities of the street ecosystem of the urban masses, under the impassive gaze of passersby. She bears no blame for having been born without rights or opportunities.
Carmen Rita Cordero

The streets that Sunday were strangely silent — an emptiness that caught me off guard, right as I came face to face again with this girl I always remember with mixed feelings. When she saw me, she smiled the cold, lifeless smile of the dead, and at once, without preamble, she began to speak the way someone does when carrying a pain too deep to keep silent any longer.

"Today, the last Sunday of May, my country celebrates Mother's Day, and I've come back to the same traffic light where I sold flowers at twelve to help my mom — a job that ended up pushing me to sell my body in the worst way. And in this whole mess called life, I sold the rest of my peace too, and my dreams, and every-

1 *Originally published in the anthology* Día de las madres *(Chile: Editorial Factor Literario, 2025).*

thing innocent I had once held in my young heart," this street-soul tells me.

"Before you got here, I sat down on some stones under the overpass to let my mind wander and to remember the good and the bad. The good: meaning to sell flowers to help out at home and stay in school. The bad: the hook waiting to take it all from me. This place kept my childhood years for itself and tore my adolescence to pieces.

"I spent a long time wrapped up in the rush of the cars, the noise of their horns, that smell of burned gasoline soaked into the very asphalt that watched me grow up. Settled on that concrete curb, I felt the soot from the cars on my skin again, and all of it brought back the state I came home in every day.

"Strangely, for all the chaos of this place, real friendship survives here too. I remember how my friends from the streets watched out for me against any kind of trouble, and at the end of the day they made sure I had something to bring home. They were friends from the streets, and that didn't carry anything bad with it — because it didn't take me long to see that, even though they handed out the same violence life had handed them, they were true friends.

"I was born in the countryside outside La Vega, and at four I came down to Santiago with my mom, full of hope. But poverty and disappointment soon settled into my family. Crying from hunger was an everyday thing. I can swear to you that hunger hurts, and when it hits, your understanding shuts down, time stops, and anxiety takes over your mind. I remember at that age, with my lips cracked from malnutrition, asking myself questions that had no answers.

"Even like that, I was sure my only hope was to study. As soon as I could, I enrolled in a school in the neighborhood and went there in the mornings, eager to be there. The rest of the day, I helped my mom.

"My three brothers worked too, so all of us pitched in to keep the household going. They were very small for that kind of work, but my mom trained us in it. Things often turned critical, and the only food we had was a cup of sugar water. To help, I decided to sell flowers at a busy traffic light in Santiago.

"At that corner, I was the only girl. That intimidated me. *I've stepped into the territory of tough men*, I thought at first. There aren't many of us at the intersections and the corners, since most of the girls work in family homes or look after their younger siblings. That's the main reason there are fewer girls in the streets. I, too, ended up working in houses.

"At the traffic light, I made close friendships with young men older than me, who lived off informal work. It was a high-risk place. Even at my age, the propositions were constant, but I had the luck of having those boys looking out for me. It was a very hard time. I was studying and working in the streets, but the satisfaction of helping support my family eased the everyday tiredness.

"There, between cars and shouting and horns, I met a young man many times my age. He offered me a better-paying job, with fewer hours and better conditions. I didn't think twice. I accepted, and that one decision finished off whatever was left of my childhood. Bebo, my new boss, was running a commercial sexual exploitation network — something I knew nothing about. Without ever wanting it, I became a victim of this scourge that turns childhood into something to be traded for money. It is an illegal act, punishable under Dominican law, but it is a sad reality that exists and persists.

"It was true that I was earning more money in this new job, but I had to have sex with multiple men, and even with people of my own sex. I did it under the effect of drugs mixed with alcohol, so I could bear it. It became a heavy burden across my adolescence.

"When the long days were over, my soul was in pieces. Even so, I had to keep up an artificial cheerfulness so I'd be 'in good spirits' for the next session. That hell went on for some years, and in it I came to know what it is to be numb, and the weight of evil.

"The money I earned, I gave to my mom. I told her what was happening to me, day after day, but she wouldn't listen, and she didn't want to understand any of it. What she told me was to keep going, because what I was bringing in had eased the household. She even welcomed Bebo's visits to our house with courtesy. I remember the conversations I had with her, explaining why I couldn't keep doing what I was doing, but the only thing she cared about was the money I brought home. She never gave a thought to how I was breaking down, body or spirit.

"I went on subjected to the abuse that was doing me so much harm, until one day, in a fight with Bebo, I begged him to set me free from those degradations. He confessed that he couldn't, because my mom wouldn't allow it. He told me he had paid her up front — meaning she had sold me to this man. That was when I understood her courtesy toward Bebo: she was his ally.

"It was the worst day of my life. The world collapsed at my feet. Now I understood my mom's attitude, and from that day on I used more drugs than ever to numb the pain. For a long time, I felt as if she were running her own hands straight through my heart. In my innocence, I could not take in such harm.

"One day I was left almost dead, and helpless. I had no strength left to go on. I wanted to die, because I saw no way out, but my mom kept insisting I had to keep on, because she needed the money my work brought in. That was her position right up until the day I told her I would seek legal help.

"Then, frightened by my condition and by my threat, she went looking for help — supposedly to help me. She asked to speak with a social worker, and lied to her about how badly I was behaving. She told her I didn't want to contribute anything at home, that I was very violent with her, that I disobeyed her. The social worker came to our house. When she saw the state I was in, she opened an investigation that drew in several organizations working on behalf of children's rights.

"That was when I saw a light at the end of the tunnel. Acción Callejera began legal proceedings and asked for me to be evaluated by forensic doctors. They also gave me a psychological evaluation at the Children's and Adolescents' Court. The result showed severe psychological damage and the destruction of my external genitalia. The Foundation immediately filed a report with the Prosecutor's Office, and through the Public Ministry it secured an arrest warrant and a restraining order against Bebo.

"For my safety, they took me to a halfway house without my mom knowing where I was. She kept saying that everyone was getting in the way of her daughter being able to keep earning money. She refused to lift a finger to move the case against Bebo forward, and she never showed up at a single hearing — her way of rejecting everything the Foundation was claiming for me.

"I remember that, in order to get my mom to come to the final hearing, the Public Ministry had to issue an order to compel her appearance. Once she was there, the only thing she did was beg the court to release Bebo, reaffirming her loyalty to her ally.

"Lawyers from an organization that protects and counsels women took on my case and led the hearings on behalf of the Foundation. Those women, against wind and tide, kept calling for justice until they obtained a ten-year prison sentence for Bebo.

"The years have gone by, and time has not been enough to put my life back together. My mom, the whole way through, considered Bebo's arrest unjust, since, in her view, he had only done me good — she even grew angry with the lawyers who handled my case.

"Today I am perhaps another person, but life's hardships tore the innocence out of me, and I have not been able to heal or put the broken pieces of my life back together. The worst of it is that I haven't been able to break free of this addiction that's consuming me, either. And since then, it has also been impossible for me to honor the commandment to honor one's father and mother. I refuse to honor my mom, and even less to celebrate her day.

"I'll admit this has been a long, hard exercise for me, because I still keep in my heart the innocent intention with which I started out working, how much I loved studying, and how useful it made me feel to bring something home from honest, dignified work.

"Today, Mother's Day, sitting in this makeshift seat where my story began, it isn't easy for me to celebrate. Forgive me, good moms — a standing ovation for all of you. As for me, I'll keep trying to heal, to forgive, and, one day, to honor.

"I'm still planted at the traffic lights, with no hope of things getting better. Still in a haze, I wait for each change of light and watch the cars rush past. The same mistreatment from passersby tramples me, and men harass me. My back bends under the weight of all I've lived through; those miseries go on wounding what is left of the soul of the girl I once was. The soot of discouragement has stuck to every corner of my spirit, accustoming me to the indifference and the mockery of those who know me.

"I dedicate this story to the girls who work in the streets, to mothers, and to all the organizations that raised their voices for my rights. Most of all, to the educator Carmelo Mateo — witness to every step of this story, and a standard-bearer for the efforts that gave me back my freedom," she concluded, nameless, her soul heavy with pain.

When we speak of human trafficking, we picture this scourge as something far from us. But cases like this one remind us that the trade in sexual exploitation often circles in close, whispering right behind the necks of its own victims.

I said goodbye to this girl, broken on the inside, with a stab of injustice running through my chest. Her eyes, though dimmed, hold stories deeper than those her lips were able to speak. The weight of her pain — visible in her slumped shoulders and audible in the fragility of her voice — reminds me that trafficking and human exploitation are not distant phenomena. They are scourges that lie in wait in many homes, where hunger and desperation throw the doors wide open to abuse.

In the middle of the urban chaos, indifference has grown into a habit. Meanwhile, this girl's body is a living testimony to deep, invisible scars. She remains at the same corner of forgottenness, with the same soot of discouragement and a heart heavy with injustice. Leaving her there, in the same place as her hells, makes me feel like an accomplice to a deaf and silent society. As I embraced her, I noticed that the look in her eyes drifted off into the distance, and that her body spoke of what she had forgotten to tell.

Today, on this Mother's Day, while so many women celebrate it with pride, this girl finds only emptiness, anger, and pain. May she heal enough to forgive herself and to find the peace she deserves. Until then, her struggle remains a reminder of how urgent it is to protect those who, like her, have been betrayed by the very people who should have loved them. A pain that leaves the heart suspended and the soul on fire.

Born Twice

The pains of body and soul are pains of uncertainty — the kind that lives within whoever walks through it and suffers it, and that can destroy them too. But when uncertainty is taken on as an ally, it can favor a life story that, even in a hostile place, may be redeemed by hope. This account by Milagros de Jesús de Féliz, telling the life of Robinson, brings to mind Ecclesiastes — the line about how, where danger grows, what saves us grows too.

Luis Felipe Rodríguez

The story of this brave young man begins to take shape long before his birth. The fidelity of his memory recalls events it reshapes — expanding or diminishing them according to the weight he gives them. They are told through the eyes of a child, later an adolescent, who lives his life with intensity and light, but with shadow too. In this careful, almost sacred exercise, he tries not to let a single detail slip from the meticulous record of his memories.

After several years without seeing each other, he greets me with a deep voice — firm, like a news announcer's. The joy of the reunion wraps around us, and through words that twist and tangle like a labyrinth, we begin a long conversation. We decide to start with what this young man holds in his memory and keeps close to his heart:

"My date of birth is uncertain, and so is my origin. I was supposedly born around Christmas, on December fifteenth, but another document insists it was April twelfth — so I've decided to celebrate life twice a year. As for the place, I'm told it was Cap-Haïtien, but I'm not sure, because a lot of clues make me suspect it was actually in the Dominican Republic. Even so, my birth certificate says Haiti... And that was how my life began — between certainties and contradictions that would follow me through life.

"My mother is of Haitian descent, and my father is Dominican, surname Martínez. I was very small, too young to understand, when my parents separated.

"What I'll tell you is the version I hold most clearly in my memory. That doesn't mean every fact happened exactly that way, because my *via crucis* — my way of the cross — began the moment I came into the world, between half-truths and lies that hurt. Even so, I'll tell you from the heart everything I know and lived through. From here on, I'll lay bare both my sorrows and my joys.

"Almost from the time I was a newborn, I lived in the home of people I believed were my family — but who weren't. Not long ago, I learned that my parents had agreed to pay someone a sum of money to carry me across the border from Haiti into the Dominican Republic. When that person brought me over, my parents never honored the agreement, and the debt was never paid.

"The person who'd done the work felt cheated, betrayed — and decided, in revenge, to keep me. So from the time I was a newborn, I was the one who paid for a broken promise. I grew up in the home of that couple, whom I always believed to be my aunt and uncle. In truth, they were the only family I had within reach at the time.

"As I grew, I felt mistreated. I never received care or affection. By the time I was five, I had discovered the truth: they weren't my aunt and uncle, weren't even distant relatives. But there was no one I could turn to for help, because I had no idea where my biological parents were. I was far too young to know what to do with my life.

"What I do know is that God always walks beside the abandoned, and one ordinary day, without saying anything to anyone, I took off for Santiago. I arrived with little hope, but with faith enough to keep fighting — because God also sends angels into this world. In Parque Duarte, I met Alberto, who took me home with him, where they treated me with kindness. I can say with full conviction that Alberto is the brother I never had and the angel I had always prayed for.

"But I was full of unanswered questions, of sadness and accumulated pain. Carrying that weight, I became aggressive and intolerant. I would fight over anything.

"At nine, I met a woman who came up to me and said she was my aunt — but I no longer believed in anyone. She sold clothes in the streets, and she found me at Parque Duarte with photos of my birth and of some relatives. That convinced me a little. Hungry to be with someone of my own blood, I went to live with her for a time. But there was no bond between us, and I went back to Alberto's house.

"That change shook me, and I felt that life had set itself on striking me again and again. I didn't know who I was; my origin was a blur. Without the security of a biological family, I was deeply sad — too young to take so many blows at once. Even now, I cannot fully explain what was happening inside me, but it was a time that marked me deeply. I wanted to lose myself so I wouldn't have to find myself.

"Because of all this, I didn't trust the people who were supposed to be mine. At such a young age, I was already caught in a web that tightened around my soul. I remember spending whole days crying and looking up at the sky, asking God for an answer, from the blurred picture I had become. I felt suspended in nothingness, with no roots, with no mourners and no kin. *How did I come into the world? Who brought me here?* It was a feeling of emptiness, of sorrow, of misery..."

As he describes these feelings, his voice breaks now and then, remembering that he had no one to unburden himself to. With his father, he never had a relationship — and now he has no interest in pursuing one.

Robinson's memories lay bare the pain of abandonment — of parents who left him in the care of strangers. He was told they were his aunt and uncle who weren't his aunt and uncle, in a country that wasn't his country either. As he speaks of this hard truth, the young man does not hide his sorrow; on the contrary, he tells it as though those wounds still belong to the present — and perhaps they do.

What strikes me is his need to remember everything, to speak it all aloud, even what merciful forgetting strives to veil. He talks it all out as a form of release — perhaps as catharsis, perhaps as a determined effort to reach a freedom that will help him rise above old resentments. With that feeling rooted in his heart, he goes on telling his journey, his road, his life...

"At twelve, I decided to take hold of my life and follow a road that might lead me somewhere good. I moved out on my own to gain independence — but in truth, what I lost was my peace. I went on surviving in the streets of the city's historic center, in those places where people were always passing through. From that time, I clearly remember that going out to see the people walking by, being among them, gathering with others, belonging to a group, or simply staying in contact with other people — all of that validated my existence and made me feel alive, because the loneliness of my little room was unbearable.

"Because of all that, it was easy for me to learn what the street demanded of me and to take on the rules of the park. There, you had to respect the leaders, and the way to show that respect was to give them a share of the money the shoeshiners and the vendors made. Anyone who refused wasn't allowed to work. But I didn't want to be an errand boy. I wanted to be one of the bosses.

"To get there, I made myself tougher than I needed to be, more aggressive than the rest. It led to constant violence; we had to wage the fights that broke out almost daily under the shade of that beautiful little plaza of my memories.

"That was how I quickly moved up to managing the money the boys handed in — the *rédito*, as we called that mandatory payment. I say 'we' because I'd reached my goal of becoming one of the park bosses. That role still fills me with shame, but it was my reality.

"I held that role for a long time alongside *el Chino*, Stalin, Rudy, Melvin, and a few others. We were the *papaúpas* of the park — the big shots!

"In that war for power and control, there was another group: Haitian boys who refused to hand over the *rédito* from their work to the Dominican bosses. So almost every day a brawl would break out — kicks, cuts, black eyes, and other rough blows. The police got involved sometimes, but they too had to be paid a cut to let us run the place.

"In the middle of that fight between Dominicans and Haitians, I asked myself, deep down, whether I was really Dominican or Haitian. Either way, I always stayed on the Dominican side, because that's how I feel.

"At that age, with so many emotional blows already on me, I came to know the programs at Acción Callejera. I could have breakfast and lunch there for just five pesos — a hook the Foundation used to draw boys like me into its educational programs.

"I liked it from the first day, because they welcomed me warmly. There I found basic-skills training, sports, psychological and academic support, food, personal hygiene, and many other programs that, with the years and daily follow-up, sanded down my aggression and intolerance. I also found the arms of Yohanny, Carmelo, Cinthya, and Bentodina — an exceptional team of psychologists trained to work with children like me. Among them, they helped me come to terms with my emotional pain.

"The psychologists recognized the hole I carried in my soul, and how much it hurt me to live without family bonds. So through different channels, they finally got in touch with my biological mother: María.

"Meeting Mom was something close to a day of final judgment. María's eyes were full of tears in a face full of joy. Her arms longed to hold me, but I trusted no one, and in that moment, conflicting feelings rushed all at once into my heart. I felt rejection toward her, blended with a quiet, buried gladness. I wanted to confront her about so much — to ask her why she had left me alone, to tell her how much I had suffered for it, to make her account for every bad thing that had happened to me! It was a moment I could only get through with the support of the team of psychologists. That bittersweet meeting hammered at the deepest part of my guarded heart. I don't remember it bringing me joy, or sadness either. I forgot it all, because it hurt too much..."

When this young man speaks about the harshness of the road he has traveled, he does it with great honesty and without holding anything back. His memories surface unguarded, with no secrets and no disguise.

"Believe me, it was very hard for me to understand her and to accept her — but in the end, she was all I had. She carried me in her womb and gave me life, something I am still grateful for to this day. That helped me a little, but I had to keep on fighting for my survival.

"At Acción Callejera I found full support and close follow-up for a long time — for years, really. That support gave me the chance to become a collaborator in the program, and I started by serving water to the boys in the Foundation's dining hall.

"After that, I was put in charge of organizing and cleaning the dining hall before the food came up from the kitchen, which was in the basement. Because of my effort, I was allowed to become a sports assistant on the Foundation's court — a very small space where the toughest fights would break out.

"I kept growing, trying to manage the aggression I'd held on to for so many years, but I had a problem with another boy during a retreat at La Molino Blanco. There I got into it with a kid who claimed I had hit him while we were in the pool — which wasn't true.

"What happened was, the kid attacked me, and the devil got into me. I grabbed his head and slammed it violently against the wall, over and over. When he started to bleed, I let him go. That was disastrous for me. I lost the progress I had made, and the psychologists suspended me from the Foundation for nine days — but they kept watching me at school and kept watch over what

I did in the streets. On the sixth day, they let me come back under a list of conditions I had to meet.

"That was my last fight. I understood I had been wrong, and I asked my friend's forgiveness. The consequence changed my whole attitude toward life. I learned to value the support I was being given, and my change was lasting. Now I know God never abandoned me.

"From then on, I did my part to win back the trust of the people who had helped me. I served the food, collaborated with the soccer team for the boys from Hato del Yaque, oversaw the showers in the hygiene department, and worked as a sports assistant. On top of that experience, I went through the Peace Corps trainings in *Futuro con Ideales* — Future with Ideals — and a deeply enriching course to become a sports trainer, called *Deportes para la Vida* — Sports for Life — all of it guided by Dean Avery, a much-valued American volunteer. From there I went on to take courses in first aid, in masculinity through *Chicos Brillantes* — Bright Boys — and in sex education, along with other trainings that shaped me as an educator at the Foundation.

"I trained to walk alongside other children who, like me, needed help, and to guide their lives — a deeply rewarding task that I keep among my best memories. They taught me something good every day. That passion moved me so much that any training to strengthen my skills as an educator brought me great joy.

"During that time, several groups of American university students came down, volunteering with the Foundation's educational programs. In one of those groups, I met Alejandra — a wonderful young woman who changed my life from the moment I read in her eyes the nobility of her soul. Alejandra came from Fort Myers as a volunteer, and from the first instant I saw her, I felt a calm in my heart. I knew it was the good kind of love — and it seems she felt the same.

"Alejandra and I built a beautiful relationship over seven years — she in the United States with sporadic visits, and me in Santiago. We married in 2019, and we live in Florida now. I came to the United States a few months before the pandemic, and I started out washing dishes in a restaurant. There, I made progress with eagerness, drawing on everything I had learned at Acción Callejera. From dishwasher I went on to be a kitchen prep cook, and today I'm a chef at Sacred Pepper, a well-known Italian restaurant in Tampa, Florida — at your service.

"You know I've always loved cooking, and not to brag, but I cook good. As Fefita la Grande says, *la pimienta mía e la que pica* — it's my pepper that brings the heat.

"I'll close by telling you that none of that has been a gift as great as having Giuliana, my daughter, who is one year old now. She's a girl with eyes as bright as her father's, and the tenderness and the charm of Alejandra, her mother.

"Alejandra and I share Giuliana's care between my work and a master's degree she's pursuing in Public Health at the University of West Florida," this young man, once so impetuous, tells me with deep satisfaction.

"My mom lives in Santiago. I rented her a decent house, and she lives in a safe place. I love her deeply, and I always keep her present in my thoughts. I keep watch over her health, and I carry her in my heart as the mother she is. Through her I came into this world, and she became my teacher in life — for cherishing and loving Giuliana with my whole heart. Without her, I would not have learned to value the stones along the road, nor to give thanks to God for the troubles, or for the blessings either.

"Having her alive moves me to keep growing, so I can give Giuliana every day the embraces I never had. Every look from my daughter makes up for the lovelessness I once endured, and every caress from Alejandra confirms what I now know to be true — that I have found the love of my life."

A silence, heavy with emotion, marks the end of this powerful, moving testimony, poured out in a torrent of words. Looking at the man he has become, I can say that Robinson took the bitter flavors of his hardest experiences and combined them with effort, with forgiveness, and with tenderness. That is how he has made his life into something to admire — like the dishes he prepares.

God bless you, striving young man — heart of bread, soul of a lion.

I celebrate the joy of knowing you!

The Last Act of Courage

Wandy was a young man born with the wisdom of an adult. Without material wealth, he left behind an invaluable legacy. I had the joy of knowing him and of holding his generous hands. The author of this story reminds us that Wandy was a hero from the moment he was born until his early departure. He should be remembered as such, and recognized as an example of devotion to others.
Yudelka Pérez de Haddad

"Ma'am, listen to what happened to me the other day. A customer at the supermarket where I work was reading everyone's palms, and curiosity was killing me. When my turn came and I held my hands out to her, the fortune teller closed her eyes and covered her face.

"'What's the matter, ma'am?' I asked her. She told me she couldn't read my hands. I pressed her to explain why, and at the end she said: 'It's just that I don't see a future for you.'

"Listen, ma'am — she didn't see my future! That woman's not in her right mind. The moment I heard that, I pulled my hands back and walked off, because that woman's no fortune teller, not at all."

That's how Wandy told it to me, on that occasion — a month before he said goodbye to the world. A current of water carried him off while he was practicing the kind of solidarity that defined him. Coincidence or not, it turned out that his future was only his present.

I knew him when he was a child — quick, bright eyes, a slight little body, a small step, a shy but cheerful smile, restless, headstrong, and a great talker. In short: too old for his age. I never thought I'd meet someone who held so many virtues together at once and kept so much love in his heart, to the point of giving his life to save the lives of others. He is one of the people I have most admired along this stretch of life.

It is hard for me to speak of Wandy in the past tense, but the sensible thing is to face his physical absence with the same steadiness and clear-eyed vision with which he faced life.

Before he had turned six, he had already taken on the support of his household. He was born in La Cueva de Cevicos, west of Cotuí, and arrived in Santiago in his parents' arms when he was barely five months old, with five siblings beside him. They settled there as a family and, together, mapped out a plan for the life ahead.

Wandy got along better with his mother than with his father, with whom he often clashed over the heavy drinking his father did every day. He had grown tired of being mistreated as a result of that destructive habit, which he always rejected. After many difficulties, and so as not to disrespect the man who had given him life, he rented a room near the family home. At such a young age, with more courage than belongings, he set out on his own — with nothing but heart.

His mother went to heaven very young, doubling the weight on this child as hardworking as he was responsible. It was one of the harshest blows life dealt Wandy. He took on the cost of her medical care. He looked after her until her last day, and protected her so that she might die in peace, surrounded by the love of her children.

Wandy's childhood unfolded in a very humble community on the southern edge of Santiago, a place where time had forgotten to pass. His life moved along steep footpaths, foul-smelling gullies, makeshift streets and narrow alleys, ravines that gave a fine view of the city, houses pressed tightly against one another, music turned all the way up, and people both good and not so good — as in any crowded place.

There, the only services within reach are still betting parlors, the small-scale sale of substances, and pool halls. The nearest school was a half hour away on foot. Even so, Wandy walked that route with the highest motivation to be educated.

In this neighborhood, he always felt welcomed and deeply loved. For many reasons, he put down roots in that family haven he always cherished and protected. There he built his two-story house, with generous space, in the first dip of the main road, just to the left of hope, at the roundabout of his efforts, very near his dreams.

From childhood, he took on responsibilities and tasks meant for adults. He looked after his siblings, worked hard to help at home, and counseled his father about the harmful effects of alcohol. He studied with dedication in the few free hours he had. In that same childhood, he became aware of the needs of his community, and he did everything within his reach — and a little more — to help those who, like him, lived in vulnerability and at high social risk. All of it astonished the adults, myself included. The thing was, however many tasks piled up, he took them on with contagious joy.

Wandy was born with the heart of a fighter. Every day, *sin mancar* — without fail — he found a great opportunity and seized it, no matter what stone lay in his path.

His routine was relentless. He went to bed with the chickens, because his workday was long and intense for someone his age. He would get up at one in the morning to work alongside his father at the Hospedaje Yaque. There, he loaded and unloaded trucks of fruits and vegetables as they arrived at the market. He earned some money for that work, but he also took advantage of the produce the truckers rejected, reselling it at the small stall his grandmother ran. Over time, that little business grew so much that, from the salads he sold to the neighbors at the start, he went on to offer boiled eggs, hot dogs, juices, coffee, toast, and soft stewed beans. Wandy was a born entrepreneur, and into every venture he poured his whole effort.

With the household's livelihood secured, he would also head out, without losing a moment, to shine shoes and round out the day's earnings. When his shoeshining day was done, he would get ready for the local school. That was how full his days were — and yet he smiled all the more.

Some years later, he joined the programs at Acción Callejera and became part of a youth group called *Grupo H* — Group H — where many adolescents his age worked through topics like gender-based violence, social norms, social justice, the new masculinity, and other formative themes.

"Those activities planted in me values that strengthened my life and that became the foundation for helping other working children," he said in an interview with this dream-maker.

When he started high school, his life turned, and he said goodbye to the streets. He set down the shoeshine box and took up a position as a dental assistant in the Foundation's Health Program. His new schedule was in the mornings, so that he could attend school in the afternoons. I still remember seeing him arrive earlier than every other employee, his coat impeccably white, attentive to whatever the dentist on duty asked of him, and cleaning down the area each day.

He was also an enthusiastic educator at the Foundation, and received a range of trainings in integral development. He completed his secondary studies at the Liceo Roberto Duvergé Mejía, where his classmates elected him president of his graduating class — a role in which he displayed his leadership by organizing a graduation ceremony of real dignity. We all celebrated with him that day, giving thanks to God for such a meaningful blessing.

Wandy celebrated everything. Life itself was his daily festivity. He was born with joy in his heart and had a sure aim for reaching his dreams, even when he had to walk across the embers of fate.

Without losing a moment, as ever, he enrolled in the Bioanalysis program at the Universidad Tecnológica de Santiago. With new horizons opening before him and now a university student, he was happy — and he didn't have to say it, because the joy on his face gave him away. Luck stayed with him, and at his very first job interview he was hired by a well-known supermarket in the city. He took great pride in being a university student and in having gotten there through his own effort and his own savings. He loved his work and threw himself into it with passion. Three months in, he was named *Empleado Orgullo* — Employee of Distinction — and a year and a half later he was promoted to a more demanding role with greater training.

One afternoon I went to the supermarket to buy a bottle of wine. At the time, he was the wine-aisle stocker on aisle seven. He kept the beverage section organized and guided customers thoughtfully through their choices. When I saw him, I asked for his help, and very gently he recommended the right wine for me. I was charmed and delighted by the encounter. I have not forgotten the impression he made — the ease with which he explained the characteristics of that juice of grapes, and the fermentation process required to draw out the special wine he was recommending.

Clearly trained in the subject, he went on to talk about the differences among the various grape varieties. Meanwhile, I delighted in watching the most passionate of wine enthusiasts, with advanced knowledge of oenology. He was a full sommelier. In fact, I bought more bottles than I needed, just to enjoy that special moment of pride — watching him do his work with so much professionalism, enthusiasm, and force of conviction.

Wandy was also a photographer. His work was in demand among friends and acquaintances who needed photographs for all kinds of events — graduations, birthdays, weddings. It was one of his favorite pursuits, and so he became the photographer for everyone he knew.

To help the community where he lived, he also trained in several capacity-building programs in emergency education and risk management, offered by the European Union. The last course he took in this area was given by the Dominican Red Cross, on flood response and first aid. Wandy stood out for his enthusiasm in every activity in those workshops, because he was always thinking of how to protect his neighbors and family from any natural disaster. He had been born with solidarity tucked under his arm.

His path in the community where he lived — his effort and his example for the young people there — reached the ears of the Sala Capitular of the Ayuntamiento of Santiago, the city council.

There, he was honored with the Premio Municipal de la Juventud Santiago Apóstol — the Santiago Apóstol Municipal Youth Prize — in the category of Personal Achievement, 2011. That award belonged to all of us. We celebrated it, I think, more than he did, aware that Wandy was living through the best of his moments.

On the night of November 19, 2012, less than a year after that recognition, it was raining torrentially in Santiago, with violent lightning. The sky closed in, heavy and dark. The moon and the stars wept in sheets, with tears of dark omen. A call from the community at midnight stunned me and left me without breath. They told me Wandy was missing, and they urgently needed high-intensity lights to help in the search. He had fallen, alongside a three-year-old girl, into the strong current of a drainage gully. Both had vanished into the darkness of the night.

We alerted the fire department, and they arrived in time with what was needed. Wandy had braced an improvised ladder of rough wooden poles against a tree standing inside the gully. He carried people in his arms and climbed the ladder with them, leading them up to the high side that gave onto a road where they were out of danger. That was how he had evacuated an entire neighborhood — and every life saved was a trophy of honor for this brave young man.

The flood surged in fury, like a vulture circling to devour its prey, while the rain hammered down and the wind howled. Even under those circumstances, Wandy went on saving the lives of adults and children. On a final attempt, he took little Amerly into his arms — but this time the ladder gave way and crashed into the waters with him and the girl.

The community awoke searching downstream for any sign of this beloved young man and the little girl, but every effort was in vain. The fury of the waters, together with the logs being dragged along, had cowardly swallowed up these two souls. His body and the child's, still in his arms, were found in the Yaque River, near La Herradura, southwest of Santiago.

His life was short, and his last hours were too long. Death struck him down and stalked him in the darkness, to immortalize in our hearts the gaze and the courage of a boy who was never a boy, and of a soul that never let itself be brought down. His departure still hurts. His example endures in every act of courage, on the face of every working child, in the sunlight of his community, in the joy he offered each of his companions, and in the hearts of those of us who had the privilege of knowing him.

Wandy stands at the head of the inventory that makes up an honored pantheon of champions — those who walk the paths of love behind the brave footsteps of their devotion to the service of others, weaving new reasons to live under the umbrella of that solidarity-bound love he professed until his final, fateful night.

His body was held in vigil at the school where he had worked. That painful departure polished the shields of soul and spirit that this young man left to us, like a fertile seed sown in the earth of his own life. The young people raised murals with his face on them, and the community still weeps for him, remembers him, and — like me — misses him.

At the wake, his sister, filled with love and grief to the very marrow of her bone-deep conscience, took the floor with honor and, in a voice broken by tears, prayed the Our Father aloud, and several Hail Marys.

We said goodbye to him with the highest honor and the deepest respect. The young people of the community carried his body to that humble dwelling of peace, reserved exclusively for the great.

I Found God at the Far Edge of Pain

"He spoke to me of God as a healer of lives, and I held on to that faith with all my strength, all the way to today. After years of struggle, daily temptations, and a great deal of prayer, I left drugs behind." The author introduces us to Rafael, alias Tachón, who found an angel in his path: Betania, a young Spanish volunteer at Acción Callejera. In acts of solidarity, we lend our hands to God, and we become the necessary miracle.
Raúl Martínez Trémols

Meeting up again with these boys puts my heart in brine. With *Tachón* in particular, the feeling is one of a kind. The last time I saw him, he was a working teenager, facing head-on, in full sunlight, the difficulties life had laid upon him. Crossing paths with him again now is like opening a box of surprises — meeting the unexpected with an intuitive joy that surfaces alongside a certain uncertainty.

From somewhere along the foothills of Cotuí, a child of about eight, maybe nine, made his way to Santiago. They called him *Tachón* because of the deformity that marked his cleft lip. But behind that nickname there hid an extraordinary being, with large caramel-colored eyes and a small, delicate head that seemed to hold in silence a sorrow too great for his tender heart. His curly hair, bleached blond with peroxide, framed cheeks weathered by soot and by all the rough edges of street life. I remember him as gifted, quick-witted, and with the instincts of a natural negotiator.

Tachón read with a clarity of diction that astonished the educators. His ability in sports and in the small everyday negotiations — above all in the unceasing search for food — was proof of a sharp intelligence, a capacity that kept him on his feet against the harshness of the streets. He was a misunderstood child — he always said so — but the truth was that his family had never accepted him. Even after multiple visits to his parents, his grandfather would pronounce his sentence:

"That boy is the devil set ablaze. We don't want him near us."

When he sat with the educators, *Tachón* always spoke with a disarming frankness. He would tell us that his mother was a prostitute and his father was in prison for drug trafficking. At his house there was nothing but an immense emptiness. Coming home from school, he would find his little siblings without having eaten. On one occasion, he confessed that he had taken to stealing in order to feed them, looking out especially for Nani, the youngest.

"My mom was always drunk and in a foul mood. She'd taken over the drug-selling business my dad had left behind, and she trained me to sell little packets of that poison. I learned to do it discreetly, so as not to draw attention.

"But there were days when the buyers would steal the merchandise off me, and when I came back empty-handed, my mom didn't believe me. She'd give me terrible beatings — they hurt me more than the blows the buyers dealt me when they refused to pay. Those were very hard times, and to forget all of it, I started trying the drugs myself. I wanted to be happy, even if just for a little while."

Rejection followed him beyond the walls of his home. On the streets, he was "the whore's bastard and the little drug dealer." He was always fighting other boys, and school offered no refuge. He remembered how a man once stole a packet of drugs from him and broke his arm. Desperate from the pain, he went home looking for help, only to be beaten again by his mother. She grabbed a broom handle and struck him so violently across the back that she broke two of his ribs.

He relives that double pain as if it were happening now. His grandfather was the one who took him to the hospital, but no one came to see him during the whole week he was admitted. Only the little nuns of the hospital looked after him. When he was discharged, his ribs still broken and a few pesos in his pocket, he got on a bus and took off for the capital.

"In the streets of Santo Domingo, I came to know the cruelest face of life — drugs, fights, humiliations, deaths. Rainy days were the worst. It's hard to sleep under a drainpipe or a stubborn leak, but the indifference of people hurts even more. When you sleep just anywhere on the street, people with sick minds try to take advantage of you, and many of them get what they want, because when you're alone out there, no one will lift a hand for you.

"I wanted to die many times, but I never had the courage to take my own life. So I would pick fights, hoping someone else would do it for me. Believe me, to take your own life takes real courage, and I didn't even have that. I didn't even have the strength to die. I was destroyed. Before I was fifteen, I had been locked up twelve times, and I was sick of myself.

"My life began to change when I heard about an organization that helped boys from the streets. I saved up the little I could and made my way to Santiago. That's where I found Acción Callejera. The Foundation opened its doors to me and processed my birth certificate so I could enroll in school. It was the happiest day of my life, because I had always loved to read. I remember waiting for the newspaper every day, eager to learn what was happening in the world.

"Through them, too, I was taken to a medical mission where they operated on my cleft lip. The first time I looked at myself in the mirror, I felt like a different person. But the fight against the drugs was constant, and however hard I tried, I always relapsed.

"In time, and thanks to the support of Betania, a Spanish volunteer, along with the educational programs at Acción Callejera, I got back on track. Betania spoke to me of God as a healer of lives, and I held on to that faith with all my strength, all the way to today. After years of struggle, daily temptations, and a great deal of prayer, I left drugs behind.

"Today I'm more than seven years clean. It's still a daily battle, one in which I keep choosing to say no. Everything I am today is because at the far edge of the deepest pain, when death was circling me, I found God."

With a serene smile, Rafael — alias *Tachón* — confided that he had found a new purpose. He now lives with an aunt in Santo Domingo, who received him with open arms. He works cleaning water tanks and as a gardener. Through steady effort, he was able to buy a modest pickup truck and train two of his cousins in both trades. The three of them now work together as a family, carrying out their responsibilities with consistency and care. Looking at his face now — calmer, still marked by the same dimple he has had since childhood — it is easy to see that his life has changed.

"My mom died during the pandemic. And though her absence hurts, I know she found rest from her demons. My dad died in prison seven years ago. They killed him because he was very violent. I was left an orphan, but I don't feel alone. I have God, and that is more than enough."

When I asked him about his siblings, he told me that his two brothers now work at a cinder-block factory in San Cristóbal, and that Nani, his younger sister, lives in a Carmelite convent, preparing to become a nun. As we said goodbye, he asked me to convey his gratitude to all those who had supported him through those years of hardship.

"Please tell Cecilia, Patricia, and Jochy at Acción Callejera that I am grateful to them for believing in me when I couldn't even stand myself."

I watched him walk away, his step firm. In his eyes there was no longer a trace of the child marked by abandonment. In his place stood a man who, against the odds, had rebuilt his life. His story stayed with me — a testament to the courage it takes to face the past and claim a future with dignity.

We embraced one last time.

"Until next time, *Maestro*!" I said to him, deeply moved.

UNDER AN OPEN SKY

Here, childhood has no walls. It lives out in the open — it works, it begs, it wagers itself against life, it endures, and against all odds, it keeps on dreaming.

This is how they face labor far heavier than it should be, and how they make their way through nights that run too long, under fragile shelter and a sky that seems to hang too close above them.

Faith Made Flesh

Neither the darkness of the nights nor the endless days that consumed Madoché's life could break him. The hope of seeing the light in his mother's eyes gave him the strength to walk hard roads, accompanied by another soul as defenseless as his own. That was how they made their way from Plaisance to Santiago, to live a new story — one no less shadowed than the last, which the author renders in moving detail.
Carolina Enriqueta Pérez

Meeting up with the young people I once knew as children — now adults — brings me far more than nostalgia. These encounters wake a joy in me, but a quiet uncertainty too. After so much time without knowing what had become of their adult lives, I feel a small startle in the soul, accompanied by the deep hope of finding them fulfilled as people.

I admit I feel a kind of relief when I hear how these young people have managed to carry their lack and their hardships, facing a road full of obstacles. It fills me with satisfaction to discover that they have become useful, persevering people, still pursuing their well-being. I am even gladder to learn that they have finished their studies, that they keep on chasing their dreams, and that they have built their own families — moving forward with courage and celebrating life.

The sum of all those feelings was what I felt as I sat down to talk with Madoché Noralus, a young man of Haitian descent — slender, soft-spoken, with his education tattooed on his skin. He crossed the border at a very young age and has woven his life through storms as well as small victories. As a child he was hard-working, shy, and always responsible, eager to learn whatever came within reach.

We arranged to meet for dinner at six in the evening, and we chose a table for two at a pleasant spot in the city. The first lesson he offered me was that Madoché eats healthy food and doesn't like junk food. While he had a wholesome salad and a fresh juice, I devoured a pizza piled with every topping I could find.

Over the course of our conversation, the two of us slowly pieced together, in detail, the years we had spent without seeing each other, and used the moment to catch up. We walked through his childhood, lingered a long while over his adolescence, and took joy in each accomplishment along the way and in the simple fact of having found each other again.

In our exchange, Madoché set himself to summoning that past in which we had first known each other, with a maturity that exceeded his twenty-five years. He looked back from the place between memory and the forgetting of certain sorrows he had decided not to carry. Though he is still shy, the peace in his face shows a man satisfied with what he has built. As he spoke of certain passages of his life, I listened closely, careful not to wake his ghosts or call his old fears back to life.

With calm steadiness and impeccable diction, Madoché tells me he was born in the summer of 1998 in Plaisance, north of Cap-Haïtien, in Haiti. His parents separated when he was very small, and they began to look for ways to better their lives. Madoché longed to grow up beside his mother, who was already living in the Dominican Republic — and to do that, he would have to cross the border.

Set on his purpose, he and a cousin laid out a plan: they would walk up to the border crossing and pretend to be shoeshine boys. Equipped with the wooden boxes of the trade, they offered their services to the soldiers patrolling the area. After shining their boots, they walked off discreetly, as though they already lived on this side. Without any visible hurry, but with their hearts boiling with fear, they moved away from Haitian territory and began to make their way through the illegality and the demands of the road ahead. With little money and barely ten years of age, they walked themselves to exhaustion along the edge of the highway, with no guide and no orientation of any kind.

"I remember we had to avoid the militarized checkpoints, which made the road much longer and more anguishing.

"Hitching rides and eating a few mangoes that I'm sure God placed within our reach, we followed an improvised route. We went through a great deal of hardship and hunger, along with all the other troubles we faced as we kept moving forward.

"Along the way, we shined shoes in the small towns we passed through, and with whatever we earned each day, we could eat something. We also met good people on the road who could read the hunger in our drawn faces and offered us food. That helped us a great deal.

"The nights filled me with anxiety and unease, because we never knew where we might rest or sleep. That frightened me very much. I remember my cousin came down with a terrible flu and ran a fever several times, but we felt God was there with us, and that He never abandoned us in the middle of a fear I still wouldn't know how to explain. Just remembering it tightens my heart."

That was how they finally arrived in Santiago. Madoché tells me of the relief they felt when they caught sight of the lights of the Monumento a los Héroes de la Restauración, the place where their relatives were waiting for them. They arrived with their feet blistered and their bodies badly dehydrated, as if they had come back from a war, still wearing the same clothes they had left Haiti in.

"From the moment my mom held me in her arms, I breathed deeply and felt the peace I had needed so badly. That same night, all of us prayed, and holding one another, we gave thanks to God for being together. I remember that, for an instant, the world transformed and became something else. To this day, that has been the best moment of my life," Madoché said, his gaze deepening.

As he summoned these memories, still engraved on him, the wetness in his eyes revealed the immense weight of the anguished crossing he had endured at such a young age.

With the pride of a grateful son, he tells me his mother is a hardworking woman, an honest entrepreneur who for many years has worked as a street vendor — selling socks, T-shirts, men's underwear, and other goods, and who also weaves hairnets. His brother works at a restaurant in the city, while his older sister sells secondhand clothing on the street. The whole family works hard to meet the needs of the household in the Bella Vista de Pastor neighborhood.

When Madoché began a new life after crossing the border, he started shining shoes alongside his cousins, who already knew the trade, so he could help with the household expenses. As was usual among boys in his situation, he began working in Parque Duarte and on the streets of the city center.

"There I learned to fight, to take any problem head-on, and to withstand many beatings from the ones who thought they were the 'bosses' of the park. If I didn't hand over part of what I'd earned, they'd beat me until they'd taken almost everything I had made. Coming to terms with that injustice was very hard for me.

"The language barrier made me feel deeply frustrated. Since I didn't speak Spanish, it was hard for me to find customers. I also didn't see the dangers and the threats of the street, or the ill-intentioned adults who hung around that crowded area," says this good-hearted young man, with a heart made of *pan de agua* — soft bread.

"Not long after I began working in the city center, I came to know the educational programs at Acción Callejera, and I started going every day. The skills department impressed me, and I was filled with joy when I found a small basketball court there. I also had the chance to play my favorite sport: soccer. There, I joined the team *Los Halcones de Acción Callejera* — the Acción Callejera Falcons. I remember that sports were decisive for my development and my self-esteem, because through sports we played, we planned strategies, and we pulled off feats that made us feel like world champions.

"Under the guidance of the educators Yanelis Peralta, Mercedes Pérez, Yohanny Rodríguez, Cinthya Lora, Carmelo Mateo, Melanie Benoit, Bentodina Jiménez, José Ramón Taveras, and others, I learned to read and write at the Foundation — an achievement that opened the door for me to enroll at the Escuela Juan Ovidio Paulino.

"That is why Acción Callejera will always be my home, because it was there that I was shaped to face life. The tools I received and God's favor are the ground I stand on in every circumstance. The psychological guidance program was very important for me, and working in its different departments strengthened my self-esteem and helped me heal the emotional gaps I'd carried from different parts of my childhood. If I had to define Acción Callejera in one word, it would be: 'guide.'

"To improve my income, I balanced my studies with work in the area around the Monumento a los Héroes de la Restauración, at night and into the early hours of the morning, because it was an excellent spot for finding customers. There I offered flowers, water, mints, phone chargers, and cookies, in addition to shining shoes. At thirteen, I sold compact discs in restaurants, on street corners, and at bars. I also sold boiled corn from a pushcart at specific stops.

"I worked as a collaborator in Acción Callejera's programs, and for a time I worked as a delivery driver for a well-known supermarket, where I also stocked and organized merchandise.

"In the Monumento area, you could even triple what you'd earn at the park, which made the place very attractive — despite the exhaustion and the abuse and humiliation we suffered, those of us who were migrants most of all.

"The police carried out raids constantly, and I had no papers. I remember more than once running off at lightning speed to hide in streets and alleyways until the officers had gone. When we saw the immigration agents, we'd warn one another, and we'd hide wherever we could — even in the storm drains in the streets, in the trash bins outside a business, or in nearby corners.

"I see now that, because of my humble look, the way I talked, and the color of my skin, it was very easy to identify me as a migrant. I still carry a discouragement I haven't been able to shake, but I trust in God. I carry that obstacle and its consequences with me until I'm able to put my papers in order.

"People tend to think that street vendors are bothersome, but it isn't so. Behind each one of us, there is an urgent need that drives us to survive. When hunger presses in, instinct forces you to look for a way out. And if you're a child, you throw yourself into whatever task is within reach, simply to keep going.

"Working in the streets is a bitter experience, and doing any kind of work at night multiplies the risk for children. Many adults make dishonorable, deceitful propositions that can lure any child who lacks affection and lives in a vulnerable condition. It's also fair to say that well-intentioned people do appear, people who want to help improve the conditions of the children who work in the streets — but those are the fewer.

"Getting through the daily challenges, by the grace of God, with the support of my family and the guidance of Acción Callejera, I finished high school and graduated in French from the Alianza Francesa de Santiago. Today I'm a designer at a company, and I have many projects in mind — among them, pursuing a university degree to strengthen my knowledge, if it pleases God.

"I live here, with my family, and every day all of us pray for Haiti to recover. Together we ask God for mercy for my people, and above all for the relatives who stayed behind." That was how Madoché closed his story, his face touched with sadness and his faith unshakable.

Before ordering dessert to close out the evening, I thanked him for sharing with me so many lived stories and so many precious memories.

By the end of our conversation, I felt I had traveled through Madoché's life beside him, like an attentive passenger watching and admiring him through a loving window as he made his way through the various stations where he had so bravely stopped.

At some of those stations, I was not present. At others, I listened as he described the dangers of the road — always courteous, quiet, kindhearted, and cheerful. It was a privilege to ride with Madoché through one car of his adolescence, and I confess I never foresaw seeing him so mature, so whole.

With my heart warmed and grateful to God for bringing us together again, I placed my hands on his shoulders and said:

"Thank you, Madoché. Your life is a gift from God — you know that? Knowing you is a joy, and learning from your story is a great privilege."

"I know," he answered, smiling with the same eyes he had in adolescence.

To This Very Day

In a devastating opening line, we meet Frank, whose hard reality lands with such force that one might wish to stop reading. The author shows us how and why miracles happen, making clear that faith, values, and a meaningful maternal presence can overcome adversity. Seeing Frank lean toward the calling of an educator, without resentment, reveals to us a glimmer of forgiveness and a renewed hope in humanity's capacity to rise again.
Edward M. Butler

"Mom, Mom, we just got out of the car and you forgot to pay the driver the fare," Frank said to his mother as the two of them stepped down from a route-K car.

His mother looked him up and down with a fearsome calm and, as casually as she could, answered him:

"I didn't pay the fare because the driver is your father." And she kept walking briskly toward the only front door of our house.

Frank stood frozen, as if suspended in midair, trying to hold on to the profile of that man he had barely glimpsed from the back seat of the car. That was how he met his father, when he was six years old.

His story begins with that scene, a moment he remembers down to the smallest detail. His childhood and his adolescence, like part of his adulthood, are full of bravery, daring, an attachment to life, and an unshakable faith in God. He grew into manhood listening to his intuition, between courage and audacity.

I came to know him through the byways of life, and I never forgot his bright eyes or the two dimples in his smile, which stood in contrast to a shyness that lived just under the skin — a shyness he overcame, a little, through his talent for painting and for sport. Having known Frank as a child is one of those gifts I treasure. When I saw him today walk through the doorway of my house — neatly bearded, with the bearing of a leading man, and those same eyes that gather moons full of promises and hope — I confirm what he so often repeats: "God is with me, and He always was."

He learned hard work as a child. He came to the edge of many kinds of abuse, and he saw death pass close by. The sum of those experiences, together with the severity of the streets, tempered his character with rigor.

He was born on *Día de la Raza* in 1997, on a Sunday at dawn, under a nickel-bright moon resting in the gray sky over a hospital in Los Mina, Santo Domingo. The young woman in labor — a girl with broken dreams but full of hope — gave birth to Frank, her firstborn. Seven daughters by four different fathers would come later.

He is the only child of the route-K driver, whom he saw only on the day his mother made that astonishing revelation, and one other time, when his father invited him to his home. On that second occasion he was received by his stepmother, who never spoke a word to him. The echo of his own steps on the cement floor still resounds in his memory, along with the cold walls where there was nothing but silence for him. Because of that cold reception, he set aside the possibility of returning, with a feeling of relief and peace — not knowing that would be the last time he would see his father.

His father died twelve years ago — the same length of time Frank has spent wishing him light from on high. He absolved him of every fault and every grudge, so as to face life with less weight on his shoulders.

This boy lived in Los Mina until he was five, in a house with many rooms and few resources, under the care of his maternal grandmother and surrounded by thirteen other members of his family. For reasons Frank cannot recall, one day they left the big house, and his grandmother, his mother, and he set out for Santiago to settle in La Otra Banda. There he spent some time without doing much, under the protection of those two women.

Once they were settled, his mother began working in private homes. Frank, aware of his role as the eldest son, understood that he, too, had to help support the household. The boys in the area shined shoes in the city, and so he decided to do the same in Parque Duarte, a well-known landmark in Santiago, set in the very heart of the city's historic center.

"As a shoeshiner, I learned a lot of little tricks at the park. I even realized that if I moved around the area, I made more money than if I stayed sitting on a bench in the plaza. So I'd spend the day going round and round, offering my services from seven in the morning on," Frank says, his gaze drifting.

"At the park, I only had to fight once — to defend a kid who was new there and smaller than me. He was shining a customer's shoes when he splashed a little polish on one of his socks. The customer, an aggressive bully, slapped the defenseless boy so hard he turned his face. The kid started to cry, badly frightened, but the man kept hitting him. Watching that mistreatment, without thinking about the consequences, I smashed my shoeshine box into the man's face. When he squared up to come at me, nine of the others arrived to back me up.

"So now it was eleven against one. In their hands my defenders had knives and sharpened bottle ends. Two of them were sizing him up with guava-wood clubs, ready to take him on as he deserved. When he saw the fury in our faces, the bully took off running, and I haven't seen him *hasta el sol de hoy* — to this very day."

So Frank came to know some of the injustices and rough edges of life. By day he worked as a shoeshiner; at night, he washed windshields at the city's "hot" intersections. The night work was more dangerous, and a greater threat to the dignity of any child. The abuses that take place under those conditions are so many that listing them all would add several volumes to this story.

"Washing windshields, I think the devil himself invented it," this good young man says — speaking from experience.

"Apart from the fact that a car can run you over at any moment, you're up against the temptation of the drugs, the insults of the people, the brawls that break out, and the propositions from immoral adults who size you up like an object. They think you're a means to do bad things, or that you're something useless.

"The humiliating insults, full of bad words, that the drivers used to throw at me cut me very deep, and they kept echoing in my ears, all of them at once, for a long time. There comes a point when you start to disqualify yourself, when you start to believe that it's true — that you're trash, a nuisance, good for nothing — especially when those words come from grown people, who are supposed to be the guides and counselors of children.

"I don't know if people realize how a child's face changes when he is insulted. If they would stop and look, they'd see the harm they're doing. But it's also true that only by facing those difficulties do you learn what you're capable of, because, as the saying goes, necessity has the face of a heretic.

"My eyes would light up when someone gave me ten pesos for cleaning a windshield. I always asked the drivers' permission, and I never threw the sponge without their consent, although a lot of the time that didn't help either. I felt that people rejected me anyway, but at least I'd earn some three hundred, four hundred, even five hundred pesos a day if it didn't rain and there was a lot of traffic on the avenue. When it rains, the cars move slower, and you take advantage of that to clean the glass or to ask for help.

"One night, while I was washing windshields, a man driving an SUV invited me to talk, on the pretext that he lived very alone and had no family. He told me he would treat me like a son, that he would buy me dinner and give me anything I needed. Intuition told me not to go with him, but I accepted on the condition that two of my friends came along. The man told me there was no problem with that, so I went and got the other two.

"The three of us got into the back seat, and he took us to a big empty lot, full of weeds, on a major avenue of the city. It was a very dark place where you couldn't see anything except the high grass and a path where a few vehicles would pass. When we arrived, some men were waiting for us — men with a strange look about them — but we never managed to make out their faces clearly.

"From the moment we pulled up in the SUV, the man who had invited us unlocked all four doors. A group of men appeared at once and, without saying a word, set on one of my friends, the one sitting next to the window, with baseball bats. I was stunned at the rage with which they were beating him. My other companion and I took off running like blind roosters, not looking back, knowing the men were after us. I jumped a fence twice my height.

"As I jumped the fence, I felt a supernatural force lift me up and over the wire without so much as brushing the posts, and I can tell you it was God who lifted me at that moment, because I felt His help. Once we were on the sidewalk, we kept running until we reached the police station, but when we came back to the place, the men were already gone. My friend was lying in the brush, badly beaten, twisting in the dark, dying from the blows to his head, almost gone.

"We rushed him to the hospital, which was very close by, but after almost a month admitted, he died. That event marked my life, and for a long time guilt ate at me. Now, looking back at that moment, I am sure those men were thirsty to kill someone — it didn't matter who.

"The killers never paid for what they did. The death of a windshield washer isn't news to society. He passed away unnoticed, with the world's back turned. We were never able to reach his family, because he had never told us anything about where he came from. That is how many of these boys die — and their families find out long afterward.

"After that horrible event, back at the traffic light, an elegant woman twice my age came up to me. Very well put-together, by the way. She offered me a lot of money to throw acid in the face of a woman she hated. Out of jealousy, it seemed. Of course I didn't accept. That experience helped me understand even more clearly the harshness of the streets, what a risk it is for any child, and how those of us who go out looking for a better life are taken advantage of.

"When I realized that these horrors were not happening only to me but to almost all the boys, I gave up washing windshields for good. God helped me make that decision in time.

"At fourteen, I came to know the educational programs at Acción Callejera, and I was placed in the care of Cinthya Lora — a psychologist with a strong character but a very sweet one. She guided me and enrolled me at the Escuela Mercedes Batista in La Otra Banda; she helped me see the importance of education. Her teachings marked me so deeply that whenever I would drop out of school, Cinthya's lectures echoed in my ears, and I'd go straight back to class.

"At Acción Callejera I was formed in values, I discovered my talent for sports, and I trained in different areas — tools that will be with me for life. There I received the loving support of Bendodina Jiménez, a psychologist who taught me to see life from another angle, with new possibilities. I also remember the advice and the close attention of Yesenia Rodríguez, an extraordinary woman who guided me, as did Yohanny Rodríguez. I will never forget the struggle, the trouble, and the trips to Santo Domingo that Heidy González made with me to obtain my birth certificate when I turned eighteen. Nor do I forget the kindness of Carmelo Mateo, and his faith in what I could become.

"I count it a real blessing to have met this team of professionals at the Foundation, because from their hands I learned the value of taking care of myself, of tolerance and respect for others — among many other lessons I carry with me.

"With the backpack of life-tools I received at Acción Callejera, I worked for three years at another foundation devoted to children's welfare, where I trained to guide and care for children who, like me, run into sharp stones along the road. Alongside my work, I joined an evangelical church where I found spiritual nourishment, an oasis of peace, and an answer to all my needs.

"This year, when I finish high school, I plan to enroll in the university to study educational psychology. I'm very drawn to that field, because I know that with that knowledge I'll be able to guide other people in their human development and in their life experiences.

"At the moment I'm a coach and a player on the Escuela de Fútbol Santiago Junior team at Parque Central. Soccer is my favorite sport, though I also enjoy running. Since the very first *Santiago Corre*, I've taken part in every race, breaking records in my category. Recently I traveled to Colombia for a tryout as a soccer player, and I went back in May of this year with the same purpose. I work for a construction company, and I still live with my mom and my grandmother — two good women who support me in everything I take on."

Before our conversation comes to an end, Frank says that there are no excuses for doing things badly, that he doesn't regret the mistakes he has made but tries to rise above them. He believes firmly in prayer and in God, and he insists, too, that he wouldn't change a single one of the stones he found along the road, because every one of them taught him to keep going.

The two of us, sitting in a corner of the patio of my house, brought the Sunday to a close, both of us pleased to have had the chance to be together — but I wanted to end with a simple question:

"In one word — what does Acción Callejera mean to you?"

Frank smiled and, without thinking twice, answered with certainty:

"Family!"

Heavenly Conversations

"Heavenly Conversations" presents an angel who, with love, receives boys and girls from Gaza, Israel, Ukraine, the Congo, and the Dominican Republic, embodying the worldwide tragedy of child abuse. The author evokes the hope of a God who, in the midst of pain, extends His hands to heal wounds both physical and emotional, on Earth and in Heaven, still believing in His creation: humanity.

Rosa María Cuesta

At the news of yet another conflict, a barefoot, smiling angel — a guide of the souls of children — welcomes into Heaven the many boys and girls now arriving from Earth. The angel, with a retinue of seraphim and cherubim in white robes and gentle faces, stands ready to receive the latest innocents fallen to war.

The guiding angel and the retinue are tiny beings, with no particular skin tone, just as we are shown in our churches — where, by the way, there are no Black angels. Their faces are smiling, even though they suffered in their earthly lives. They wear ivory-white tunics that wrap around the torso and cross between their four wings. Two wings cover part of the body; the other two help them fly.

"It is October 2023. We have a great deal of work today," the guiding angel says to the retinue. "Come with me."

They all rise into the air and glide swiftly toward the luminous, arched gateway, because a great number of children are on their way from a place in flames.

"*As-salamu alaikum!*" the guiding angel calls out, welcoming the group now arriving at the gates of Heaven, their faces full of wonder, their bodies badly bruised.

"*Wa alaikum as-salam!*" answers a group of hundreds of children killed in the bombing of the Al-Ahli Hospital, in the Gaza Strip.

The angel looks with sorrow at the children's grief-stricken faces. The boys wear *taqiyahs* on their heads, while the girls arrive crowned in glorious *hijabs*. The angel is horrified at the sight of those innocent souls, their clothing reddened with blood, their bodies burned or mutilated, many of them missing vital organs, all of them with faces drawn tight by terror.

With great compassion, the angel receives them, trying to bring calm to their hearts. But shaken by this genocide, the angel asks them:

"What happened to you down there on Earth?"

The children, their voices faint and rising in a discordant chorus, answer that they had no time to understand anything. Some people had been hooked up to monitors; others had only a fever. More than a thousand people had taken shelter in that hospital, which suddenly turned into an inferno.

"There, the doctors were performing surgeries without electricity, and they operated on me without anesthesia. In the middle of that painful ordeal, I woke up here, in Heaven," said Bilal indignantly. He was a twelve-year-old boy who had stepped forward to address the angel.

"In Gaza, more than fifty percent of the population is children. We don't know much about the hatred that lives in the hearts of adults, but even without understanding it, we pay dearly for the consequences of war, because we don't know how to defend ourselves.

"My name is Amira. In Arabic it means 'princess,' and I want to tell you what I remember. Last week, my parents were murdered, and I was left an orphan. The neighbors took me to a nearby hospital, the only safe shelter in the area. There I found many other children, and although we were afraid, from time to time we would play in the basement of the shelter, and on Fridays the adults would gather us for the *Jumu'ah* prayer. But on the dawn of the day no one expected, everything changed, and life froze all at once. As we slept, an explosion shook us, and I felt my body begin to burn.

"Then a rocket struck. Even though no one now knows who launched it, we all suspect who was responsible. The blast destroyed the hospital where I was. Even though I was badly hurt, I saw many people, bloodied and mutilated, being carried on stretchers through the darkness. I didn't want to keep seeing such horrible images. That is why, since arriving in Heaven, I feel better," the girl explained to the guiding angel, who wanted to understand what had happened in that hellish place.

While Amira was telling her story, other groups of children also in transit drew near, this time from Israel. One of them raised a hand, asking for a turn to speak.

"*Shalom!* My name is Shadi, and I'm from Israel. I was five years old, and I lived with my parents on the streets of Sderot, very close to Gaza. Suddenly, armed men came into our house with hatred on their faces and gunned us all down, the neighbors too.

"I recognized the bodies of many people I knew, while everything around us burned, even our little garden. That was how I set out for Heaven, and here I am, looking for peace," Shadi said.

Deeply saddened by the vulnerability of children, and seeing how distressed they all were, the guiding angel first invited them to drink a tea of linden and valerian, before taking them to see every corner of infinite harmony there is in Heaven — the very harmony we are told abounds up there.

They had all grown calm when thousands of cherubim arrived from Ukraine. "*Pryvit, pryvit!*" they called out in greeting. But because of how long they had been in Heaven, all they remembered was that they had been bombed by order of a short, malice-filled little man with a certain resemblance to Ivan the Terrible. They could not recall his name, but they knew he was still ordering massacres, not caring whether the dead were children or adults.

As they shared the tea, Hassan, a boy from Gaza, watched a large group of seraphim playing with a globe, turning it with some difficulty. He noticed that those angels had no hands, and many of them had no feet either. It was clear they hadn't been born that way; they had been mutilated. Even so, they floated with grace and joy, and that astonished him. Curious, he asked the host angel who they were. The guiding angel answered:

"They all come from the Congo, and most of them are girls. They have been here in Heaven for many years. From around 1885 to 1906, more or less, Leopold II reigned in Belgium. That evil king set himself on seizing the riches of the Congo at any cost — above all, its great reserves of rubber.

"That sadist, Leopold II, hoodwinked the international community as malicious rulers know how to do, and managed to bring the Congo's population from twenty million down to only ten million, through a long catalog of abuses inflicted on those forced to harvest the rubber — a slavery that took up all twenty-four hours of their day.

"Behind a veil of supposed philanthropy, King Leopold II made the Congo his private colony. At the altar of his own riches, that beast of the Belgian monarchy imposed sadistic punishments on the harvesters, among them boys and girls. If they failed to deliver the minimum required, they were whipped, or the girls were sexually assaulted. Their hands and feet were cut off, until whole tribes were left without hands and lame. And tragically, the Congolese knew that their land held mines heavy with riches they themselves could never touch. Humiliated, they walked barefoot over the carpets of their own wealth, by then seized by wicked hands."

As the children listened to the angel's explanations, questions began to surface, one after another, among the new arrivals — especially as they discovered stories so much like their own.

"Guiding angel, forgive me — why are there so many girls in that group over there?"

"Ah, yes," the angel answered sorrowfully. "They died in the process of having their genitals mutilated."

"But more keep arriving — do they still do that to them?" asked one of the new arrivals.

"Yes, sadly. More than two hundred million girls around the world have suffered some form of genital mutilation, and they cannot withstand the pain or the infections this procedure causes them," the host angel acknowledged.

Along a luminous path lined with white lilies, there is another group of angels with shoeshine boxes in their hands. Some still hold a sponge for cleaning car windshields, while others walk along with trays of sweets and small treats balanced on their heads to sell.

A boy from Ukraine asks the guiding angel in surprise:

"Who are those children who, even though they're working, dance all the time here in Heaven?"

"They are children who lived their lives in the streets of one of the two countries that share a beautiful island in the Caribbean. They are from the Dominican Republic, where people dance to a rhythm called merengue. Dominican governments have signed countless agreements promising to guarantee children's rights, but once those in power take command, amnesia comes over them. That is why so many children get by however they can in the streets. The ones who die arrive here in Heaven carrying a heavy load of social injustice.

"Many of those children lose vital parts of their bodies doing dangerous work in high-risk places. The one who dances all the time is called *Buche*. From the time he was very small, he sprayed agricultural plantations in his country with substances that ruined his health, and he died of lung cancer. The other one, the one with the tricolor maraca, is Javier, who lived for many years under the traffic lights of his city. He was killed, and we believe no one missed him, because not even he himself knew who had stolen his life.

"The good thing about that group is that they never lose hope that, one day, everything will change in their favor."

After this tour of Heaven from top to bottom, night fell. The celebration the angels organized every day in that paradise was about to begin.

The boys and girls of Gaza changed out of their bloodstained clothes and tried, hopefully, to put on the delicate ivory-white tunics, but the fabric still let their wounds show through. The children of Israel, still shaken by that sudden massacre, managed to hide the stains on their tunics with their wings.

The cherubim from the Congo had been in Heaven for a long time, and they did nothing now but sing — for, having no hands, the only instrument they could play was the instrument of their voices.

The mutilated girls, still skittish, carrying their pain on their backs and a sadness that pierced through their wings, sang Allegri's *Miserere* in chorus, together with Psalm 51, to ease their sorrow.

And because wherever music, dance, and rhythm are spoken of, Dominicans show up at once, those angels who had lived their lives in the streets asked, without hesitation, for *güiras* and *tamboras* to be brought to them, so they could impress Saint Peter and liven up the celebration with slow little steps.

As the concert began, the guiding angel said goodbye and handed command over to Saint Peter — now the conductor of a great orchestra of millions of innocent children, and keeper of the key that opens the gates of that paradise we have been told about since we were small.

As the sound of celestial music thundered around them, the children sang and danced. And little by little, the scars began to heal. Each one, from their own culture and their own story, offered a singular tribute to paradise.

The cherubim from the Congo sang with untamable joy. The children of Gaza and Israel shared songs in Arabic and Hebrew. And the Dominican girls and boys carried the rhythm of merengue in their bodies, like heartbeats keeping time with their hope. Despite their losses, in Heaven they all found a refuge where their differences merged into a single song of peace.

These conversations keep turning over in my mind, and in the end I conclude that the world is mortally wounded, and children, of course, are its most defenseless victims. Millions of tender lives are cut short while the powerful violate rights, justify bombings, and divide the blame among themselves.

Every child killed in Gaza — more than 13,000 in less than a year — every small life lost in Syria, in Ukraine, in the Congo, in the streets of the Caribbean and so many other places on the map, reminds us that war defeats even the one who wins.

If there is any consolation, it lies in the certainty that all of them will find an eternal refuge in Heaven — because we have already given them hell here on Earth.

Farther on Down the Road, There Are People[1]

In this true story, as difficult and as hard as the lives of so many, Milagros de Jesús de Féliz brings out the courage of Robenson, her protagonist, along with his admirable capacity for resilience — moved and steadied by a powerful and unshakable faith in God.
Yesmín Haddad

"I am brave, and I do what I have to do!" Robenson said to me when we greeted each other warmly while I was pouring myself the last of the coffee. That was how our meeting began — a long talk to catch up on the life and the small miracles of this young man, as deeply loved as he is admired. We were both happy to find ourselves together again after so much time.

It was a Friday afternoon, the air cool and pleasant. Robenson wore a beard that accentuated his maturity, made him look like a gentleman, and he carried a smile so wide and so honest that it filled the room. I listened closely to every detail of his story,

1 Originally published in the anthology *El niño que no fui* (Cuba: Editorial Luminaria, 2026).

told with the ease and the wisdom of someone whose experience seemed to double his thirty-four years.

I took advantage of a pause in the conversation to ask him how he was feeling. As if he had been waiting for the question, his coffee cup still in his hand, he answered me with light in his eyes:

"I'm very well. I have a woman I love and two children who are my greatest treasure," he said, with a proud and happy face.

After that answer, the conversation continued without pause.

"I was born in Fort Liberté, in northeastern Haiti. My parents were of Haitian descent. I have an older brother, André, who is a Catholic priest, and a younger sister, Widelene, who sells secondhand clothing. They both live in Port-au-Prince, but I've spent the last twenty-four years in the Dominican Republic, and I love this country."

With a grateful smile, and a touch of mischief, he begins to fill in the details.

"For as long as I can remember, I've been aware of a particular gift I carry: I can read people's auras and pick out their intentions before their words or their actions give them away. I believe deeply in the signs of the zodiac and in the omens that fate sends my way. So if I leave the house and stub my right foot, I stop, turn back, and rethink my path, because I know the day won't bring good things. But if I stub the left, I keep going with confidence, sure that everything will fall my way.

"My dreams have always been a kind of secret compass, showing me what's coming and saving me from running into trouble."

After speaking about his beliefs, Robenson paused briefly, perhaps to put his memories in order before continuing his story.

"My dad was a merchant, and my mom was a wonderful homemaker. She was the one who made all of us happy. I had a good childhood while she was at my side, but she died when I was ten. My world fell apart, and my life changed in fundamental ways for a child of that age. Sadness took over the house. My brother and sister were just as sad as my dad, and everything began to go wrong. I couldn't bear that atmosphere.

"My dad was a good man, but he was always working and never had time to look after us. That was part of why I decided to run away from home and live on the street. For me, that was the biggest decision of my life — I couldn't sleep thinking about it, and I dreamed about dying. I thought I might die, because in Haiti danger is something you grow used to, and killing a person is common. They bury you and that's that.

"So I told my friend Luis what I was planning, and I packed a backpack to leave from the school we both attended in Haiti. Luis and I went first to Port-au-Prince. The people who saw us warned us about the danger we were in, because by then there was already a lot of violence in the streets, for adults and children alike. Following their advice, we decided to cross the border into the Dominican Republic. We knew that life was better here.

"For a few months, we did whatever work we could in Dajabón or in Juana Méndez, and we changed what we earned back into Haitian money, because that way it stretched further for us to survive on. So we'd wake up in Haiti and, very early, cross over into this country without any trouble from the authorities, because in those years 'the guard didn't mess with you the way they do now,'" Robenson explains with evident conviction.

"One day, my friend Luis and I made the decision to stay in the Dominican Republic. We set out on foot from Dajabón with the idea of reaching Santiago, where, we'd been told, you could earn good money. The journey took us almost a month, because we didn't have enough cash to make the whole trip by vehicle. So we went from town to town, working at whatever we found along the way. That gave us enough to eat and to move on faster, paying for the occasional ride.

"I remember that the people were good to us, and generous. They gave us work, food, even a place to sleep in some houses. We were so grateful that we'd say goodbye to them with hugs that brought my mom back to my mind. I feel that God walked beside us all through that journey.

"Luis suffered from *pecho apretao* — a tightness in his chest. Every so often it would come over him and he couldn't breathe properly. Thanks to a few homemakers who looked after him with great love and care, he didn't die. Now I think God sent us those angels so we could survive.

"In the end, after going through a lot of hardship — colds coming and going — we made it to the Monumento a los Héroes in Santiago. There, many older boys and younger ones were waiting for us — boys who, like us, lived their lives in the streets. They had gone through the same thing to get from Haiti to Santiago, and they knew how to manage there.

"Phew — this new city dazzled us! So many lights, so many people in motion, and friends willing to help us. We felt as if we'd reached glory itself. The boys at the Monumento gave us their support right away. They showed us where we could sleep and, most important, they explained the *menéutica* of life on the streets to us. They set aside water, sandals, clean clothes, and *pica pollo* for us.

"My first night I slept with the others in an abandoned house on Avenida Francia, almost at El Ensueño. Very near that place I got work at a mechanic's shop whose owner was an exploiter

— a truly bad man who, for two years, gave me only breakfast, lunch, and fifty pesos a week, after I'd put in ten or even twelve hours a day from Monday to Saturday. I remember that if he gave me dinner because we had to work at night, he'd take it out of the weekly pay. That man and Satan had the same heart.

"I grew up and came to see this tormentor's intentions for what they were. So I set myself to gaining experience as a car mechanic. I quickly found work at Bojolo's shop, a good man who even let me sleep in a room of the shop itself, and who paid me as a night watchman on top of my mechanic's wages.

"It was a dream of a place, because don Bojolo bought me a comfortable bed, a decent bed of my own, and I was always grateful to him for it. At night I went to school, and on weekends I took driving lessons to get my license, until I had it.

"One Christmas, don Bojolo had a heart attack and died. I felt it deep in my heart, because he had always treated me with kindness. He used to spend time with me, telling me about his life and listening as I told him mine. After his death, his sons took over the shop, and the first thing they did was let me go.

"I thought back to what don Bojolo always used to tell me: 'Robenson, remember always that *más pa' lante vive gente* — farther on down the road, there are people, and they're good neighbors.'

"Two months later, don Bojolo's sons called me back to the shop to take up my old job, but this time it was I who turned them down, because I understood that their intentions weren't good. I already knew that the new job would include selling 'little packets' of the kind of thing that brings in money — and trouble. Easy money is very dangerous."

When Robenson spoke to me of his efforts, the light in his eyes lit up like that of someone proud to have sidestepped so many obstacles. He kept telling his story with a luminous calm in his face. I felt I was sitting across from a man who had lived, fallen, and risen again as many times as it took.

I didn't want to interrupt him, but I was struck by how, despite a life with so many scars woven into it, he had kept his soul clean and his dreams intact. With my heart lifted at being across from this brave young man, I went on listening closely and asking him a few questions, which he answered without hurry or strain. He, unaware of my thoughts, kept telling me his life in stations, like the litany of the Holy Rosary.

"With determination, and focused on reaching the goal, I kept on with my studies," he told me. "I got a new job as an assistant on a truck that delivered food, but that job had me out almost until daybreak, and since I needed sleep so badly, I decided to look for another way to earn my living.

"For two years, I bagged groceries at a supermarket. It was decent work, but it didn't pay a salary — I only got the customers' tips. At one point, I decided to change the way I made my living. Since I'd always behaved well, when I told the personnel manager I was leaving, she referred me to a company as a valet.

"I started parking cars at the restaurants in the area around the same Monumento a los Héroes that had taken me in when I first arrived in this city — and I've been doing that work for almost six years now. I like working as a valet, though you have to be careful with the various propositions people make you. You have to keep your head on straight to say no to easy money, and on top of that, being responsible for someone else's car keys is a real responsibility. I give thanks to Yohanny, from Acción Callejera, who used to tell me: remember, you have to be honest every day.

"In the end, I feel that God has walked with me. He has given me a beautiful, healthy family. He has also given me the grace to work hard, but with joy and complete trust in Him. I'm very happy to tell my story, because maybe some young man will read it and understand that you can get ahead without doing what you shouldn't."

Cónchole, Robenson, how much I am grateful for your story! In telling it, you have given me a lesson in life that I will keep with great respect and admiration. Your efforts carry a powerful truth: that even after crossing borders and facing so many difficulties, you were able to build a life with dignity, step by step, and full of purpose.

"Remember, ma'am, what I told you," he said as he rose to leave. "I didn't do it alone. God walks with me, and He always has." That was how he said goodbye, with the same bright eyes as ever.

With Rhythm in His Feet

The author tells us the story of Derlyn, a working boy from the streets "with the soul of bread and the heart of a lion," who at a very early age clothed himself in steadiness and generosity to carry himself through hard circumstances and the byways of life — abandonment, scarcity, mistreatment, responsibilities far beyond his years. His goodness and his strength of spirit are a gift to life, to our lives.
Irenarco Ardila Estupiñán

I have known Derlyn since he was very small, and the chance to spend time with him over the years is a gift beyond measure for me. Life brought us together at different stages of his life, and I bore witness to his growth, his effort, his daring, and his courage. He is one of those young men who wear their soul on their face and their goodness right at the surface. Derlyn meets life with the force of his magical character — the kind capable of turning any difficulty into an experience that shapes a life, an opportunity to be born again.

In the patio of my house, with green grass for a carpet and a shy sun filtering through the shade of a *higüero* tree, I had breakfast with Derlyn — the fighter of a young man I have admired since he was a boy. His big, sudden laugh announced his arrival. When I caught sight of him in his uniform — the shirt the color of his soul, the company logo beside his heart — I recognized the joy of sharing that table laid out for one of life's small banquets. Before we began breakfast, he took the lead in talking, like someone who feels both pride and urgency about telling his life and the barriers he has overcome.

To talk with Derlyn is an experience that lifts the spirit. His story inspires, and it confirms that courage is a decision, often made in childhood. That is what defines this admirable young man with laughing eyes and an open smile.

He was born with music in his soul and rythm in his feet. He is a hard worker and, to round out the picture, a true artist as well. He first saw the light in Carbonera, Montecristi, the eldest of ten siblings — six on his mother's side and three on his father's. The reach of poverty, the abandonment of his biological father, and a chain of misfortunes brought him to Santiago when he was seven. At that same age, he started school, full of hope.

With ease and joy, Derlyn remembers some of the episodes that marked his life.

"My mom worked away from the house, so it fell to me to make the meals for the others. She'd leave me the rice already measured out with the water, and I'd cook it for everybody. We went through a lot together. I remember we were going through the worst stretch of our lives — we were *en olla*, flat broke. We didn't have money to cover the basics, not even what we needed most. In the middle of all that hardship — more than you can imagine — a thief came in one night and took the little we had. He took the few pennies my mom had been paid, and other things, and the gas tank too. That was almost everything we owned. I thought right then that we couldn't just sit still and do nothing. With no other choice, we went back to cooking the rice on a charcoal burner.

"That event made me think hard, and I decided to help carry some of the financial weight off my mom and improve things for the family. That was how, at twelve, I started shining shoes in Los Guandules and later in Parque Duarte. The change brought in more income, but it was a great challenge, too, because the park was a place where violence lived and slept. With this new arrangement, I'd study in the morning and work the streets in the afternoon.

"I know what life on the street is, because I lived it from very early on. In that world, people respond badly to anything. There are a lot of ill-intentioned people, violent ones, ready to impose their will on you whether they're right or not. Because of all those dangers, I always tried to make sure my brothers and sisters didn't end up the way I had — and I would never want a son of mine to work or live on the street.

"People tend to generalize and to call every boy they see in the street a thief or a bad kid, when the truth isn't like that at all. That way of thinking hurts a lot. I was a working child who wanted to get ahead, to fulfill my dreams, and to protect my family. Since my father didn't do it, I felt the responsibility to take on that role."

That is how this young man, mature beyond his years, speaks.

"I was a calm kid, but I had to wise up when I realized that the ones who didn't were the ones who got mistreated. In the street we were supposedly a team, but when the time came to fight, they'd leave you on your own. And you had to fight; it was the law of life. So I decided not to bother anyone, and to respect the others so they would respect me — though that didn't always work.

"On the street there are many kinds of violence. I remember seeing my friends fighting savagely over five pesos," he tells me, with sadness. "Many friends from those years died, and almost no one missed them. Living your life in the streets is a deep, unjust burden for a child to carry.

"On one of those hard days, exhausted from the grind of the street, my friend Ruddy told me about the educational programs at Acción Callejera, and I started going every day. There I found guidance, respect, training, and a welcome among the educators. I liked the atmosphere of trust and shared understanding.

"After some time, they started a group that we chose to call *Futuro con Ideales* — Future with Ideals. I was selected to work formally at the organization, and I worked in the areas of Reception, Sports, Hygiene, Food, Kitchen Support, and Dental Assistance. Preparing for the formal job interview was part of the training, and I worked hard to get there," he tells me proudly.

"Acción Callejera also took on the work of getting me my identity documents. I'd reached nineteen without having a single one, and because of that I had access to nothing. I will always be grateful to the educators for helping me get my birth certificate and my *cédula*.

"Maybe a lot of people don't realize what it means not to have a registered name, not to have ID — but that condition shuts you out of so many basic rights and opportunities. You can't open a bank account, you can't get health insurance, you can't get married, you can't benefit from any government program. A person without ID simply doesn't exist. So getting that paperwork was something huge and precious to me. I remember the day I held it in my hands. It was as if I had been born again that very afternoon.

"With my existence finally recognized in the census, I started applying for work. They called me in for an interview at a supermarket, scheduled for two in the afternoon. The day came, and I dressed *con buena pinta* — sharp — in the only sneakers I owned. From a quarter past one, I was waiting on a corner near the supermarket when a tremendous downpour caught me by surprise and flooded everything, even under the overpass where I'd taken shelter. I couldn't show up looking right, or on time, the way I'd been taught. I arrived fifteen minutes late, and the head of Human Resources, with an authoritative look — and rightly so — told me the interview slot was over. And then I remembered what my grandmother used to say: *the one who's about to mess up doesn't see it coming.*

"With more faith, I kept on dreaming about working in that big, clean, air-conditioned place, because I knew my dreams were unbeatable.

"Three months later, I went back and applied for the job at the same supermarket, and this time they gave me the chance to work in parking-lot security. Grateful to God and to my superiors, I've been there eleven years now, and a while back I was promoted to camera monitor. Doing my job well, taking responsibility seriously, holding to good values, and bringing passion to whatever I do — all of that has helped me a great deal at work. I feel valued and respected by my superiors and my coworkers. God has been good to me.

"I finished high school, and recently I completed a two-year course at Infotep as an electrical technician, and I've already completed the required internship. When that training is finished, I'll take another course on installing solar panels.

"Two years ago I married a good woman who studied medicine — she graduated from UTESA. She's done her hospital rotations and is now waiting on her formal residency. For a long time she ran the washing-machine rental business I have with my brother as a partner, at my mother's house. It's called *Lavado-*

ra Los Martínez — Martínez Rentals. We gave it that name to lift up our family's unity."

Derlyn had a hero who has always taken him by the arm and helped him discover the paths of hope. She has gone on clearing the thorns from his road, and even today she gives him smiles to set against life's sorrows.

"My mom is the hero," Derlyn confirmed. "Right now she works as a janitor at a gas-bottling plant in the morning, and in the afternoon she runs a *colmado* the brothers all own together, *Colmado Los Martínez.* I dream of a chain of colmados in different parts of the city, run by my own people, with the vision of building a beautiful family portrait.

"I also bought a piece of land, and that's where I'll build my house.

"I'm an artist, and my stage name is Lirikal. I sing, I write songs, I do musical arrangements. I feel blessed, because God is crazy about me. And I'm a witness to that!"

Go Well!

The author tells us the story of Joel, someone who invites us to pause and witness how childhood rises again with strength every time it finds, in some act of generosity, the chance to bloom. A single gesture can open that door. "Life tapped Joel on the shoulder," and in doing so, it tapped ours too. Let us focus on what really matters and walk the path of goodness, setting aside that distracting illusion of "believing we possess."
Marión Pagés

That was the farewell of a boy of about thirteen, whom I came to know in this tangle of life. We were heading off on an outing to the mountains with a group of working children. The joy was contagious, and in the middle of all that excitement, Joel sent us off with his best wishes:

"Go well!"

He said it with his face lit by joy. He didn't go with us because he couldn't miss work. With that smile he wore seven days a week, he said goodbye, wishing us every good thing. That was the last time we saw him.

His life stays in our memory through that farewell, and through the legacy of pure love that his noble feelings reflected.

The years have trained my eye and sharpened my soul's sensitivity. Often we are not aware that, at any moment and without warning, life taps us on the shoulder so that we will turn around and look at others. Then we discover ourselves reflected in the people around us — people whose burdens and weariness move us — and we come to understand that they were true teachers of life. They came into the world to teach us how to live, how to give thanks, how to value what matters, even after they are gone.

That, in part, is what happened to me as I remembered Joel, and in this story I allow myself to share it briefly.

I met Joel when he was a boy shining shoes in the city center — a place that welcomes so many defenseless souls and, at the same time, lays dangerous traps that wound their dignity. On any bench in the park, you could come across this boy with his pants down to his knees, his hair turned blond by the force of the sun, scars on his legs, and on his soul too.

Joel was rough-edged, with cinnamon skin and an evasive gaze, like a squirrel's. He was distrustful, because his parents had been the first to fail him, and to that absence were added later the failures of his family and of society. But at such a tender age, Joel's anger was fixed on his mother's absence, and he used to say she had abandoned him and gone off alone to another town because she didn't love him.

"That boy was born when my daughter was fourteen. Because of the pregnancy, we threw her out of the house, and even so, she stubbornly decided to give birth to him. It was very hard for her, because Joel was born terribly thin and small, and she was left badly malnourished after the pregnancy. That child's arrival in the world was always a heavy burden for her and a disgrace to the whole family," his maternal grandmother would say during the home visits we made to her house.

"We never knew where my daughter went. She worked in private homes with her son always at her side, but it seems she grew tired, and without telling anyone, she abandoned him. We never knew the whereabouts of either one," the grandmother told us, with very little remorse and a hardened heart.

With the weight of that unexpected abandonment on him at such a young age, Joel set himself to shining shoes and came to the Foundation in search of guidance and support. A dedicated team of educators helped him through therapy that slowly mended his emotional wounds. They managed to locate his family, brought him back into the school system, and, through steady follow-up, encouraged him to move along a better path.

He stayed in school, showed important progress in his emotional life, softened the edge of his violent temper, and began working while he kept up his studies.

On the minibus route that ran from the city center to Hato del Yaque, Joel found humble work as a *pícher* — the fare-caller who rode standing at the door, one foot on the outer step and one hand gripping the bus for balance. He had no salary, only the right to fill the *palo de la cotorra*, the narrow bench tucked behind the driver and the front-passenger seats. That space, turned into his only property, became his livelihood. Every time he managed to place a passenger there, the full fare belonged to him.

The boy accepted the challenge and was an efficient *pícher*, until the day luck looked away while destiny lay in wait — on a restless weekend. The buses were packed with passengers, and the revelry in the streets was impossible to miss.

To sell that seat, Joel always moved half bent over, holding on precariously to the strip of aluminum between the bus's roof and the door. The day promised good earnings, but on that somber afternoon — one that cut straight across the best years of his childhood — the minibus bounced suddenly into a trench the driver could not avoid, and Joel fell face-first onto the pavement. The others riding with him feared what that dull thud of his body against the ground meant.

"His spleen burst!" — that was the news that spread quickly, before he reached Heaven.

The people in the neighborhood where it happened called for an ambulance at once, and it came to his aid with urgency and care.

The boy was complaining of severe abdominal pain. Heavy bleeding made him lose consciousness again and again, and his condition was very grave.

On the way to the hospital — gravely injured, rushed through streets that beat without a pulse, just like his heart — he asked the paramedics to tell his mother that he loved her, that he was grateful to her, and that he forgave her from his heart, perhaps so she might be freed of her own burdens and her days might be lighter.

The paramedics, visibly moved, told us of that final message, which shook them even though they were used to situations as painful as this one.

Joel saved his last gesture so as to leave no accounts unsettled — and surely, without that weight, the flight of his soul was that much lighter.

As soon as we heard the news of the accident, we went to help him, but we arrived too late. Joel had already gone, leaving us a moving message — a sorrowful symphony that, even today, many years later, still echoes in our memory.

Joel left us the key to a dusty album where so many boys like him rest, boys who, in their struggle to ease their sorrows, never had the chance to say goodbye to a world that still owes them their lives.

WHEN JOY APPEARS

Lives that, even marked by fragility, find moments of celebration and rest.

Four accounts in which faith, perseverance, and the presence of people touched by grace open up paths that are possible. Stories that remind us that God also lives in the streets and walks with those who keep going, even when joy is brief.

Caps of Dignity

Blessed are those who can find happiness in simplicity, fullness in goodness, and love in self-giving. Sometimes, the lives we hope to touch by offering a little of our time end up transforming our own forever. This is what Milagrós de Jesús de Féliz reveals to us in this beautiful story of dignity and hope.
César Román

At the end of January 2024, I had the privilege of attending the 119th Commencement Ceremony of my alma mater, the Pontificia Universidad Católica Madre y Maestra. In more than six decades of academic life, this institution has given the country and the world 98,059 professionals, and each graduating class, like this year's, renews a commitment to knowledge and to society. Its commencements, filled with symbolism and solemnity, preserve intact the rituals that remind us that education is an inheritance that transcends time.

At PUCMM, the academic authorities dress with strict formality, and the colors of each gown carry a meaning that denotes the degree of the person who wears it. The students also attend impeccably dressed, joining their joy to the formality of the occasion.

When I heard the notes of our national anthem, my heart stirred, and I remembered those graduations we used to hold in Hoyo de Puchula, a humble neighborhood in Santiago, located very near Estadio Cibao. Because of where it lies, beneath the avenues that surround it, people may pass by many times without realizing that the large buildings perched at the rim of the hollow are only a façade. In reality, they cover the upper edge of a funnel of poverty, densely inhabited by families living in deplorable conditions, who came in and settled on the land.

Right there, in that place where the sun hid the misery and the moon settled over the foul waters of a contaminated drainage gully, we set out to support children with educational tools and prevention programs. This meant designing strategies to offer a new direction, one capable of challenging poverty.

Through these educational spaces, the children and young people who came to those rooms received literacy instruction, skills training, recreation, reading, flute lessons, talks on pregnancy and drug-use prevention, first-aid training for key members of the community, and many other offerings essential to their formation.

Holding the graduations was never simple. I will never forget how willingly the families embraced that meaningful ceremony, which marked the close of the school year. They rented dresses for the girls and proper clothes for the boys so they could arrive dressed for the occasion, though no such thing was required. The only true requirement was to have attended the small room on the second floor of a church that pleaded with God for the souls of those families.

The girls, with eyes the color of the sky at daybreak, dressed in whatever colors were within reach, and the boys did the same. So that nothing would dim the splendor of those celebrations, each child was given a short red gown and a cap as white as their soul. Footwear was varied and unrestricted at those peculiar, unforgettable graduations, from sneakers to flip-flops.

The mothers kept watch over their children as they paraded eagerly along the street leading to Hoyo de Puchula, then descended a dangerous open-air stairway of dirt and cement, one the students knew by heart.

As soon as the procession began on the street above, the musicians of the Municipal Band would strike up songs suited to the occasion, and the graduates would make their way down the slope to parade along the community's main street. Then, in a well-ordered line, they climbed to the homework room, the educational space that welcomed them from Monday to Friday.

Once everyone was gathered in the crowded room — boys and girls, fathers and mothers, teachers, and relatives close to the graduates — the notes of the national anthem were sung. It was a very special moment, one of astonishing solemnity, that seemed to still those in attendance, along with the people of the community who had come to witness that great miracle. The residents, enthralled by the supreme spectacle of a celebration honoring the present and future of the neighborhood's children, found places for themselves wherever they could throughout the hollow.

Those graduations remain sealed in my memory. Each graduate represented a torch of honor, and each gown, a challenge to poverty. Together, they formed a rosary of voices, a new tribe whose shared dwelling celebrated the first footprints of education.

So that nothing would diminish the splendor of that grand celebration, a member of the community would take the floor to close the event. At the last ceremony I attended, the mother of six graduates, wearing a scapular on her chest, took the microphone, moved and with her eyes wet. With gratitude settled in her gaze, she managed only to say, "Thank you, thank you, thank you." With those words, one of the most meaningful graduations I have ever attended came to a close.

In those humble rituals, where the children sang the national anthem with their hands over their hearts, where the families showed their gratitude, and where the faces of those present reflected joy, the musicians, who played their instruments with such dedication while balancing their way up and down the slopes, remain in my heart like confetti at a celebration of gowns and caps of hope.

When the emotional ceremony ended, after each graduate had been called by first and last name, the air filled with joyful commotion, and we toasted with cake and red soda to the future those children longed to reach.

I remain seated on those worn steps, lit only by the faith and hope of those who believe in the transforming power of learning.

As I consider the contrast between two worlds — the solemnity of a university and the humility of Hoyo de Puchula — a deep truth is revealed: education, when it is genuine, becomes an invisible thread that weaves the dreams of a community into a firm fabric through which poverty cannot slip.

Today, as I call those moments back to mind, I celebrate with gratitude the dignity, the courage, and the unbroken desire to rise of each boy and girl. In every anthem sung and every gown worn with honor, a promise of change rises. If one lesson remains with us, it is that with perseverance, what once seemed impossible can indeed be transformed.

The True Gospel

In this story, the author invites us to become sowers of goodness, inspiring others to cultivate compassionate hearts through concrete gestures of solidarity and humanity. Only in this way can we help sustain the world the Almighty created for all, and ease the injustices and inequalities human beings themselves have raised against one another.
Mercedes Carmen Capellán

I recently visited a well-known, crowded shopping mall in Santo Domingo. The plaza was overflowing with people moving in haste, packages slung over their shoulders. It was Christmas, a season when everything feels urgent, in direct contrast to the true meaning of these days dressed in green and red. At one point, I stopped to watch the people coming and going along the stairways and corridors of the mall, and I felt as if we were moving at the bottom of a giant fishbowl. When I mentioned this to my husband, I think he was as struck by it as I was, so we decided to quiet our spirits and have lunch together as a family.

The place where we ate was a kind of privileged box seat, from which I could observe the urgency of the shoppers, the faces of the artisans offering their goods, the music confirming that we were indeed in Christmastime, and the grace of young people in their fashionable clothes. I spent a long while entranced, watching the Christmas decorations rise and fall from the mall's atrium for the delight of the little ones, amid all the rushing about.

Suddenly, very near where we were sitting, a young man of uncertain age came in, his face as drawn as that of the dead, his almond-colored eyes hungry for compassion, his clothes mended, his hair turned blond by the sun, his hands weathered, his lips dry. With desperate gestures, he was asking those present for something to eat. His physical appearance and his worn-out sandals said everything. I remember his dull, hopeless gaze, a look that pleaded more loudly than his voice. What caught my attention was that he was not asking for money, but for food, irrefutable proof that he was hungry.

Before long, one of the guards who watched over the plaza called him over politely and invited him to leave. I gathered the guard was lecturing him with some lines from the rule book about the prohibition against begging in the mall, but all I could see was the guard's hardened face and the terror-stricken expression of that young man, son of nowhere. Apparently, the boy obeyed and disappeared for a while.

Less than an hour later, he slipped back in from another side, carrying the same sadness, trying to stay out of the guard's line of sight and persisting in his request, because he needed something to eat. The people, busy with their lunches and distracted in their own worlds, looked at him and shrugged, a bad sign for his urgency.

After pleading at nearly every table, a compassionate family helped him in his hardship. It was a man with two girls who appeared to be his granddaughters, all seated at the last table in the dining area. The man wore formal clothes — worsted trousers, a checkered shirt — and a smile as open as his sparse silver hair. The presumed grandfather ordered him a full combo meal, drink included, a gesture of solidarity that offered the young man, with dignity, the happiness he had been longing for.

The young man sat at a table a fair distance from ours. I saw his eyes grow wet. The instant our gazes met was magical, and we both rejoiced in what had happened. With such a feast laid before him, set out for him alone, the young man recovered his good humor, and his face burst into joy. I could see that he was almost laughing to himself. At the first chance he had, he gave me a victory sign with his index and middle fingers spread apart. Instinctively, automatically, I returned the gesture, as if to say, "You deserve it, young man!"

In silent complicity with what had happened, and wanting to honor that gesture of solidarity, I approached the Samaritan and, touching him on the shoulders, expressed my gratitude — a forwardness on my part, since I did not know him.

The grandfather, with the unhurried bearing of a magnificent rector, smiling and visibly pleased, explained to me in a gentle voice, without surprise, that he did this often in order to give his granddaughters an example of solidarity.

"I want to leave them that legacy: that they be generous with the most vulnerable," he told me, with an impeccable smile.

He kindly thanked me for my words and, with the good kind of joy, took one granddaughter by each hand and continued on his way. He left without expecting any reward beyond that of teaching by example. I followed him with my eyes until he reached the stairs. Most likely, he carried a beautiful light in his heart, the kind that lights up when we understand what Christmas is really about.

That brief episode was one of my finest gifts during that festive season, for I too, like his granddaughters, received a little of his altruistic legacy.

The young man and I never said anything to each other, except when our joyful gazes crossed. And in that deaf and wordless exchange, heavy with empathy, I witnessed that God is everywhere. Then I remembered the well-known phrase attributed to Saint Francis of Assisi: "Be careful how you live; your life may be the only Gospel many people will ever read."

That young man's eyes remained in my heart as an eternal dialogue of joy, and as a standing ovation for those who, like that grandfather, preach the Gospel through their example, as the living Jesus did, the Jesus in whom I believe.

A Possible Happiness

In this story, the author reveals to us how care and love for our fellow human beings turn, in turn, into a deep satisfaction and a genuine happiness for ourselves.
María Victoria Menicucci

I sat down comfortably with part of my family in a charming restaurant that, in addition to its good cuisine and the way every table has its own intimate atmosphere, has a spectacular view, set as it is, and has been for many years, on Calle del Sol, at the foot of the Monumento a los Héroes.

Around an elegant table, we enjoyed the imposing lights that filtered through the beautiful windows of that great mass of marble, while we talked about the bustle of the cars along that artery of the city where the sun rises. We talked about a thousand topics, the kind that come up spontaneously when families gather.

We ordered a tray of appetizers to share, and each of us chose the main course that appealed to us. As I always do, I suggested to the person sitting next to me that he order something I would like to pick at, in case my own dish didn't quite suit me. My family knows this little quirk of mine and indulges me.

Just as we were beginning to enjoy our main courses, I heard a timid voice rising from the sidewalk, very close to our table: "Give me something, I'm hungry!"

A fine drizzle was beginning to fall. I looked over and saw that it was a child of about eight, no more — the same age as one of my granddaughters, who was there with me. The boy was looking at my table, at the dishes laid out on it. He had eyes that begged for pity, ashen lips, threadbare clothes, very weak arms. In his right hand he held a shoeshine box, and with the other hand he was rubbing his flat belly, signaling that he needed to eat.

I sat watching him closely. In less than a minute, one of the restaurant's waiters shooed him off with contempt, as if he were a fly hovering at the edge of the place, or a piece of trash someone wanted to sweep under the rug of misfortune.

Almost running, the boy crossed the street, dodging the cars, and sat down, ashamed, on the green grass of the wide esplanade of the Monumento, which took him in without reproach. He gathered himself, placed his shoeshine box close beside him like someone caring for his only treasure. Music was playing from the open trunk of a car parked across the way, and the boy watched the people passing without quite letting them see he was watching, his hand all the while moving over his belly.

For a long while I stayed with my eyes on the boy. Then I saw another child come up to him — probably a friend, or a brother. The boy offered him a plastic bottle half full of water, and the smaller one drank it down in a single swallow. The newcomer sat down beside him and they began to talk — perhaps about the good fortune of being alive.

By one of life's coincidences, I had recently read a passage that struck me. The humanist Erich Fromm, in one of his books, explains that human well-being depends not so much on what we receive as on our capacity to love. According to the author, taking an interest in our fellow human beings, practicing compassion, and giving without expecting anything in return are exercises that strengthen that capacity. When those attitudes become part of everyday life, he argues, the possibility of building a better world opens up to us.

Watching this hungry child in the middle of so many people pretending not to see him, I doubt that we can reach that *possible happiness* in the face of a childhood that — born in a country where its rights are not guaranteed — grows up with the worst stigma there is, the stigma of hunger marked on its forehead.

What Fromm said is something some people seem to intuit. Thanks be to God, the boys waited long enough, without losing hope. In the end, from the hands of a Good Samaritan, they received the plate of food they so badly needed. Without grabbing or asking too many questions, they shared it between them, while they stayed seated on the same green and welcoming grass that had taken them in without prejudice.

Eternal Traces

Most of us tend to think that transcendence is born of grand gestures and acts that make noise in the world. Yet this story reminds us that simple, brave, silent gestures also leave deep traces and indelible memories. Reading this story, the first thought that comes to mind is that God dwelled in the home and in the heart of that great woman.
Excélsido Féliz Mustafá

There are gestures that hold up the world in silence, and for that very reason they reach an immense greatness. Near the Cathedral of Santiago, in the busy heart of Parque Duarte, where the streets served as an uncertain refuge for many boys, there lived a woman who turned the living room of her home into a daily act of love.

In the early 1990s, doña Vilma Guzmán Taváres made her house a safe harbor for working children who lived much of their lives in the streets and came to the programs at Acción Callejera.

Every afternoon, Monday through Friday, this great woman opened the door to hope quietly, without ceremony. Her living room filled with timid steps and with eyes that, little by little, learned to trust. Faithful to her generous routine, she always left something ready on the table — and what she set out, for them, meant shelter, care, and a silent gesture of generosity.

"Served with dignity, the table always held fresh water, juice to share, and often freshly baked bread from the bakery on the corner," Jochy and Juan *Oreja* recalled, remembering those days that marked their lives.

So those details remained engraved in the hearts of that army of boys who dreamed of a different future. Berto, one of them, has never forgotten the way doña Vilma called each child by name, and how that melody tasted to him like the home he had never had. In that living room, every chair offered a welcome, and every greeting was an act of recognition.

Today we know that doña Vilma dwells in eternity, and lives on in the grateful memory of those who found refuge, dignity, and welcome in her home.

Even now, that gesture of calling them by the music of their own names continues to rise through time, reminding them that every life deserves to be recognized and embraced with the dignity we all long for.

7

THE STATION OF SILENCE

Before entering this station, it is worth pausing for a moment.

Seven stories open a small crack through which we glimpse the lives of girls and young women from whom violence stole their childhood and dreams. Some are no longer with us; others made their way through. In each one beat truths that press in on us, and memories that refuse to be forgotten.

Their voices rise so that violence will not become a habit. They wake the conscience so that these lives are not buried in indifference. To tell their stories is also a way of refusing to let silence have the last word.

Alone in the Crowd

Magdalena, alone in the crowd, torn in body and soul, shares her ordeal after having been "given over to be raised" by a couple who promised to offer her a better life by taking her to the city. The author tells us, with deep emotion, how child slavery persists in our society, disguised as the appearance of a "better opportunity."
Vicky Pappaterra de Read

From 2008 until the end of 2014, I had the privilege of seeing, up close, the work of the International Labour Organization (ILO-IPEC), a program with the difficult mission of eradicating the worst forms of child labor. The effort is grounded in the terms of Convention 189, adopted by our country to help eliminate this scourge that still wounds the most vulnerable children.

It was a profoundly enriching experience. I came to know in detail the various forms child labor takes. I met children who developed cancer from spraying pesticides on rice fields, boys who lost parts of their fingers in mechanic shops, and others who were left sterile from carrying merchandise too heavy for their age.

The work also addressed a form that remains hidden from view: domestic child labor. In those programs, the ILO turned its lanterns toward revealing the vast scope and the implications of this harmful practice, lodged within the culture not only of our country, but of many other nations.

Boys and girls who have not reached the legal minimum age perform dangerous tasks in other people's homes — without set hours, without anyone to mourn them, without anyone to speak up for them. They become invisible creatures, swallowed up behind those walls where, according to what the culture tells us, their lives were supposed to improve.

According to UNICEF's global estimates, in 2021 there were 97 million boys and 63 million girls working: a total of 160 million. But it is not enough to stop at the figures. We have to consider the conditions under which child labor takes place — generally tied to poverty, to family dysfunction, and to the lack of opportunities in their communities, among other hardships.

A few days ago I met with one of the participants from that program, in which we identified so many girls in this situation. Today, now an adult, she feels ready to bear witness to the danger of handing our sons and daughters over to be raised by others.

I will refer to her as Magdalena, but it is easy to gather that this is not her real name. To preserve the privacy of those involved, in this story everyone goes by a pseudonym.

Magdalena and I met in a pleasant place in the city, the kind of welcoming setting that invited a calm conversation. I arrived early and hung my rain-soaked jacket on the back of a chair. I took a seat by a window and ordered a hot chocolate while I waited for that girl — now a woman — whom I would surely recognize by her eyes. Before long she arrived, and our reunion brought me immense gladness.

Magdalena is taller now than the last time I saw her. Her skin remains as fresh as the rain, and her smile is the same shy one

I remembered from those years. She is now a woman of dignified bearing and serene presence, who speaks unhurriedly and with the same restful gaze of her adolescence.

From the moment she heard I was gathering stories from those years of work with children, Magdalena got in touch with me to describe what she had lived through. She insists on sharing her experience as a warning to families who hand off the raising of their children, giving them over to others. Many parents do this, convinced that this way the children will have more opportunities, when in truth they are being exposed to grave dangers — the girls especially.

Magdalena had always been someone who let you in close, so it didn't surprise me when she gripped my right hand in hers and began to unburden herself. You could see her urgency to tell it all. Her eyes fixed on mine to make sure I was listening with care.

That girl, today a woman of strength and grace, remembers that at ten years old her parents handed her over to be raised by a couple — doña Casilda, a teacher with an austere air about her, and her husband Miguel, a military man with a gaze so imposing he might as well have been called Lucifer. The couple had a summer house in the hills near where Magdalena lived with her family.

She and one of her sisters used to help the lady of the house with the domestic chores, which gave way to a relationship that seemed sound but would end up collapsing into the worst of nightmares. In that corner of the countryside, even though the family went without much, Magdalena found her happiness among her own people. Yet her parents, dreaming of a more promising future for her, decided to send her to the city under the protection of this new family — without ever suspecting the ordeal that awaited their daughter.

"The day my dad entrusted me to those two people, he laid out a list of conditions about my care, and only doña Casilda heard him out. The military man, by contrast, slipped out of his responsibility by going out to the patio to look over his vehicle — like a sign of bad omen," Magdalena recounts.

Her parents knew that she would have to help out with the chores around the house, but they trusted that she would also have better educational opportunities alongside the schoolteacher Casilda, in addition to access to other benefits of the city that they could not provide for this girl with her beautiful face. None of that came to pass.

With careful clarity, she remembers the day she left her people behind. And, like someone with a presentiment, she said her goodbyes through tears. That same sadness traveled with her to the new house, and with much grief she still remembers those difficult moments...

"What I found there was a quantity of tasks that went beyond what a girl my age could physically handle, and along with it, an abuse that took over my daily routine. I was very shy and never said anything. I just obeyed without complaint, the way my parents had taught me. But often, even at ten o'clock at night, I was still working.

"Doña Casilda was very harsh in giving her orders, because her husband was harsh with her too. From the time I arrived at the house, I witnessed mistreatment — first in words, then physical too. The husband was a beast with a military rank: a career abuser who lived embittered because his wife couldn't conceive children, an absurd excuse for putting into practice every devilry that crossed his sick mind."

Magdalena tells me that, six months after she arrived at the house, Miguel violently took her innocence from her, and threatened to kill her if she dared to say anything. At that very young age, she felt deeply shaken, and although she asked her parents on several occasions to take her back, she did not dare to reveal the true reasons. So she went on at the mercy of that uniformed beast, trained in the darkest hells.

"I remember that I went back to my little ranch less and less, and that began to break the beautiful bond I had with my family. It was very painful, because the world I had grown up in and the one I was now living in were completely different — and on top of that, my feelings of abandonment kept growing.

Magdalena says that the moment she crossed the threshold of the house, Miguel would threaten her again, immediately, again and again. She remembers with sharp clarity the day after the first time he raped her. Her abuser had his chin smeared with shaving cream. He stood naked from the waist up in front of a small mirror that hung on the wall beside the sink. With the razor in his hand he was threatening her, and she, broken by pain and fear, was trembling uncontrollably. Inevitably, every time she saw him, terror took her breath away. Even today, that image follows her like a shadow.

So time passed, inexorably. That girl went on facing all the horsemen of the Apocalypse that were trampling her life before its time. Against doña Casilda's wishes, at eleven she enrolled in night school. But that only worsened her way of the cross, because it gave the wrongdoer the most convenient chance to follow her and force her into seedy motels, where he crossed the limits of cruelty and his sick way of seeking pleasure.

When she was thirteen, the predictable happened. She began to feel different and noticed that her belly was growing. She had not menstruated for three months. Her abuser suspected a pregnancy, and that was enough for him to take her to a clinic that was known for abortion tourism, in order to protect the "honorable" name of the man who would pay for the procedure, this woman told me with her voice breaking.

"That little room — suffocating, with poor hygiene, reeking of blood and unwashed bodies — served as both a surgical room and laboratory of death. Hard as I fought with everything I had, four people held me down and tied me to a filthy gurney, and they forced me to inhale a substance that left me without strength, at the mercy of the savage who would carry out the abortion.

"After that butchery, the uniformed beast told his wife that he had taken me to the countryside. But in truth, he took me to the home of some friends near Canca La Piedra, in Tamboril. There I became gravely ill from hemorrhaging. Now, with the awareness that the years bring, I understand the enormous risk I ran.

"The abortion was horrific. To remove the fetus, that savage of a man-midwife crushed my bladder and my urethra, which gave me pelvic inflammatory disease. In that brutal procedure, the man-midwife — or rather, the devil's butcher — tore the tissues between my vagina and my rectum so badly that I was never able to conceive children, just like doña Casilda.

"I remember that when the massacre was over, I woke in a pool of blood, with the feeling that I couldn't breathe. My body was shaking. I felt a great weakness in my legs and a desperate need to lie down, but they made me walk.

"I felt I was dying — and I swear to you, in that moment, that was exactly what I wanted.

"I was a helpless witness to the murder of my own child, and that is something I will never forget," she says, the full weight of the sorrow still on her shoulders.

"I came out very badly, and I tried to take my own life twice. I had more desire to die than to go to school. I forgot how to smile. I was skeletal, and I had horrific nightmares. I was destroyed, above all emotionally — it was unbearable. A shame I could not forget tortured me, followed me everywhere. I trusted no one: I hated the world, and I felt disgusting. It was painful, too, to discover how unprotected I was, because my visible deterioration never stirred any compassion in the schoolteacher. Perhaps she was in denial in the face of something her own experience let her sense. She did not even show suspicion at the sudden trip to the countryside.

"I could find no reason to go on living that way. So one day, when the military man and I were alone, I cut him along the chin with a piece of broken bottle that I had kept hidden near my bed, to defend myself. When he saw himself bleeding, he struck me with his elbow, and I had a pounding headache that lasted the whole night. But it seems that taught him a lesson, because he came after me less and less.

"A few weeks later, the news arrived at the house that the monster had died in a shootout, in which he lost his life and I gained my freedom. When the news came, doña Casilda and I looked at each other in silence. Without summoning any witnesses, we felt the first signs of release," Magdalena says, with profound sorrow and wet eyes.

In the middle of that crisis was when the girl learned of the existence of the support programs. There she received psychological care from an interdisciplinary team of professionals who walked beside her in the process of healing, at least in part, the wounds of what had happened at such a young age. With time, Magdalena completed a course as a commercial cashier, which opened a door toward independence. Thanks to that training, today she works with dignity at a supermarket in the city.

The years have passed, but they have not erased those moments of hopelessness and abuse that marked her so deeply. As I listened to her, I could see in her face that remembering her story was opening a wound still alive. So I chose not to ask questions, and limited myself to listening with respect.

Magdalena married a good man. She has not been able to bear children, but her husband has a daughter from a previous marriage, whom she loves and protects as if she were her own.

She speaks of her past with a serene dignity and holds an absolute faith in God. What she lived through has given her the capacity to walk with empathy alongside pregnant girls who need guidance and support.

Today Magdalena is a beacon of hope for other girls and women crossing labyrinths like the ones she lived through. Although the scars remain, she has been able to turn them into strength and into service. Every time she extends her hand to a girl in need, her own wound seems to heal a little more. Her life is a testimony of resilience and of redemption.

"Girls must be believed," she says. "When they speak, it is not because they are lying. It is because they need someone to save them."

Heaven Has the Answer

The author presents us with a child who seems to have neither past nor future, wandering the streets with a hunger he was born with, while two happy children play and eat beside their mother. Moved by aporophobia, the mother draws her children away from this faithful representative of such a "crime." A shoe lost in the samán tree creates a fleeting bond, bearing witness to the meeting of two childhoods set worlds apart.
Thelma Amparo Kunhardt Javier

Once again, among so many other times, the boy had gone to sleep on an empty stomach, curled up in the backyard of an abandoned house in the historic center of the Heart City — that city of broken hearts for the children who survive in its streets.

As the morning wore on, hunger pushed him to beg along one of the main avenues, very near a well-known fast-food restaurant. Sitting on some curb of oblivion, the boy waited for what never seemed to come: a coin, a glance, a gesture of humanity, anything.

In the midst of his hungry solitude, he saw a car approaching. A well-dressed woman parked there with her two children. As she stepped out of the vehicle, the boy gathered his courage and asked her for help, but she did not even look at him. Instead, she gripped her children firmly, as if she had to protect them from some imminent danger, and led them into the restaurant. The boy remained standing and watched as the youngest child got out of the car, and a shoe slipped from his foot and fell onto the pavement. Neither the mother nor the older child noticed, and they continued on toward the place where food and games were waiting for them.

The boy sees the shoe and thinks of telling the woman, but something stops him. He is certain she will assume he is insisting on asking for money and will reject him again, without compassion. He stays there, thinking, looking at the shoe on the ground: a forgotten object, like him.

In a rush of frustration and anger, he picks it up and throws it with all his strength toward the sky, as if that gesture might bring him an answer, or some divine relief to quiet his hunger and his pain. Then he notices that, as it falls, the shoe has come to rest in the branches of a *samán* tree that has been watching him in silence, just as it has watched the hardened heart of that elegant, soulless woman.

The shoe remains in the tree, a mute witness to his presence in a world that ignores him. And while the city continues on its way, he walks off slowly — at the pace of one who is still a child, and clings to his dreams.

Full of hope, he thinks that although his life may resemble a forgotten object, he will not always be invisible. In his heart, he holds on to the hope that perhaps, one day not too far away, the wind will carry his story beyond the hardened hearts, and someone will answer the silent call he sent up to Heaven today.

In the Navel of Hell[1]

Milagros gives us a firsthand portrait of Juancho, a child born with the address of hell engraved beneath his arm. The road to Heaven is long and difficult for those who carry the mark of the worst poverty of all: orphanhood. Long or short, the orphan's life is a constant search for shelter, for the loving wing that life has denied him.
Altagracia Salazar

On a beautiful island of the Caribbean, "set squarely in the path of the sun" — as our great poet Pedro Mir put it — one of those innocent country roads of the deep south wound through a landscape where *guazábaras* grew alongside the goat-thorn tree, sister to the spines of the cacti. There, amid the parched terrain dotted with *guayacanes*, a few cabins rose up that seemed to fuse with the surroundings. In that forgotten corner, a business operated in which young women from the area, and others who had come from far-off provinces, sold themselves, drawn in by the promise of *an easy life*. A bait as cruel as it was bitter in the days that followed.

1 Originally published in the anthology *Cuentos de autores latinoamericanos* (Chile: Editorial Factor Literario, 2024).

By then it was common for outsiders to ask after the place, and to receive the same instructions:

"Keep going straight, and at the first curve you'll see a sign that says *Colmado Ramírez*. Keep on until you come to a big *samán* tree with a public water tap. Turn right and there are the cabins."

"Are there signs?" they would often ask.

And the answer was no.

In truth, no sign warned of that place that looked like paradise at first glance and was hell to those who lived there. Anyone who wished to reach the cabins had to come in through a stone backyard, fenced in by leafy trees. From there one stepped onto a wide terrace that overlooked a ravine with a striking view at the back. There was a bar, decorated in the local style, well stocked with every kind of drink and substance, music until dawn, and many tables to choose from. There were also very young women — many of them underage.

That place ran by its own rules and a system of strict orders, as if it were a school. One of those rules established that each woman had a handler — what in our local idiom is called a *maipiolo*. This figure took charge of finding the clients with whom the woman would have her sexual encounters, generally illicit, acting as the go-between and as the supposed guardian of her interests. Each of those encounters generated a payment, which would then be reported to the owner of the cabins, or *cabaré*.

Another rule was that all the women had to be young, beautiful, slender, and graceful. There was also a woman in charge of watching over the girls — a kind of guardian, heavily built, of great physical strength and harsh character. A single look from her was enough to inspire terror. Her specialty was handling the difficult cases and imposing the cruelest punishments on anyone who dared step out of line. *La Robot* was the nickname of this disciplinary mayor, who had once worked as a prostitute herself. Her experience had earned her this position, which gave her license to mistreat the *employees*.

It was not unusual for one of these women, in her constant relations with different men, to end up pregnant. That was what happened to one of these young women, who, like her companions, had lived for years in the same hell. As a result, a beautiful boy was born to her — amber eyes, curly hair, a wide smile: Juancho, the protagonist of this story.

Juancho never knew his father, because his mother did not know him either. She had never bothered to ask, since for her it didn't matter. The boy grew up in that place, always at his mother's side and with *La Robot* as godmother — a piece of luck that ended up saving him, because pregnancies were forbidden in that place of music and misery. At the brothel, Juancho's mother did the work she had been hired to do, but in the early hours of the morning she always came back to the bed to wake up beside her boy.

Some years later, his mother had a daughter who did not look like her brother. Katia was born with light skin, large almond-shaped eyes, fine features, and a strong build. She was Juancho's joy, and the two of them protected each other as best they could, aware that staying there was a hateful necessity, given how violent the place was. They were the only children at the cabins, which was probably owed to their mother's good standing with the owner of the business and to the bond of *comadre* she had pledged with *La Robot*. On top of that, she got along with the *maipiolo*, who served as a kind of father to the two children.

Juancho did not trust anyone, nor did he share his secrets easily. His past stayed sealed shut, and so did any mention of his origins. Speaking of his mother was an open wound that tore him apart from within: it brought tears he could not hold back and threw him into violent fits of vomiting. That anguish was reason enough to avoid a subject that pierced his soul with every memory.

I came to know him along the byways of life, and the two of us extended our trust to each other at first sight. He valued having someone offer him a friendly hand, and so the two of us bet on a sincere friendship, with no expiration date. With time, less on his guard, he decided to reveal a part of his past. That was a grim and painful burden that pursued him to the end.

"My mom was a *cuero*, and we lived right at the same business where she worked," the boy said, his head down.

"My sister and I are siblings of two different fathers, and we never knew either of them. The man in charge of the *cabaré* was like my mom's owner," he went on.

"He managed the money she earned at her trade, you know how, right? That man was also like a dad to us. He was a good man. And even though he wasn't our real father, we felt like a family under his protection.

"One day, without giving any reasons, my mom took my sister Katia and handed her over to a family to be raised. That was very hard for me, because she was my company; but I understood that it was better for her to go somewhere else and not stay at the *cabaré*. The music deafened her and made her cry until dawn. My little sister could not get to sleep because of the noise of that place — a place of music and drinks and arguments and danger.

"My mom was good, and she loved us a lot. She would go out with men, and many times she came back drunk, but she always came to wake up beside me, to protect me from a place that wasn't easy. I remember that almost every night I'd wet the bed. Every time it happened, she would scold me so I wouldn't do it, but it would happen anyway.

"One day, almost at dawn, I felt the bed wet and I thought I'd peed myself, but no. My mom had bled to death, and she was lying on top of me, dead. Someone had taken her life with knife wounds, and she came to die beside me. That's what I think." His voice broke, and the boy could go no further.

He could never describe what he felt in that moment, but he said it was very painful. His mother's death saddened the man in charge of the *cabaré*, and that sadness sank him into a deep depression. Before three months had passed since his mother's death, the man who had protected Juancho throughout his life in that place hanged himself.

When Juancho came back to the house at the close of the afternoon, he found his stepfather hanging in the very room where the two of them used to sleep. To the devastating image of his protector suspended in the air was added the indelible memory of that other tragic day when he had lost his mother. At only eleven, he was left abandoned and broken, in the navel of a hell that offered him only promises of suffering and terrible memories that dragged him to the abyss of his own sorrow.

As if by God's hand, a regular client of the *cabaré* — owner of a butcher shop nearby and a friend of his mother's — gave Juancho a job and took him home to live, in exchange for helping him in the early-morning hours to slaughter and dress pigs, goats, and cows for selling the meat early in the day. The boy accepted, and he became an expert at killing those animals. He developed agility and skill with the knives and with scraping the hair from the carcasses. He also became an expert at the proper cuts of meat for sale to the public. That was how Juancho found a new profession: butcher.

Some time later, Juancho came to know with certainty who had been his mother's killer. It was a client of the brothel, a man Juancho knew.

"The killer never paid for his crime, because my mom's death didn't matter to anyone, except me, who was her son. There was no wake and no prayers when it happened, and the *cabaré* went on with its normal activities as if nothing had occurred. We took her to the cemetery, my stepfather and I, along with three of her companions — among them my godmother, *La Robot* — and there she was buried, that woman I loved and respected," Juancho would tell me, with wet eyes and grief written on his face.

A short time later, his younger sister came back to him. At the house where she had been taken in, they were mistreating her. By good fortune, a family from that area, moved by her situation, took her in as an act of solidarity. That was how the girl was able to begin attending a school that, even though it was somewhat far away, she never missed; every day she walked the long way there with great determination.

Meanwhile, Juancho worked hard at the butcher shop, putting in every effort so that his sister Katia would lack for nothing and could continue her studies. Yet life seemed to have made an example of him, dealing him low blows again and again, as if it were constantly testing the limits of his endurance.

One day, on the way to school, the same man who had murdered his mother brutally raped his sister and bragged about it to the four winds, like the depraved creature he was. In Juancho, feelings beyond words built up against that monster who was devouring his family.

At thirteen, he took advantage of a moment when his quarry was drunk, and he collected the debt for his mother's death and his sister's rape. Without thinking twice, and with all the rage he had been holding in for so long, Juancho killed the murderer and rapist with as many blows of the blade as he could land, wielding the knife with a master's skill — a skill he had been practicing for a long time in his trade, and which let him kill the man like one more pig.

No one knew who had killed him, except his butcher friend. Once told what had happened, the man protected him and gave him some cash so he could flee that same night to another city. And so Juancho did.

He caught a ride on a truck loaded with pigs that was heading to Puerto Plata. During a stop in Santiago, he decided to stay there, dazzled by what he saw.

They had arrived at night, and Juancho was struck by the great number of people in the area of the Monumento a los Héroes de la Restauración, the favorite gathering place for everyone. With an instinctive nose, he sensed that the great city gave birth to boys and girls who, with no one to grieve for them, wandered the streets at night, begging for something to eat at the restaurants nearby.

Juancho arrived in that unknown city carrying in his chest a tender, young heart already broken by the horrors of his past — without family, without friends, with little money, disoriented and full of fear, uncertainty, and confusion. Sorrow was eating at his soul at barely thirteen years of age. He had to give his age as whatever number was needed, because he had never been given a birth certificate. The only document he kept carefully in a small pocket of his trousers was his mother's death certificate.

He used to tell us that the day he arrived at that giant marble obelisk with its many steps, what he saw was a great commotion of people walking from one side to the other, as if they were all floating in the same place. Many children begging for food; others asking for money or working until midnight. Girls being prostituted, police chasing migrant children, who hid or fled in panic — all of it set against many lights, lively music, and smiling people.

When I think of how he described that first night, I picture a Marc Chagall painting, in which all the figures hover like sprites in the same painted space.

Because of his past, Juancho knew he had to avoid crowded places. So he hid himself, dead with sleep, in a drainage tunnel of the Monumento, at the far end of Calle Restauración. In the days that followed he found work at a mechanic's shop, where they let him sleep in exchange for keeping the place clean and watching over it.

Juancho walked the streets cautiously, afraid the police would arrest him for what he had done — though he had it in his favor that he came from the far south, and that in Santiago they would hardly recognize him.

But this was not the end of the hard times. In this new life he began another way of the cross, for he had only lived through the antechamber of a future he could not have imagined.

Juancho did not know some of the dangers that lay in wait in the streets, and one of them was the use of certain harmful substances. At the time, what was in fashion was *cemento* — PVC glue, an inhalant with psychoactive effects that alters the senses. *Your sorrows will be wiped away and you'll feel happy* was what they told him when they handed him the glue to inhale. No one warned him about the brain damage it caused, and the consequences were not slow in coming. The boy quickly lost many of his abilities and faculties. He spoke very slowly, and his vision often clouded over. The only thing that remained intact was his nobility.

Juancho, even still very affected by the drugs, went on being helpful, an extraordinarily hard worker, a faithful friend, and a defender of the weakest; but he would flare up immediately at any little thing. His emotions were deeply eroded by the harms he had suffered.

The street consumed his life with mistreatment, sexual abuse, hard labor, drug use, indignities, illness, addictions, and everything else that environment drags in its wake. Even so, and despite so many difficulties, this boy stood out as an exemplary worker.

He had a great deal of physical strength for his age. He had developed his muscles in the butcher shop, in the mechanic's shop, in construction work, and in various jobs he had taken on after arriving in Santiago. A respected urologist told him he would never have children, because having borne weights too heavy for his height had damaged his testicles.

He got into street fights and was caught up in robberies that often landed him in jail. When he was arrested, he would cut himself, generally on his arms and his wrists. Because he bled heavily, they would rush him to the hospital, and in this way he would escape the punishment for the harm he had done. He repeated the same pattern so many times that he turned that self-injury into a habit, looking to free himself from negative feelings and strong emotions like rage, sorrow, rejection, despair, and emptiness. Even so, he had fewer scars on his skin than wounds in his soul.

With time, hardened by the things the street demanded of him, he discovered that, instead of begging at the traffic light —

where it took a whole day to make any kind of money — he could earn more by letting men seduce him in exchange for sexual favors. He figured it was better to spend two hours on this than to spend the whole day enduring the humiliation of passersby. So he got involved with men and young men in that environment, and he ended up working as a prostitute — a trade he had known from birth.

Even though he already had a partner whom everyone recognized as violent and abusive, on one occasion, Juancho began a relationship with a young man from Dajabón who had been flirting with him. Word about the new relationship traveled to every corner and traffic light. His partner found out and invited him to use drugs together one Friday night, like any other, without showing his real intentions. Juancho fell into the trap, and they shared as they always did, until he fell asleep. His partner took advantage of that moment, and, full of jealousy and the basest instincts, he doused him with gasoline and lit a match, leaving him to burn until his soul was scorched.

The boy who summoned the cowardice and the courage to commit that terrible act disappeared, and has not been seen to this day. His guilt dissolved among the crimes that no one pursues and that the world does not care about.

Wrapped in flames, Juancho ran out into the street, desperate, tearing his clothes from his body as the fire devoured his skin. That was how he made his way to the hospital, more than six blocks from where the tragedy had taken place. The burns were extreme, and it was urgent to transfer him to the capital, since at that time Santiago had no burn unit.

Quickly transported by ambulance, he was admitted in the early hours to a hospital in Santo Domingo. He was received professionally by a team of surgeons who were already waiting for him. The surgery was delicate, but the doctors were determined to save that life — though they warned that it was a very complicated case. The first measure was to attend to him at once to stabilize his breathing and his circulation.

Before going into the operating room, he said: "Thank you for everything... let me go, I'm tired." No one answered. They were all looking at that swollen body, visibly burned, with skin scorched, white and waxy; the face deeply inflamed, almost unrecognizable; the heartbeat low. In that moment, all of us commended his soul to God, while the boy writhed on the gurney in spasms of agony.

About half an hour after the surgery began, the doctors brought the news that Juancho had gone. He left at twenty, after a life badly lived through no fault of his own. Death carried him off, taking him to the other side of the world, away from his terrible nightmares.

His employer, the owner of the shop where this beloved boy had worked, in a gesture of gratitude, paid for the wake so that Juancho could go with dignity to that promised Heaven he had always longed for.

Judging Juancho is no easy task. From inside our bubble, the easiest thing would be to call him a precocious murderer. But, as I unspool his life, I find no proper word to contain him. I think he was the sum of many wrongs that battered his existence, from being born in a small-time brothel, through the long and tragic litanies of his childhood, to his last day, as he lay dying, charred, in a hospital. I think that, in the depths of his heart, Juancho was waiting for something more. Maybe what he was looking for was not justice, but a truce with life, a moment to catch his breath — because, even after he had survived all the blows, life still owed him a measure of hope, a ray of light that never came.

My children remember him still with affection, for having shared so many moments of Christmas Eve, Christmas Day, and June 24 too — his saint's day, since he never knew his own birthday.

Unlike his mother's wake, his burial was attended by many companions who, alongside him, had lived their lives in the streets. All of them dressed in their Sunday clothes, they kept honor guard over his body for an entire morning — a distinction Juancho deserved.

His sister Katia came to the wake. Juancho's friends gave her the humble chain he had always worn, with a medal bearing the letter K, in honor of her name. She lifted the white sheet that covered her brother's disfigured face and bent over him, remaining there as long as her heart needed to say goodbye. With her face marked by an immense pain, calling him by name in a voice broken and seeming to rise from the bottom of a well, she hung the chain around his neck so it would rest against his chest, the way it had been since they were children.

The boys carried Juancho's body from the shop where he worked all the way to the cemetery at El Ingenio, walking slowly and trading off the weight of the humble coffin. They all moved forward in silence, with gestures of inwardness and a deep sorrow on their faces.

His burial looked like a procession of the faithful on the feast day of a venerated saint — but wrapped in a collective silence. All you could hear was the echo of footsteps dragging with grief over the gravel of the road as they crossed corners, paused at traffic lights, and walked the same pavement that had watched him grow up, until they arrived at his last destination, very near the grave of his friend Chiquito.

Juancho, the boy with amber eyes, who once survived in the navel of hell, became a man who, although made invisible by the city, left his mark on those of us who came to know his story. This boy spent his short life stumbling against the cracks of fate. He received love from his mother and from others who supported him, but violence wounded his noble soul so many times that, in the end, it claimed his body.

That much-remembered boy learned to earn his living in the streets of Santiago, where nights were as cold as the hearts of those who looked at him sidelong from the corners of his fate. Although the weight of his tragedy never left him, he chose to carry it with dignity until his last day. The memory of his mother and the longing to protect his sister Katia gave him the strength he needed not to fall. Remembering his face, I feel that in his gaze lived the quiet resistance of those who, although broken, remain standing.

I'm One of the Lucky Ones

To lack what is necessary, to carry a heavy cross, and still know oneself to be a beloved child of God: that is the true definition of faith. It is the assurance of things hoped for and the conviction of things not seen. In these pages, the author shows us that Saúl, far from having lost everything, has in truth gained. He is an illuminated soul, one who rises above the misfortunes he suffered from the womb and the lack of recognition on earth. His life reminds us that wisdom always surprises us, and that it often springs from the most unexpected places.
Giselle Sánchez Almánzar

"I don't know where I was born. I don't know my mother, and I don't remember who took me in when I came into the world. I don't know who fathered me. I only know that I am a beloved child of God."

With that brief declaration, Saúl began our conversation after years without seeing one another. We met on the very day President Luis Abinader was beginning his new term. While the entire country was listening to his speech, I remained captivated by the presence of that wise young man, marked by life and yet possessed of a deep spirituality.

Saúl is missing a hand and overflowing with optimism. One pale morning, when he was barely eleven, an iron barrel severed his left hand while he was working in a mechanic shop, and that devastating blow split his life in two. I met him around that time, when he was attending a homework room in one of those communities where extreme poverty, fractured families, orphanhood, migration, and lack of access to education, among other ills, push children into the street and strip them of innocence.

He is twenty-three now. He is single and completed the fourth grade, an achievement he carries with pride and with the desire to keep learning. His smile is still the same as it was in those years. His attentive eyes, lit by a calm wisdom, reflect an inner peace that disarms. Despite his uprooted beginnings and a past clouded by uncertainty, Saúl embraces the present with absolute freedom: an invaluable legacy he offers, at the price of opportunity, to those of us who have drawn near to his noble heart.

"I live deeply grateful to God for the gift of life. God dotes on me. The circumstances in which I came into the world were apparently very difficult. The story I have been told, though at times I doubt it, is that I was born in a hospital in San Pedro de Macorís. They tell me my mother's name is Magdalena, and in my mind I associate her with that good, though flawed, woman the Bible gives us. My mother abandoned me there, and it seems she never came back for me. That is why I do not know who my father might be either, but God knows why, and He knows what He is sparing me from.

"That means I do not know who my parents were, though I confess I have dreamed of them. I have seen them in my dreams, both of them, but they always appear with their backs turned. In those dreams, my mother is light-skinned like me, and my father is darker and short in stature. Lately, though, I dream only of my mother, and I have a feeling my father died not long ago. In any case, on the days when I dream of them, I wake up very happy, as if I can feel them near. Despite their absence, I am fortunate, because along the way I have found many people who have helped me, though I have also met those who try to humiliate me because of where I come from and the fate I was given.

"Apparently, when my mother abandoned me, a compassionate nurse took me in, but she never registered me officially. That is why I had no birth certificate. It was at Acción Callejera, after many years of effort and many trips, that the educators managed to obtain that essential document for me, the one that opened the doors of citizenship. With my birth certificate in my hand, I finally felt like a person, because when you do not have that paper, you feel as if you do not exist.

"Maribel, the nurse who adopted me, died when I was four years old. After that, a supposedly compassionate family took me in. My memories of that time are vague, and I cannot piece everything together clearly. What I do know is that Maribel was good to me. Although I do not even remember her face, I have always had the feeling that the only embraces of my life came from her.

"That new 'Samaritan' family still specializes in finding children with disabilities, renting them out, and passing them off as children or close relatives at traffic lights. Under those terrible circumstances, designed to stir pity in passersby, we begged on the corners of streets and avenues.

"I spent a long time lying and begging in the streets beside boys and girls I did not know, but with whom I had to pretend a forced brotherhood. It is a ruthless business, well known to the authorities, who should eradicate it instead of ignoring it. I remember a little boy from Bonao who suffered severe seizures. It was very hard to see him during those attacks, when, without knowing what he was doing, he would wet and soil himself in the full sun.

"I accompanied those children for a long time, and more than once I saw on their faces the withered smile of a wounded childhood. The same questions always came to me: How can families rent out their disabled children, knowing the torment that awaits them? How is it possible that the authorities do not investigate these cases? Why do people walk on by, ignoring such cruel abuse? I remember that, on several occasions, more than three children with those conditions would be gathered together to be trafficked, then placed far apart from one another on different corners.

"That was how I grew up: serving as a guide for the blind, pushing children in wheelchairs who could not walk, and dragging along others with visible brain damage. All of that stained my childhood with sorrow and helplessness."

Saúl remembers this as the most painful stage of his childhood. He was forced to beg for unscrupulous people who used disabled children as a way to make money under the disguise of charity. It hurt him not only because of the cruelty involved, but also because of society's indifference.

"When I grew older, I began unloading trucks at the market in the capital, and there I met many drivers who traveled to the Cibao. That was how I arrived in Santiago. In this city, I survived in the streets as a working child for two years and three months. I slept beside other boys on a central lot near the José María Cabral Hospital. I worked hard around the Monumento so I could rent a room in El Ejido.

"Today I share that space with a friend who works in a free-trade-zone company. Between the two of us, we cover the rent and food. I look after the cars parked in the historic center, work I can do easily with one hand. There I have a network of friends I consider family, because we all take care of one another.

"I don't have a mother, and I don't know who fathered me. I don't know what it is to have siblings or blood relatives either, but I've got friends to spare. The priests at the church are my buddies. People greet me with affection and miss me when I don't show up in the street. Some of the neighborhood women give me food and even used clothes that belonged to their sons. Some trust me with their houses when they go out, and I always keep an eye on everything in the neighborhood, even the garbage truck when it comes by. Besides, if parking is slow, I help sell sweets at a stand on Calle Restauración. And on top of that whole banquet, I have the love of God. If you look at my story from back to front, you'll realize I'm one of the lucky ones."

Saúl repeats the absence of his parents like a sacred mantra with which he invokes some divinity. Those words stir his vague memories like a heavy burden he has carried all his life. And yet he says he accepts and understands his parents. In that reflective, unhurried way, he finds a way to ease his pain and quiet his good heart.

"I am grateful to Acción Callejera for teaching me to read and write, for guiding me at the right time, and for accompanying me for so many years, until I obtained my birth certificate, my *cédula*, and other documents that have allowed me to access certain rights," said this young man, who was born without knowing what color his future would be.

Saúl and I never really said goodbye, because his way of seeing life took a seat in my heart. He found meaning and purpose in the midst of adversity. His story, marked by scars and open wounds, is a testimony to the human capacity to resist, to love, and to live with gratitude, even when life turns bitter.

As he was leaving, he called out to me from the corner with a mischievous smile. He turned his head toward me, his body half turned — a gesture that revealed his blend of mischief and charm. Then he let it out, as if casting a secret into the open air:

"Ma'am, I forgot to tell you I'm in love! I'm killing it — I've got a girl!"

And his laughter disappeared down the street.

Saúl has that savoir-faire, as the French call that rare ability to manage when life tightens its grip. It is a quality that inspires one to believe that, even in adversity, a path can always open.

Runway of Shadows and Absences[2]

The author tells us the drama of a woman whom life
wrung dry and robbed of all her smiles.
Freddy Ginebra

It was high noon, beneath a smothering sun that threw off sparks without mercy. Its glare hurt the eyes as it struck full-on the zinc roofs of those shacks made from tin, precariously clinging to the crest of a steep ravine near a foul-smelling stream.

They were little houses like single-slope huts, each with only one window, through which the polluted air drifted in from the stagnant current. From the highest point downward, houses of many colors seemed to hang in balance along twisting paths, with clothes hung out to dry on low, scraggly trees. In that clay-heavy earth, only sparse vegetation survived, touched here and there by a few traces of green.

That was the landscape that met us from the top of the rise, where we paused before entering this forgotten community — a place of dwellings that looked more like a row of lean-tos sus-

2 Originally published in the anthologies *Cuentistas latinoamericanos de amor y seres humanos* (Chile: Factor Literario, 2025) and *Frag-mentada: La violencia no es un cuento* of the Festival Grito de Mujer (Dominican Republic: Rosado Fucsia Editorial, 2025).

pended in midair, inhabited by people and domestic animals moving among them.

From that point, one could see the hamlet surviving unsteadily among the red earth, the stepped paths cut from that same broken soil and mud, all scattered along a cordon of poverty and neglect. It looked like a landscape drawn from surrealism.

On the earthen steps of those paths, dogs lay in the sun with an astonishing calm, their movements unhurried, as if filmed in slow motion. Each muddy hill was crowned by a tiara of small rooms, dwellings of misery for the people who had settled on lands buried in a ravine lost to the world, without horizon.

"Families live there," the residents of the community told us.

And it was true.

In one of those little houses, a young woman was scraping out a life, her gaze somber, her skin sallow, wrapped in an aura of sadness. Her dream was to be a runway model, to walk and show her legs. The truth was that, since the age of twelve, she had not been able to walk, and her condition kept her condemned to a wheelchair, with which she moved with great difficulty through the small room she shared with her family. On her face, one could read clearly that life had stolen her smile, and neglect had taken part of her very white teeth.

Neighbors say that this young woman, twenty-three years old and living with a motor disability, was left paralyzed when her mother threw her down a precipice. The fall damaged her fragile spine when she was twelve. To complete the punishment, María never received medical care. She was sentenced to a wheelchair forever, and for that reason she never went to school. Yet as an adult, she liked to leaf through magazines filled with advertisements for women's fashion, because since childhood she had dreamed of becoming a model. She could not read or write, and she never obtained identity documents, which also kept her from gaining access to social programs.

With Abelardo, her companion, she had a beautiful little boy with amber eyes, the color of the sun, and hair in honey-colored curls. In that grace particular to childhood, he liked to hide whenever strangers came to the house, only to appear suddenly afterward with a mischievous smile. When we arrived at their home, the boy, overcome by shyness, wiped his hands by rubbing them against his pants and, smiling from ear to ear, came forward beside his friend, a dog he handled at will. The child moved with difficulty, and rather than walk, he dragged himself across the floor, imitating the movements his mother had made before she obtained a wheelchair.

"This is my son Joel. He is three years old," the young woman pointed out when two Catalan volunteers and social workers visited her, leaving their hearts in those muddy places where the lives of so many people splashed about.

Her twenty-eight-year-old companion also could not read or write and, like Joel and his mother, had no identity documents. Abelardo worked gathering materials in garbage dumps and suffered frequent skin infections because of it. He seemed affable enough, a short man with a soft walk and an evasive gaze, but under the effects of drugs or alcohol he became very violent. Whenever he consumed either substance, he changed, and usually ended up assaulting María.

He worked hard in the dumps from very early in the morning until late at night. Then he repaid his exhaustion by mistreating his companion, without caring whether his son or the neighbors were present.

"Abelardo loses his mind when he drinks," María would explain, referring to her companion. "He hits me and he is very jealous, but deep down he loves me, because he supports me, bathes me, and cooks for me too. That is why I love him as well, and I do not hold his outbursts against him. I love him very much," she would insist, "and I do not want him arrested. Instead of arresting him, I would like them to help him leave behind the violence and the vices."

Abelardo gave her the basic care her family had never offered, but he did so abusively. He even forced her to have sex in public whenever he wanted, as often as he pleased, along with other terrible violations.

Another aggravating factor was his jealousy over his own brother, who lived next door. Abelardo knew that while he was away at work during the day, that brother also forced María to have sex, certain that, because of her disability, she could not defend herself. When this happened, the brother, fully aware that he had crossed the boundary between evil and pleasure, found a small amusement in letting Abelardo know, which only intensified the cycle of beatings against her.

Given the situation, the family was assisted by a multidisciplinary team of professionals, who enrolled the boy in a nearby school. María, though late, was helped to receive quality medical care.

The doctors concluded that there was no longer any way to reverse her condition: the time that had passed since the fall had closed every possibility of recovery. The consequences of untreated infections and illnesses had worsened the damage, and although her legs still retained some capacity for movement, the lack of immediate treatment had condemned her to paralysis. She also carried an untreated brain injury. Even so, María remained attached to the hope of walking again and dreamed of one day appearing on a runway.

In her world without letters or numbers, maps were her favorite pastime. When she was alone, she would abandon her household duties completely and sit at the edge of some ravine, watching the star-filled sky.

The cycle of violence remained intact, and only a few days after the volunteers began visiting, Abelardo gave her a brutal beating. The psychologists helped her find the strength to step out of that whirlpool of abuse. María took courage and filed a complaint with the prosecutor's office, denouncing the mistreatment she had endured. Through the Unit for Attention to Gender-Based, Sexual, and Domestic Violence, the prosecutor's office promptly moved María to a shelter for abused women.

But the shelter offered no real solution for María. The facilities were not adapted for people with disabilities, nor did they have staff who could care for her, so she remained there only a week. After that, she had to go to her parents' house, protected by a restraining order against her aggressor. The decision to place her with them, in the same community, was based on her condition and on the hope that someone would care for her and the child. Yet even there, her ordeal continued.

In that place, María's cross grew even heavier. The surroundings were far from a safe refuge. Her father was an alcoholic, and when he was drunk, he tried to force himself on her, beating her if she resisted. Added to that violence were the man's deeply aberrant behaviors, including acts of bestiality, according to the neighbors, accounts I was later able to verify alongside members of the prosecutor's office.

María told us how cruel and difficult it was for her to be forced into sex with the man who had fathered her. Overwhelmed by such extreme abuse, she decided to return to Abelardo, her companion and aggressor.

She held on to the hope of building a new home and asked not to go back to the shack where everything had begun, but to move somewhere else, far from her brother-in-law, in order to avoid his abuse.

That was how they decided to leave for the mountains of San José de las Matas, a place guarded by pines, varieties of ferns, pastureland, and timber trees. The area offered lush vegetation, with a beautiful variety of wild trees, paths, and roads flanked by ferns. It was a leafy paradise, preserved inside a bubble where time seemed to have stopped, amid a varied geography that seemed to coexist in a single neighborhood.

Amid that solitude, she, Abelardo, and Joel joined the birdsong and the ritual of the mountain crickets, carrying their hopelessness with them, along with a bed for the three of them, a table, a few vessels, two magazines, some cooking stones, and a wheelchair, her eternal companion. Together, these belongings made up the whole of María and her small family's meager household estate.

It was a place of beautiful greens, but so remote that the child was left without school. María was left in much the same condition: with no one to answer for her, no relatives nearby, nothing but the fresh breeze the mountain offered to soften her sorrows. There, she aged terribly fast.

To support this family, we made one last visit to the area, but we could not find their house. By fortune, we came upon Abelardo on the road, working in a corn plot. He led us to their new home, built on a small rise from rough poles cut in the bush and the dried sheaths of nearby palm trees. Sweating, he guided us along, grumbling and cursing life and the family fate had given him. With his index finger, he pointed toward the shack and returned to his work.

After walking along a long, narrow, muddy trail, we found María more deteriorated than before, far more neglected both physically and emotionally. A short while later, Joel, her son, arrived with his clothes wet from a recent bath in a nearby river. His eyes said everything, and we could see that he, too, had lost his sunny brightness, and that the beautiful, timid smile of earlier days had frozen over.

We shared a few moments of joy with the two of them and confirmed that bitterness had hollowed out María's life. Instead of smiling, she made a twisted grimace, with every muscle of her face yielding to it.

A few weeks after our visit, her heart filled with sadness from having been so violated, abandoned by every social program, eaten away by several untreated illnesses, and abused by her own family, María fell ill there in the middle of nowhere, very tired of fighting. This time, the illness was grave.

Abelardo brought her to Santiago, and the doctors recommended admitting her to the hospital to treat her illnesses. But her family and her companion decided to take her back to her parents' house to wait for death, because no one had time to care for her in the hospital.

At dawn on a Sunday, in the midst of suffocating heat and the abandonment that had always accompanied her, her frail body surrendered. There were no farewells, no ringing cries, only the whisper of the wind dragging dry leaves around her father's shack.

She waited for death in the same bed where her father had abused her so many times. Joel, her son, remained silent, seated in the wheelchair that had once been his mother's throne. María laid herself at the feet of the Lord and said goodbye to Abelárdo, her companion in mistreatment. She departed without noise, without a wake, without a holy hour.

Because she had no identification, no grave, and no money, her body was buried, probably against her will, in a common grave. From there, she set out "for Heaven," dressed in helplessness, with buttonholes of deep sadness in her soul, and a tulle veil draping her body in every shade of pain.

Joel must have been about twelve, the same age his mother had been when his grandmother threw her down a precipice, condemning her to die slowly. María's parents are supposedly still alive, perhaps carrying the full weight of the abuses they committed against their daughter.

Drugs strangled Abelardo. They consumed him so completely that today he does not even know who he is, nor does he recognize his own son.

As for María, I do not know whether she rests in peace. She departed without seeing her dreams fulfilled, leaving behind a life marked by cruelty, neglect, and a broken hope that never came into bloom. I sense that God reserved for her a box seat lit by Heaven on some runway of justice, and that there she models a life that must never be repeated.

One Less Rose, One More Thorn

Rosa reveals the ordeal many women endure at the hands of violent, narcissistic, controlling men, trapped in a pathological jealousy that intensifies when, out of machismo and cowardice, they feel they can no longer manipulate or subdue their victims. In this story, the author leads us step by step through the harsh reality of those who live under this scourge, allowing us to understand the depth of their pain and the urgency of breaking the silence.
Mildred Dolores Mata

In a humble neighborhood in southern Santiago, doña Tona and I rocked back and forth in two well-woven palm-frond chairs, each of us holding a cup of coffee. The aroma of the coffee seemed to open a path for memory. Doña Tona is Rosa's mother, the mother of that little girl with the angelic smile whom we all knew and will never forget.

She remembers her daughter with the wounded tenderness left behind by memories of extreme poverty. Rosa was born in a house where fourteen people lived and where there were only two thin mattresses set on blocks, incapable of offering rest. The damp dirt floor and the *tejamanil* walls that wept whenever it rained were the world into which that girl first opened her eyes.

Even so, Rosa was the small spark that lit up the family. Many mornings she woke up soaked with the urine of some sibling, or had to wait until the very end to use the single toothbrush shared by the twelve children.

Life passed without papers or rights, since none of the twelve children had been registered, making them invisible before the law and closing the doors to assistance programs. Rosa, the youngest, learned to face those deprivations with discipline. She went to school even without breakfast, in the same clothes she had slept in, and ran downhill so she would not arrive late. She embodied the wounded innocence of a childhood that never should have had to carry so much poverty.

This is how doña Tona tells it, remembering the everyday conversations she had with her little girl.

At Acción Callejera's little school, Rosa is remembered as a beautiful child with a round face, honey-colored eyes, rosy cheeks, slightly arched brows, silken hair, and the smile of a mischievous angel, a girl who came eagerly to the community school.

There, waiting for her and for many other children from the area, was Cecilia Gossetti, an Italian teacher with expertise in social risk and vulnerability, and also a loving, empathetic educator. Everyone delighted in the way she spoke, in a clipped Spanish without an accent.

It was not an ordinary little school. It was a center for learning and services, offering an innovative, traveling educational program: on a playground court, in the street, or in a room provided by the community itself.

Its purpose was not only to teach the children who attended to read and write, but also to watch over the improvement of their lives, including the lives of their family members.

In time, Nina Valdez, a young and devoted teacher from the area, replaced the Italian teacher. Nina was trained in the mission of the little school, and it is she who holds in her heart the best moments of this story I am telling you about Rosa. She is the one who narrates the following memories.

From the first time she saw Rosa, the educator sensed from the child's appearance that her situation needed attention, and she decided to visit the family to see how she might support them.

During that home visit, she found a humble *tejamanil* house, made from a mixture of sticks, palm leaves, and cow dung, a practice commonly used in the southern part of the country, where the family came from. The floor was made of packed earth, and the house had two rooms in which that large family was distributed. The greatest danger was that the house stood at the edge of a ravine, which helped explain Rosa's appearance and behavior.

Even in such poverty, the family picture held hope, because this was a united family. So, without delay, teacher Nina began guiding them in matters of hygiene, good practices, and health. She carried out an assessment to identify the family's most urgent needs. Certain habits had to be improved; the legal documents they needed had to be obtained; the dirt floor had to be replaced with cement; and the roof had to be changed, since whenever it rained, water not only ran across the floor but also poured in streams through the gaps of a useless zinc roof.

With help from members of the community, the floor was completed, and the roof was improved with used zinc sheets that were still in good condition. Immediately afterward, the teacher began helping this large family with the process of obtaining their identity documents.

Rosa's mother was a woman of strong character who ruled over her twelve children. Her father worked as a watchman, which is why he was known in the neighborhood as *el Guachimán*.

From the time she was very small, Rosa wanted to earn money to help support her large family. At twelve, she began washing dishes in homes around the community in exchange for a small monthly allowance. She continued her studies at the same time and earned excellent grades.

She also assisted the teachers with extracurricular activities, and everyone marveled at her intelligence and her ability to learn. This young girl always stood out for her leadership, her good heart, and her desire to rise above her circumstances.

Nina, the teacher, still remembers the hug Rosa gave her when she finally obtained her birth certificate.

Over the years, Rosa had grown into a radiant adolescent who dreamed of pursuing a university degree and building a luminous future. Although several young men in the community sought her attention, she placed her eyes and her trust in a neighborhood merchant, the owner of a small *colmado*.

Aware of the hardships that were suffocating her family, he began to draw her in little by little with promises disguised as favors. He offered her rice, beans, pasta, and other foods that eased the hunger in her home, but in return he demanded a dark, ill-intentioned love that was nothing more than a trap woven out of false hopes.

In a poor community, the presence of a good-looking young man who owned a well-stocked business was enough for many to regard him with respect.

But that man sold his merchandise with the same ease with which he sold his conscience. With the same exchange by which he filled bags with food, he seduced and corrupted vulnerable girls. That was how he trapped Rosa too, a young woman of such worth who nevertheless fell into his claws while still far too young.

Without knowing it, Rosa was beginning, in that moment, to descend a road from which it would be very difficult to return.

As many abusers do, Judas took her out of the community in order to isolate her from her family and exercise absolute control over her life. Far from those who might have helped her, the mistreatment and beatings went on for years. In the midst of that hell, Rosa gave birth to three beautiful children: two boys and a girl.

Desperate from the abuse, Rosa gathered the courage to report the violence to the Prosecutor's Office and managed to obtain a restraining order against that man who, in the eyes of many, appeared to be a generous merchant. Trusting in the protection of the law, she returned to the support of her family and devoted herself to raising her children. But the pressure of economic need continued to tighten around her each day.

Because he could no longer approach her, Judas devised a new deception.

One day he invited her to his father's house under the pretext of giving her money to catch up on child support. Rosa, despite all she had endured, had preserved the nobility of her heart. She believed him again and went alone in search of the money he had promised.

This time, the aggressor set a fatal trap for her. The forensic report confirmed that she had been raped and murdered with extreme violence.

Today, he is serving a thirty-year prison sentence, a punishment that can never repair the harm he caused.

Of what happened that day, I would rather say no more. There are sorrows words can barely touch, and wounds that need no details for us to understand their depth.

I would like us to remember Rosa as that little girl with the angelic smile, rosy cheeks, silken hair, and noble heart, the same girl who once dreamed of studying and forging her own path in life.

Her three children were left in the care of their grandmother. Her family, her community, and those of us who had the joy of knowing her continue to remember her as the cheerful young woman who never imagined the cruel fate that awaited her.

On the ninth day of prayers after her passing, the principal of the high school where Rosa had studied gave the family two certificates that belonged to her: one recognizing her as an Honor Student, and the other, her high school diploma. That belated gesture seemed to remind us that Rosa did have a future, one that violence stole from her before its time.

But it also leaves us with a painful question: how many more Rosas must fall before we learn to arrive in time?

Topató

The story Milagros de Jesús de Féliz tells us carries a foul smell... an orgy of mud, sweat, alcohol, and tears. From its pages seeps the helpless, desperate cry of a mother and the interrupted innocence of a daughter, set against the silence of a society that seems even more ill than they are.
Aida María Fernández

It was an ordinary morning in a year not so long ago when I visited a community forgotten by the authorities and stripped of even the most basic services. A ravine cuts through the place like an open wound, and along its banks gathers a poverty that horrifies. Many families survive there, exposed to the floods that, whenever the rains fall hard, enter their homes again and again, and with them, their lives.

It is a hollow, planted in the navel of Santiago, very near Estadio Cibao, an immediate neighbor to an important commercial artery. It has watched entire generations grow up; it has held their sorrows and their celebrations, their struggles and their hopes, always "by the grace of God," as doña Juana, a resident of Hoyo de Puchula, used to say. She was always grateful for our visits and lived right at the entrance to the ravine, in front of the earthen steps that led us into the living heart of the neighborhood, that same heart that beat with the innocence and harshness of daily life in that community.

On one of those visits, among so many different urgencies, I came upon a difficult situation between a mother and her daughter, something I have never been able to forget. As if time had not passed, that image remains engraved in my memory with the same force it had on the first day, and the same feelings from that morning still rise within me.

I made my way there with enthusiasm to carry out community work in the area. It was the day of the week devoted to offering family psychological support to impoverished communities. When I arrived, the team of professionals had already been meeting with families since early morning.

I was greeting the people waiting their turn when a woman of about forty stopped me abruptly. Her eyes were swollen from crying, and sorrow seemed to cloud her whole presence. With her was a slight little girl, no more than ten, with curly hair and brown skin, no sign yet of developing breasts, the look of malnutrition, and the vocabulary of someone seasoned far beyond her years.

The mother was asking for help because the girl kept running away with a *juntiña* — a little crowd — of girls from the neighborhood and boys who were doing very harmful things, things that were damaging her life. She was her only daughter, and the mother wanted the best for her, but the girl would not listen to advice or warnings.

Without wasting a moment, the frail child interrupted to explain that her mother tied her up at home with a rope. She urged me to ask her, please, not to do it.

Stunned by such a request, I immediately asked the mother why she did that. She told me she did it because the child would leave for three or four days with a little crowd of boys and girls to go to a *topató*.

Without revealing that I did not know the word, but wanting to understand, I continued the conversation in a neutral tone and asked what a *topató* was.

The girl answered openly, giving me the details:

"Oh, it's a group of about ten or fifteen young friends and girls my age, and some older than me, who gather in a motel for three days, and among boys and girls, we hook up with each other. In other words, we do a *topató* and have sexual relations without having a steady partner and without commitment."

Perplexed, I continued questioning the little girl and asked her:

"And what else do you do at the *topató*?"

With all the force of her character, and with a shrug of her shoulders, she answered:

"Well, we smoke marijuana and have a lot of fun. We drink a lot of beer, and we have a great time there."

As she explained the meaning of *topató*, flashes of lived experience crossed her face, revealing her eagerness to continue taking part in those orgies, even as her mother tried to stop her.

To keep her from losing herself in those activities, the grief-stricken mother had gone so far as to tie her up in a room. But whenever she did, the neighbors reported her to the authorities, and she was forced to release her. Inconsolable, she explained that the moment she let her go, the girl would leave for the *topató* and return home shattered, ill-tempered, drunk, and high.

The mother worked in a private home in order to provide what her daughter needed, but her sermons about good behavior only awakened in the girl a stronger desire to remain in the street, and an excessive passion for continuing to use the drugs that were destroying her body.

While the mother wept, the girl spoke of her desire to go to the next *topató*. She insisted that she was responsible for her own life and did not need anyone to care for her because she was already grown.

It was a morning wounded by sadness, in which the love of that tireless mother stood against the dark force of those psychoactive substances and the terrible changes they cause in the brains of those who consume them.

A multidisciplinary team of behavioral-health professionals addressed the case only that once. Then the two of them, mother and daughter, faded with time, leaving no trace of their struggles.

As the mother spoke, one could see in her eyes a weary urgency, a hopeless expression, perhaps born of long hours through so many midnights, waiting in anguish for her daughter to return, knowing that every passing minute gave the *topató* another chance to tear down a life so young.

This brief but tangled story is a challenge that can touch the shoulder of any family, regardless of social class. The mother's role, as always, is to seek help in order to lighten her burden, even as hopelessness and pain stalk her along the daily road of watching her most precious treasure slip away: her daughter.

That morning, I returned home with a heavy soul. The echo of that conversation between mother and daughter still resounds in my memory, reminding us of the fragility with which the lives of so many young people sway, caught in the cycle of hopelessness.

I ask myself, with a mixture of sorrow and helplessness, how many mothers will continue to face alone the battle against the demons hidden in those dark corners, with no weapons but love and anguish. In that Hollow, as in so many others, time seems to stand still while the world turns around it, indifferent to the daily struggles of those who survive there.

BRIDGES OF SOLIDARITY

We have arrived here deeply grateful. Honor and gratitude to the people, institutions, and gestures that walked alongside, sustained, and opened the way for the protagonists of these stories.

Thanks for those simple acts and firm decisions that, in the middle of the noise of the street, changed the course of lives with love, commitment, and faith.

At that necessary halt in life, someone knew how to recognize their urgent needs and to walk with them, with respect and dignity.

Hummingbirds with First and Last Names

Near the end of the summer of 2015, the moon stood as silent witness to a luminous decision. A defender of children, with a generous soul and light in his heart, learned of the financial difficulties facing Acción Callejera of Santiago, an organization devoted to protecting the working children who survive in the streets.

Without thinking twice, he decided to donate some of his finest photographic works. He did so convinced that art, too, can be an act of justice, or perhaps because he sensed, as many of us believe, that God grants us our talents and our grace so that we may place them at the service of those most in need, turning every gift received into a bridge of hope.

And so, spontaneously and in solidarity, the engineer Edward M. Butler offered a delicate collection of images featuring hummingbirds. His purpose was clear: to raise funds so that hundreds of working children could obtain the legal documents that would allow them to become fully part of society.

At that time, I received a note from the engineer Edward M. Butler, dedicated to the children. As I read it, I was deeply moved by the precise, heartfelt, and thoughtful way he expressed the intention behind such a timely and generous donation.

Because of its importance in understanding the lives of this population, and many of the stories gathered in the pages of this book, I present it here in full:

> To see one of God's creatures risk its life, working to the very edge of physical exhaustion to build a tiny work of art with the ancestral engineering of instinct, to feed, care for, and defend its young, is both moving and instructive.
>
> The birds of the sky possess nothing, and yet they lack nothing. They raise their young and fulfill their purpose in life with the resources God places within their reach. Their young leave the nest, whether in twenty-one days or, like ours, in twenty-one years, and they must be ready to face life and carry out the divine mandate to multiply.
>
> I understand that this series of photographs is closely connected to the work of Acción Callejera, which cares for young ones who, for different reasons, have fallen from the nest. Each of the boys and girls currently served by the organization has a mother who, I am certain, sacrifices her own food for them, builds them a nest with whatever she has at hand, and is willing to stand against anyone for the sake of her children.
>
> These small birds remind us that love belongs in the nest, not in the street. We must care for the young in the nest, whatever effort it may require. The support and teaching that a family can offer, whether modest or abundant, are essential to guiding the human fledgling along the path of dignity.
>
> These photographs seek to carry a message of encouragement: what is needed is not a golden nest or a fortress, but presence, devotion, and example.
>
> — Engineer Edward M. Butler, photographer

As an accomplice in this noble effort, Rosario Gómez de Domínguez — Charo — a dear friend of children and of many social causes, took charge of mounting, selling, and curating the exhibition. Thanks to the successful results of that initiative, hundreds of girls and boys finally received their birth certificates, documents as urgent as they were essential to their development and their dignity.

As of the printing of this book, many of those children now say with pride that, thanks to that opportunity, they are studying, working honestly, and contributing to society from their own places in the world.

There is an immense triumph in watching a human being set their life on its course. For there is no greater gift than restoring to a person their rights and the place that belongs to them in the world.

That generous and timely act helped many children recover something as simple and as immense as their name, their place in life, and the possibility of a better future.

God's Bridges

On the road of service to the most vulnerable, miracles happen — wrapped in simple gestures, leaving traces that cannot be erased. When solidarity is true, God builds bridges and opens unexpected doors, especially when children are at the heart of the matter.

This story belongs to that spirit of self-giving.

It was the summer of 1996, a season the working children awaited with longing, for the camps were drawing near, organized for more than fifteen hundred participants from nineteen marginalized communities in Santiago. The excitement was great, but only days before the activities were to begin, we faced a harsh reality: we did not have the funds needed to guarantee food for so many hopeful children.

Uncertainty surrounded us, and I can say that even faith seemed to waver for an instant. And yet, miracles do happen.

That was when something unexpected took place. That very Saturday afternoon, doña Benilda Llenas de Herrera called us with news that would change the course of those days: a company in Santo Domingo was donating a truckload of milk, juices, and other products. The company had decided to share that inventory with those who needed it most.

It was not an isolated gesture, because doña Benilda had always been attentive to vulnerable children. Together with her husband, don Alejandro Herrera, and with the generous support of their entire family, she had always supported numerous initiatives at a time when this reality was still ignored by much of society. At El Edén, her open and generous home, the first meetings of Acción Callejera were held, and many of the actions that would later strengthen its educational programs were first planted.

So abundant was the generosity that we had to turn to another friendly company to preserve the cold chain for that treasured cargo. In this way, those foods, which seemed to have fallen from Heaven, arrived just in time.

Thanks to that providence, the participating children enjoyed a month of camp with their meals assured and their joy overflowing. Each little carton of juice, each glass of milk shared beneath the sun of that remembered summer became a small sacrament of love for one's neighbor.

With the passing of the years, it is clear that the project was sustained by the invisible force of solidarity, woven by generous hands like those of doña Benilda. Her discreet and luminous devotion remains tattooed on the hearts of those children, who remember her still.

In Grateful Memory

This story is as special as that donation that, at a decisive moment, was received by the working children who attended Acción Callejera's programs. At its center is a mayor who placed children at the heart of his administration and who, as a steward of the city, assumed the responsibility of guaranteeing their right to a dignified education.

"Which community do most of the working children come from?"

I remember that question as if it were today. He asked it in the middle of a Christmas celebration, sharing in the children's joy, with the serene concern of someone who wished to understand in order to act.

It was 2006, and José Enrique Sued Sem was the mayor of Santiago. He often attended the celebrations held for the children who lived much of their lives in the streets. He arrived with an open smile and ready hands, without cameras or rehearsed speeches. He mingled with them naturally, listened, asked questions, and observed.

He wanted to understand that world so invisible to many, that other humanity the city so often prefers not to see.

That morning, we explained to him that a significant part of the population wandering the streets came from Hoyo de Elías, in Yagüita de Pastor. There, don Marino Morel Ochoa had donated a plot of land to build a community center that would help prevent more boys and girls from ending up at the traffic lights and in the streets of the historic center.

The mayor made that donation a point of departure and announced with determination that the center the children needed would become a reality. And so it did. Since then, thousands of children and their families have found education, protection, and accompaniment there.

The center was conceived with a protective vision of children's rights. It includes areas for early stimulation, health, nutrition, pre-primary education, recreation, psychosocial care, classrooms, a multipurpose room, and spaces for working with families. Everything was designed to care for and educate a population deserving of accompaniment and protection.

These spaces have allowed safe and continuous development of educational and community programs suited to the needs of the area. It is a work that kept many children from roaming the streets, and that even today allows others to study where before they could only survive.

I also remember that doña Benny Sued Sem, his sister, took on the ornamentation of the place with delicacy and care, bringing beauty and dignity to a space destined for those who most deserved it. My recognition goes to this woman who, in silence, accompanied the actions of this friend of children.

Today, the children who attend that center, and those who passed through it — the ones who learned to read, to play, and to trust — carry an invisible debt to this good man. And that debt becomes gratitude whenever a child remains in school, a family finds support, and the city decides to care for its children.

In the memory of those children, the name José Enrique Sued Sem remains bound to an act of justice: he placed the city at the service of its childhood.

THE ALLEY OF COURAGE

Just a few blocks from their lives, the alley of courage opens. There, those who refuse to surrender hold on. These pages speak of the inner strength of those who, though they grew up amid violence and the street, chose not to give up.

Seven stories of real struggle — with stumbles, losses, and small victories capable of changing a destiny. Lives that never fit the scenery, but that found the courage to begin again.

A Child, a Man, a Miracle

In this story, the author takes us by the hand and leads us toward the miracle as we accompany el Ruso through his dramatic obstacle course, our hearts in our throats and our souls filled with faith.
Eduardo Sánchez

Today, a long-awaited reunion is waiting for me. I am on my way to see a boy who remains engraved in my memory, now grown into an adult. As I drive through Santiago and pass before the Monumento a los Héroes, that marble giant that seems to brush the sky, I am overtaken by memories of so many boys and girls who have made their lives around it. Optimism and fear cross one another in my chest: with all my heart, I want the miracle we so often hoped for to have happened in this story.

My heart was beating quickly with the emotion of seeing *el Ruso* again, that beautiful little imp I remember as a child and whom I had longed to find as a man. Questions rose in me, though I had no idea what the answers would be.

Would he be well, or had he remained trapped in the life he had been forced to struggle through? Had those difficult circumstances corrupted his soul? How would our conversation begin, so we could reconnect with the past and arrive at the present without wounding his feelings?

Those thoughts did nothing to help me stay calm. So, instead of searching for more questions, I focused on thanking God for the gift of seeing him again.

I was already seated at a table in the place where we had agreed to meet, and while I was answering a phone call, I suddenly felt someone speaking behind me.

"Give me your purse!"

It was indeed *el Ruso*, who had arrived right on time for our meeting and who now, fully grown, really did look like a Russian.

"You rascal!" I said, and embraced him with joy, seeing him now as an adult and such a handsome man.

At once I remembered Sandy *el Ruso*, a boy who had lived for years on Calle La Paz, on the south side of the city. He had fair skin, a mischievous little face, and a beauty unusual for a child hardened by the street. I can still see him in shorts, wearing a T-shirt much too large for him, always barefoot, as if childhood and survival had learned to walk together in his small body.

"Sometimes it was true that I was hungry, but other times I made it up," says this young man, so loved and so well remembered.

El Ruso lived with three full siblings, two of his mother's children, one of his stepfather's, and another sister born to his mother and stepfather. In all, there were seven siblings with whom he liked to play and spend time.

None of them went to school except him. For his parents, going to class was a waste of time, but that rebellious boy firmly defended his right to an education. Even without a birth certificate, he remained in school.

"Many times, ma'am, I lied at home so I wouldn't miss school," he confessed to me, with a touch of nostalgia.

"My dream was to learn to write. That was my only goal, so I wouldn't live in complete ignorance like my people," he added, now grown into a good man.

"At school I made many friends, and with them I had fun playing baseball on a nearby field. I dreamed of becoming a ballplayer. I believed I had the makings of one. But those activities bothered my parents too. They considered them another waste of time, or an excuse not to work.

"At noon on an ordinary Thursday, my father came home drunk and, for reasons I still do not understand, gave my stepfather's son such a terrible beating that by early Friday morning the child had died from the blows. For that horrible crime, my father was sentenced to thirty years in prison, and that marked me deeply.

"After what happened, everyone in the neighborhood looked at us badly. We felt they hated us, that they were pointing us out. Some of the neighborhood bullies also wanted to beat me and abuse my sister. Because of all this, my stepfather wanted to avenge that death through me, and as a result I went to live at my grandmother's house, not knowing that there, too, the flames of a new hell were waiting for me.

"My grandmother was over eighty. She was a very bitter woman, tired of life. Widowed, impatient, always in a bad mood, and with very few resources. She lived in the same neighborhood where that tragedy, so painful and so unjust, had taken place.

Her good mornings always seemed to foretell some curse, and that very thing brought her back to life.

"When she found out I would be living in her house, she kept saying out loud that she cursed the hour anyone had thought of her as the person I should move in with. Still, she accepted me grudgingly, but not before threatening me with punishments that would grow worse and worse, because I liked the street and she could not understand why. On that point, she was right. I did not like being in her house, because the air there was always sour, full of anxiety and complaint. But it was the only place within my reach.

"I remember that my grandmother, to keep me from going out to play ball, would gather up all my clothes and lock them away. She would leave me naked, with only one of her robes, and if I wanted to go out into the street, I had to put it on, because I had no other clothes available. I didn't turn out homosexual or *pájaro* because God is great," *el Ruso* confessed, pain cutting through his voice.

This woman, with her implacable character and grim convictions, found her own way to keep *el Ruso* in at night: she chained him to the bars of the back gallery, trapping his small feet and sealing the lock with a padlock that also anchored his childhood.

So passed *el Ruso*'s nights for almost a year, until a neighbor decided to report what was happening to the proper authorities.

It was under those circumstances that I came to know Sandy. He was a restless, wary child, unable to accept affection or praise. His eyes would disappear into some fixed point, and his words were few. His face, though beautiful, seemed withered, showing no emotion and untouched by a smile. His feet, like his soul, were marked by deep scars.

His feet were a silent testimony to confinement. The skin, hardened in some places and torn in others, still bore the irregular marks of the rusted iron that, night after night, had bitten into his ankles. The scars, still visible, told a story of shackles, of flesh wounded by constant friction, of desperate attempts to free himself, the Court for Children and Adolescents of Santiago reported. Where there should have been only the soft skin of childhood, *el Ruso* had the scabs of wounds badly closed. And so he walked with difficulty, as if the weight of the padlock that had once bound him still hung in his memory, where every step hurt and every night was a new sentence.

In childhood, speaking with him was almost impossible. When we asked why his grandmother tied him up, he would answer that he deserved it because he was a bad boy. It was clear that life had struck him so hard he had learned to justify his own suffering.

In time, he was taken to what was supposed to be a better place, from which he was able to attend school, though he always missed his family. He fought constantly against his demons, remembering Calle La Paz, where he had never known peace or comfort. Later, he was taken to an institutional home, where he lived for almost two years and found refuge in faith.

One rainy night, of which he remembers only the relentless sound of water, he says he tied several sheets together and escaped through the second-floor window of the room where he slept. He fled because the day before he had failed to obey the order to clean the bathrooms, and they had punished him by handcuffing his hands for the entire day, a cruel echo of his past. He refused to return to shackles, and so his life in the streets began, learning their labyrinths and facing, head-on, every danger they held.

"I made it to Puerto Plata, and that was how I came to know the sea and fall in love with it. I was very happy those first days, because seeing the sea had been one of my dreams. I slept with the salt air and woke each morning to a different shade of blue, but with an empty stomach. As the days passed, I understood how hard it was to sleep in the streets of an unknown town, always uneasy because of the cruelty of drunken men."

His head lowered, his beautiful eyes filled with tears as the pain of remembering those times rose to the surface.

And in reverence for those feelings, I too remained silent for a long while...

"I did not sleep. I ate what tourists left behind and worked cleaning a restaurant on the *malecón*. That was how I entered the life of the night, and I nearly found death there. So I decided to return to Santiago and begin again from zero. After several months of living in the streets, I managed to get paid a little to sweep the enormous parking lot of a private company. I put everything I had into that work and did more than I was assigned, while continuing school. With my wages, I paid for a room and helped my grandmother financially. Before long, they promoted me to janitor, cleaning the company building, and gave me a health insurance card. I put my cranky grandmother on that same health plan, and in that way I was able to help her until her final days.

"I graduated from high school through Plan PREPARA, an accelerated two-year program held on Saturdays. My girlfriend was my *madrina* — the sponsor who stood with me at the ceremony — and together with my childhood friends, we celebrated that triumph with a baseball game on the neighborhood field.

"Not long after, I married, and in our second year Emmanuel was born. His name means 'God with us,' and that is exactly what he has been. I assure you, Emmanuel will never live in the streets, and before God I commit myself to loving him and educating him the way I always dreamed."

Sandy el Ruso is now a man in every sense of the word.

Seeing him now as an adult responsible for his family fills my heart with joy and my soul with gladness. He visits his father in prison regularly, helps him a little financially, and offers him hope and companionship for the day he regains his freedom.

"I can tell you my life has not been easy, but I feel that God never abandoned me. I have forgiven those who hurt me, and that has lightened my burden. I pray for my parents' peace, and I love all my siblings. Emmanuel is my beacon, and I am grateful to all my friends who never left me alone.

"Now, whenever I pass through the traffic lights, I commend every child to God, because only He knows what happens in the streets. Those corners damage many children," *el Ruso* concludes, gazing into the distance, with a certain serenity.

This is one of those stories that softens the heart when summarized, shakes the soul when written, and strengthens faith when one knows it is true. Because every step Sandy took, every wound that closed, every decision that brought him closer to life and not to shadow, confirms that God never let go of his hand.

The questions I had asked myself before seeing him were answered fully — in his words, in the way he looked at me, and in the way he spoke of his son. Wonder overcame fear, and I was deeply grateful to be able to witness the miracle we had hoped for.

It Was a Lucky Thursday[1]

The author presents Rodolfo, who with admirable simplicity recounts his battles beneath the burning sun and the harshness of streets that demanded he mature beyond his years, streets where many lost themselves to vice. He never cursed his fate. He chose instead to rise above it, to learn from every setback, and to honor those who believed in him. In time, new opportunities came, along with a university degree. This testimony of courage and gratitude reminds us that even in adversity, a path can open toward a better future.
Aura Celeste Fernández

That morning I arrived at the restaurant with my heart racing. For years I had waited for this meeting, which life, through its various turns, had kept postponing. As I drank my coffee and absently turned the pages of a book, I tried to quiet my impatience. Then, suddenly, I saw him coming down the hallway — elegant, scented with cologne, sure of himself. It was him — that working child I had known long ago, now returned as a determined young man with clear goals.

When we saw each other, we smiled as we used to. We greeted one another and looked into each other's eyes, confirming that

1 This story was previously published and received an Honorable Mention in the anthology *Hispanoamericana en cuentos, Vol. 2* (Chile: Factor Literario, 2025).

this was a moment to celebrate life. We settled at a table with welcome flowers arranged at its center.

With my heart beating in happiness, we moved past the first greetings and, between jokes and stories from the past, began to speak about life — its traps and its joys. I looked at him closely. He is taller than I am now; his voice has changed, and a mustache blends into his beard, framing a grateful smile. For a long while, we raised our water glasses to the joy of meeting.

Rodolfo is thirty-one now. He is the eleventh child of six born to his mother and four to a father he has yet to know. Unable to make sense of that absence, he gave his filial love instead to his uncle and his stepfather, both of whom he holds in deep affection. He and his siblings endured a difficult childhood, marked by poverty and by hardships that seemed to follow the family wherever it went. For different reasons, almost all of them took separate paths, the kind life imposed on them. Rodolfo, however, grew up beside his mother in Santiago, the city where he was born. She worked in other people's homes, keeping long hours that often stretched even longer. Even so, she never neglected the heavy burden of sustaining a household full of interrupted dreams.

In search of better income, she and Rodolfo's stepfather set up in Parque Duarte, selling juices and *tostadas* — pressed sandwiches. She arrived before daybreak, and often the sunset would find her still caught up in the same struggle. It was exhausting work, especially on rainy days or when customers were scarce. The atmosphere of the park, moreover, did not favor that kind of labor. Street vendors and the authorities looked unfavorably on pushcart businesses, even though they were the livelihood of many families.

Rodolfo's family lived in Barrio Nuevo, in La Herradura, Santiago, and even within the limits imposed by poverty, he attended a private school just a few steps from his mother's stand.

But during the government of President Hipólito Mejía, street vending was prohibited in the park. His mother's income fell, and Rodolfo was forced to enroll in a public school.

He was still a boy, and he was afraid. He was only twelve then, too young to face the dangers of the street: the fights, the pull of vice, the things he saw every day in the park while accompanying his mother. It was a difficult moment and a risky decision, but need, poverty, and the desire to help ease the financial burden at home pushed him forward. And so, without more ceremony, he picked up a shoeshine box and settled into Parque Duarte, a place he knew very well.

That place welcomes many visitors each day, people crossing through this charming plaza. Important buildings stand all around it, and the park is equipped for recreation; but it is also the ground of hard-fought battles, of fierce confrontations among the working children of the area. Honor and respect were earned the hard way, in bruising fights won through sheer grit, like trophies of courage and daring. Each victory crowned the "gladiator," meaning he had crushed his opponent and won the fight by a wide margin.

In Parque Duarte, conflicts break out every day. Fights erupted over food, because someone "rubbed you the wrong way," over a customer who wanted his shoes shined, over money someone stole from you after you had worked for it, over collecting a debt, or simply because someone looked at you the wrong way. The street imposes a culture of urgency, and as the word itself suggests, everything happens fast: there is no time to reflect, and everything takes on an immediate character.

"The demands of the street are very hard on children. You become a man before your time, because if you don't, you may not survive," Rodolfo says, with the experience and understanding of someone who has lived that reality.

"On the street, groups organize themselves by hierarchy. The fiercest one lays down the law with his fists, through fight after fight, and sometimes with a certain gift for leadership. The boss is respected, even when that means doing things you do not want to do and know are not right. In the street, you rub shoulders with every kind of person: those who steal, those who use drugs, those who rob people, and those capable of anything for a few pesos. You also find true friends who defend you and guide you toward the right path.

"That was where I met *Bembe*, a working child with a good heart toward his friends. He was hardworking and diligent, but also shrewd — a *lince*, a sly one, when it came to taking what belonged to others. He had become a master of quick thefts, an expert at making off with anything that could be sold. His specialty was mugging women, because they were 'easy prey.' According to him, all it took was to say in a rough voice, 'This is a robbery! Give me your purse!' and they would let go of it at once, with everything inside. That was how he spoke, with nerves of steel and an armor hardened by the harsh laws of the street. *Bembe* slept wherever he could in the streets, and that life taught him, without mercy, to survive by whatever means he had to."

As Rodolfo was remembering his life in the streets, breakfast arrived, and we were joined by Irenarco Ardila and his son, Juan Martín Ardila Gutiérrez, two veterans of non-formal education. We all ordered the same dish: *los tres golpes*, the classic Dominican breakfast of *mangú*, fried cheese, salami, and eggs.

As we ate, Rodolfo went on speaking, without pause, about his memories of the street. We listened closely the whole time, but the street has so many edges, and a language of its own that must be understood to follow it, so I spoke up for the first time and asked him:

"Rodolfo, how does a boy or girl sleep in the streets, and what do they feel in that moment?"

Rodolfo swallowed hard. Then, after a few seconds, as if a sudden flood of memories had struck him, he answered:

"I never slept in the street. I was a working child. I spent my days shining shoes in the streets and went back home when the siren sounded — the one you could hear clearly on Calle del Sol, around six in the evening. But I lived alongside many friends who did sleep under those conditions. All of them guarded the only things they had. *Bembe*, for example, slept with his pants turned backward and his money tucked deep in the pockets so he could feel any attempt to rob him. None of them slept unarmed. They always kept something within reach: a pocketknife, a sharpened shard of glass from a bottle, or a knife of some kind, ready for whatever might come.

"The boys who sleep in the streets are afraid at first. But little by little, they build a network of friends, and they all protect one another. I believe God also watches over them and helps them in the hardest moments, because they face so many obstacles before night ever falls. To sleep just one night in the street is like living an entire year for an ordinary person."

That is how this young man with a short beard and long experience describes it.

"They live through hard moments during the day, but the night is even crueler — when hunger tightens its grip, when they are driven out of the places where they camp, when it rains and their only roof is the open sky, or when the police chase them, especially the migrant children," Rodolfo added.

"It is difficult, for example, when one of them gets sick in the middle of the night, in some alleyway or unsafe corner.

If a boy feels ill, he tells his friends, and they do everything they can to help him, without hesitation. They take him to the hospital if they have to, whether he is Dominican or foreign. They never leave him alone. Solidarity lives in the street too.

"I remember one afternoon when a very sick boy arrived at Parque Duarte from Haiti. He could not have been more than eight years old. He told us his name was Wilson, but many Haitian children invent nicknames so they will not be identified by their real names. He told us he had walked for several days to cross over from Haiti and reach Santiago, making his way through hills and brush in the middle of the night — a journey far too hard for a child his age. He was a migrant child who had crossed the border alone.

"He arrived dehydrated and in terrible condition. His feet were raw, his skin cracked, his lips split, and he had a high fever. The boys brought him water, but he could barely take a few sips because he could hardly swallow. They also gave him something to eat and a pill to bring down the fever. When night came, they carried him to an abandoned school near the Cathedral, where many of them slept.

"At midnight, Wilson began to convulse and to rave in Creole, saying things no one could understand. His body shook uncontrollably, and his stomach seemed to leap. Seeing him like that, everyone got up to help. They knew it was an emergency, and that Wilson was gravely ill. They turned the sacks they slept on into an improvised stretcher, and each boy held a corner. When one of them grew tired, another took his place. In this way they ran through the streets, bound together by the urgency of solidarity, until they reached the hospital. Wilson was treated immediately and admitted because of his critical condition.

"Some time later, the doctors decided Wilson could be discharged, but he was still very weak and unable to walk. The boys explained that he had no family and nowhere safe to stay, and since the street teaches you how to negotiate, they offered to sweep the hospital parking lot every day until he regained his strength. After several conversations, the doctors agreed. For eight days they arrived before dawn to clean and to visit Wilson, until at last he was able to walk out on his own. And, as if by God's hand, something good also came from that effort: Tachón, one of the boys, ended up being hired as a sweeper at the hospital, a job he still has today.

"That is the solidarity I came to know in the streets: giving of yourself without asking for anything in return. People tend to generalize, to think that all boys from the street are *tígueres* — hustlers, streetwise troublemakers — but that is not true. Many of them are noble, honest, and hardworking, carrying family responsibilities, as Waily did when he supported his grandmother and paid for his sisters' schooling.

"Almost all of them have their time accounted for. Some work from very early in the morning, go home at noon with what they have earned, attend school in the afternoon, and help at home at night. I can testify that there are boys who are fighters, boys with good intentions, whom life dragged into the street as a last means of survival."

Rodolfo remembers those harsh years clearly, the years when he had to work in the street. With pain and helplessness in his voice, he explains that in those days, there were not as many drugs within reach of the boys as there are now. The most common were PVC cement and paint thinner — the same kind used for paint.

"Today there are many more options, and there are drug-selling points everyone in the city knows about. I know one very busy place with only one street in and one street out, a grim place where more drugs are sold and consumed than water. And like that one, there are many others in plain sight.

"In that sense, it pains me to see the boys using *piedra*, a drug whose effect lasts barely sixty seconds. Once they try it, the brain asks for it again and does not let them go until they are addicted. Then they have to use it again and again. They work only to buy that poison, which ends up consuming their lives. The worst part is that the *tígueres* who sell those drugs do not even use them, because they know they would lose control. Their business is turning boys into addicts, and God will have to punish that.

"The boys who make their lives in the streets are always thinking about how to increase their income, because life swallows up the little they produce. In my case, I shined shoes and earned two or three hundred pesos a day, though sometimes there were better days of five hundred or even six hundred pesos. To increase what I made, I also worked as security for other boys. In other words, I prevented fights and beatings by protecting them from the others. At the end of the day, they paid me a fee for that service, and that helped improve my earnings.

"I also bought cheaper supplies — brushes, liquids, and other tools the boys used to shine shoes — and then resold them to make a little profit. I did other jobs too, like arranging chairs and tables at events. People often hire children for work that requires a lot of energy, and at thirteen, I had plenty to spare.

"Over time I grew tired of shining shoes and, together with *Bembe*, decided to wash windshields at the traffic light on Estrella Sadhalá and Juan Pablo Duarte. That place was hot. Everything was organized, and each group had its territory marked off, with boys ready to defend it down to the last penny. The arrival of anyone new was seen as a threat. *Bembe*, who had never known fear, convinced me to try that work so we could increase our earnings, but it turned out to be a bitter experience.

"The veterans of the spot came down on us with blows. There were six of them, and only two of us. I ran at the first beating, but *Bembe* stayed and faced them bravely. He did not win the fight, but he hit several of them hard. I watched from nearby, reflected in a car's rearview mirror, and felt ashamed for leaving him alone among those lions. That was how *Bembe* earned the respect of the block; from then on, whenever they saw him nearby, they respected him.

"Washing windshields also requires a thick skin, because you have to endure the contempt of many passersby and drivers. Sometimes they speak to you as if you were worth less than nothing. I remember once I cleaned a windshield and the driver tossed ten pesos at me with contempt. I caught them in the air, and he said, 'Take those ten pesos and use them to get yourself drugs.' That wounded me deeply, and from that day on, I never washed windshields again.

"After fighting so many battles, after splitting two or three boys open, after putting up with so many insults and feeling deeply humiliated on more than one occasion, I developed a great deal of anger. It is an unpleasant emotion, one that works as a natural response to the threats you feel, but that often becomes a problem when you do not know how to control it. At my age, I did not even know what was happening to me. When anger came over me, my breathing grew short. It was an irrational rage that made me breathe faster and set my heart racing. I felt the need to fight, as if that were the only way to calm myself.

"That condition led me into many episodes of violence. At barely thirteen, exhausted after months of fighting battles in the street, I decided, almost without hope, to join the educational programs at Acción Callejera. The psychologists and educators at the Foundation welcomed me and taught me breathing techniques and other exercises that, through long therapy sessions, I still use today to control my anger.

"The Foundation's programs helped me see life in another way and brought me back into Telésforo Reynoso School to continue my primary studies. There I received school supplies, emotional support, and constant encouragement without missing a single day. I also took part in the homework rooms and helped in different areas: reception, the dining room, sports, the kitchen, and hygiene. During that time, I belonged to a group that marked my life, *Futuro con Ideales* — Future with Ideals — a program that addressed rights, emotional management, gender, masculinity, and violence. That was when I hung up the clothes of a shoeshine boy and left the shoeshine box behind.

"Later on, the Foundation trained me to look for work and recommended me for a job as a bagger at a well-known store in the city. I completed the three-month trial period and was hired permanently. That was how I spent two years working during the day and studying at night.

"My life was different by then. I had the same problems, but I faced them in a different way, because I felt I had the tools to improve my life.

"I helped at the Foundation in the mornings, studied in the afternoons, and passed my courses with good grades. Little by little, I began to face life with optimism and discipline, until I graduated from high school. That was a source of great joy for me, for my family, and for the Foundation. That celebration pushed me to continue my studies, first with God's help, and also with the Foundation's constant support, with faith in myself, and with the tremendous financial, emotional, and loving support of my sister

Carolina, who sacrificed much of her working life so that I could make my way forward. To her, I owe my gratitude and recognition.

"In 2013, I enrolled at the Universidad Nacional Evangélica (UNEV) to study Accounting. As I moved forward in the program, I worked in different stores and supermarkets, beginning as a cashier and later passing through several positions until I became an area manager, a role I held for four years.

"In 2019, I graduated with a degree in Accounting. That day, I celebrated with gratitude to God, because the road had been hard, but it was a dream I had pursued for a long time.

"With my degree in hand, I worked conducting surveys for a project of the Oficina Nacional de Estadística (ONE). I also spent some time working in a lottery bank, but I resigned when I understood that the environment did not align with my values.

"After that, I decided to become independent and worked as an Uber driver. On one of those rides, I met the woman to whom I am happily married today. With her I have Alma, my daughter, who took possession of my heart even before she was born.

"Later, I looked for stable work in keeping with my profession, and today, for more than three years now, I have worked as the head of Water Resources at a well-known industrial park in Santiago, where I manage drinking-water and wastewater systems and coordinate a team of operators. I like working as part of a team and always looking for ways to improve things," Rodolfo said with pride.

Rodolfo had to be at work by noon that Thursday, and it was time for him to leave. We said goodbye with the promise that we would meet again, and I know we will. Without intending it, that breakfast had become a tribute to the iron will that shaped his character amid so much hardship. In his words, nostalgia and pride live side by side, as if each memory carried with it a lesson in strength and, at the same time, an invitation not to judge life in the streets without first understanding its nuances and winding paths.

On the way home, I carried with me a renewed admiration for those who, like this graduate of the soul, have found a way to reinvent themselves with a spark of hope that does not go out.

I raise my glass high in a toast to the courage of all those who, like Rodolfo, dare to defy adversity and build a dignified future with the little life has given them.

Onward, graduate.

Redemption

The author movingly tells the fate of a girl whom violence made into a woman and, sadly, marked forever.
Freddy Ginebra

She was my friend during our early school years, and her figure still floats among the brightest of my memories. She had the morning sun in her eyes and smiled seven days a week, like an orange tree in bloom. She was the companion of my first discoveries in life, but her life changed when the moon began following her steps, on those star-poor nights when she sold her body for the price she believed it was worth. From an early age, she carried the weight of injustice on her tender shoulders and was marked as the neighborhood prostitute.

We were both teenagers in that June of 1975, when news spread of a protest in which one hundred prostitutes had occupied the Church of Saint-Nizier in Lyon, France, to draw attention to their working conditions and the discrimination they endured.

These women lived under constant pressure, forced to work in secrecy. As an act of protest, they remained in that church for eight days. That event came to be regarded as the starting point of a movement demanding recognition of the rights of sex workers.

Since then, every June 2 has been commemorated as International Sex Workers' Day.

I was just beginning college when the news reached our country, where the language used to speak of that struggle objectified sex workers. People believed their protest set a bad precedent, and they referred to the event in derogatory terms, as a way of diminishing the importance of their demands.

In my generation, sex workers were called prostitutes, women of easy virtue, *cueros*, or whores. Since there is no word in the dictionary of any language that can justly define the reality of these women, I prefer to call them, and to treat them, simply as people.

Prostitution is defined as a personal service, not as work. It is a cruel exercise of violence against women. By definition, it consists of negotiating a sexual encounter in which one person obtains a specific sexual gratification from another in exchange for an agreed payment or benefit. But that definition presents, in very simple terms, a reality with many edges. There are countless stories of young women who, for different reasons, fall into prostitution.

In my adolescence, I had a friend more or less my age who entered prostitution in the 1970s. I will keep her name to myself, just as the two of us kept affection and tenderness between us. She had a beautifully proportioned body, hair so long it reached her slender waist, honey-colored eyes, shapely legs, and the aura of a goddess. She walked with the rhythm of a runway model, and, knowing she was beautiful, flirted with ease, like a creature out of fable.

She had a prodigious voice and could play a few notes on the guitar. Before she began selling her body at bargain prices, in hidden sales, she sang high, sustained notes in the church choir. That was where I met her, when spring had planted only flowers in her soul.

She was a sweet, innocent girl who smiled with two dimples in her rosy cheeks. I remember that the nuns always chose her to portray the Virgin of Altagracia, a role she performed with a purity reflected in her eyes. Under the guidance of those same nuns, she acquired refined manners that made her beauty stand out even more. She was beautiful and had the gifts to pursue any occupation other than prostitution. But her life took a merciless journey, slipping violently through the cracks of fate.

Years passed, and before long, along with her innocence, she lost the light in her eyes, and her sense of modesty too. People said she was crazy, and I am certain she never was. She came to know sexuality in the worst possible way, and far too young.

It was an open secret that a trusted uncle had raped her and used her sexually for a long time. The abuse took place with her parents' consent; in return, the abuser paid part of the household expenses. She grew up knowing she was the object of that exchange, feeling "sold" for a few coins, and this deeply wounded her self-worth. She came to understand that this was simply the rule of life's game and, without giving it much thought, devoted herself to selling sex to the highest bidder. Later, she would grieve all of it, when she realized she had lost not only her dignity, but all the dreams of her childhood.

She was violent because she had been violated, and with that same aggression she demanded payment after each encounter. For that reason, the men in the neighborhood decided not to do business with her. She carried the weight of criticism on her back and became the recognized, duly labeled prostitute of the place. Once she chose that life, she felt the accusing finger pointing at her as such, and she carried the weight of that unappealable verdict for the rest of her days.

I was forbidden to talk to her because she was considered a bad influence. However, knowing her noble heart, sharing the same age, and being born in the same month, I continued to speak with her in secret. During those clandestine conversations, as she shared details of her life, our friendship remained protected, and at times, we even embraced.

In the midst of her painful stories, she confided to me that calling women who chose prostitution as their occupation "women of easy virtue" was a myth.

"I have no words to explain so much humiliation and abuse," she told me one afternoon, her eyes wet with tears.

She told me she had worked in a brothel in the capital and that she had a boss, whom I understood to be a pimp. She decided to leave that place because of the intense pressure he exerted on her and her companions, even demanding that they be sterilized so there would be no chance of pregnancy.

She always regarded that demand as abusive, because she understood that they were chosen for being women, only to have others try to deprive them of the very thing that distinguished them: the power to carry life within.

One day, sick of having been made to abort so many times, she confronted the pimp. The wretch gave her a beating that nearly cost her an eye. That episode pushed her to flee and take refuge in a brothel that still stands at the entrance to Salcedo, governed by other rules and other exchanges that, in any case, continued to stain her dignity.

Before she lived publicly as a prostitute, we had a friend in common who had been in love with her for years, since the two of them were almost children. Still, he knew very well what the consequences would be if he threw himself into that love. He knew he risked being cast out by his family and shunned by society itself. Even so, he always dreamed of rescuing her from that harsh life. Because that never happened, their story remained trapped in the realm of the impossible.

My friend confessed to me that she was in love with him too, but she never dared reveal her feelings, sensing the rejection that would come from the young man's family. He did not take that step either, convinced that such a gesture would bring consequences too heavy for them both.

The two of them carried on a beautiful relationship made only of exchanged glances, until one Christmas Eve, the moon gave them permission to empty their hearts and reveal the feelings they had kept since childhood. With no witnesses to that miracle, morning found them still together. They waited for the sunrise, confessing the love they had kept hidden for so many years.

For her, that was her only true holy night — the only good night of her life. For him, the release of long-contained desire and the light of feelings kept hidden for years. Each of them told me separately about their happiness, their eyes filled with a quiet joy, and I promised them both I would keep their secret.

I am certain they never managed to make their dreams real, because he died very young and she wept in silence, discreetly, beyond anyone else's hearing.

After these events, I heard nothing more of her, for life led us down different roads. Now, as I revisit this story that has always remained in my memory, I have learned that she died some years ago. I sense that she must have earned heaven by suffering in advance the hell she endured in living flesh. Her sister told me she left behind a son with serious emotional disorders, wandering the same streets and footpaths of that small town where we were both born.

Today, I pause to remember her with the dignity she deserves. Her figure stirs in me a mixture of feelings, each with its own color, and leaves me fully convinced that no term — least of all a derogatory one — can encompass the ruthless and violent stories of women like her.

May Heaven receive you with the tenderness this world denied you.

Still Standing

The author recalls the quiet magic of a look that returns unexpectedly during a chance encounter in the Caribbean. There, with the salty sea breeze stirring around him, Juan feels an unforgettable past awaken again in his grateful heart. Among the warm currents of a tropical cove, beneath the soft light of the moon, that memory rekindles, defying the relentless passage of time.
Reynolds Pérez Stefan

This past May, we spent a week as a family at a hotel in the magical eastern part of the country. It was one of those resorts that makes life more pleasant, offers you the sea on a silver platter, and lets you share time with your own people while surrounded by every attention. After several days of being treated like royalty, anyone would rather not think about the day's menu, the supermarket shopping, or returning to life with a cleaning cloth in hand, tending to the house and to the thousand small duties that domestic work carries with it.

At these hotels, the evenings offer splendid dinners, drinks, shows, and every kind of entertainment. One night, with my platoon of children, granddaughters, and husband, all dressed for the occasion, we made our way to a French restaurant, already imagining and savoring the delicacies that awaited us.

In complete anonymity, never imagining I would find someone I knew in that enchanted setting of greenery and carefully tended trees, we passed near a young man who stopped to look me over from head to toe. That gaze caught my attention, and almost by instinct, I looked back at him. He was wearing the hotel staff uniform, and his eyes followed us closely as we approached the restaurant.

Just as it was nearly our turn to go in, the young man stepped forward and placed himself in front of me. He apologized to my husband for the unexpected gesture and greeted me respectfully by my full name. Such precision startled me, so I barely managed to return the greeting and confirm that, yes, that was indeed my name. Something whispered to me where he might have come from, but my mind still could not place him clearly.

The employee, smiling but somewhat reserved, introduced himself as Juan and said he had known me since he was a child, back when he worked in the streets of Santiago. He also told me he had been at La Molino Blanco, that place so many boys carry tucked into a corner of the heart. I listened closely, and without wasting time, he told me he wanted to do something special for us and, if possible, speak with me about his progress and what he had achieved.

His face seemed filled with all the colors of morning. Once I understood his eagerness, I felt a breath of joy move through me. So, without thinking twice, I accepted.

In that moment, I tried to match his calm, steady voice to someone in my memory, but I could not be sure I was looking at the same person I remembered. My mind lit up like a flash, searching for his face among my memories, trying hard not to let him feel like a stranger before me.

To be honest, I could not find his name in that vast inventory I keep in memory, filled with the girls and boys I had the privilege of accompanying during twenty-six of the most intense years of my life, along those paths God sets before us.

Still uncertain, I asked him what he did at the hotel and what time he would be free to talk. Quickly, he handed me a personal card that identified him as a housekeeping supervisor and included his contact number. He told me he would be working until three o'clock the next afternoon, and we agreed to meet then in the hotel lobby.

My heart was brimming with excitement at the thought of seeing him again, and that eagerness made me arrive before he did. As I waited, caught between joy and anxiety, I began removing dry leaves from a plant in the great hall, rooted in an enormous clay pot — a long-standing habit I have never quite managed to overcome.

A short while later, Juan arrived, along with the salt scent the sea carried in. We greeted each other again and sat in the hotel reception area. I took a corner of the sofa, and he, this time out of uniform — wearing jeans, a striped shirt, and impeccably clean shoes — sat across from me. Kindly, he offered me something to drink, and I chose a hot tea to steady the expectation of the moment.

Because I still could not fully remember him, I stayed attentive, hoping his words would bring my memory into focus. I addressed him naturally with the familiar "tú" to break the ice, and little by little he began to relax. His eyes moved across the hall's indoor garden, planted with blooming anthuriums, and one simple comment was enough for him to begin telling his story.

"Dad drank almost every day, until he was drunk. He was very violent with my mother, and with me too. When he attacked her, she would leave the house to escape the abuse, and I always went with her. That alone was enough for my father to call me less than a man and use other terrible names that still echo in my memory as if it were happening today," Juan tells me with deep sadness.

"That was how I earned his contempt. Every time he drank, he would start fighting with me for no reason at all. There were three of us at home, but all the hatred fell on me. My presence enraged him, and I always felt he hated me to death. Many times, I wanted to disappear from my own house.

"When he was drunk, he shouted terrible things at me and beat me without mercy. But even when he was sober, he humiliated me with very harsh punishments. I remember one day in particular when, after giving me a beating that left welts all over my body, he slammed me against the wall with the force of a wild animal, and I was left almost unconscious.

"If he sent me on an errand to the colmado and, for some reason, I could not do it, he would throw something sharp at my face, whether a glass or a plate. Other times, he beat me with the buckle of a special belt he kept only for that purpose. If something displeased him, he would whip me with a hose folded in four until I was left almost without strength. No one could intervene until he had emptied all his fury onto me.

"To keep from running into him, I would go to bed very early and pretend to be asleep. My father had no interest in my studies, and even doing my homework at night was enough to upset him.

"Deeply marked, both physically and emotionally, I looked for a job that would let me spend long hours away from home, so I would not be there when my executioner arrived. It was through that job that I learned about a foundation that supported abused children, and that was how I found my way to Acción Callejera.

"I arrived at Acción Callejera, and God sent me Cinthya Lora, a psychologist and social educator who, with the soul of a guardian angel, helped me stay afloat and learn to love life again. All the abuse I had suffered had taken away my desire to live.

"Cinthya would come to the school where I studied and encourage me to keep going. She also visited my house and even confronted my father, and he had no choice but to respect her. One day I showed her my bruised back, and with great courage she warned him that she would take him to the Prosecutor's Office for abuse. He got scared, like all cowards do, and for a while he stopped hitting me.

"But that did not last long, and I continued to be mistreated for a long time, as part of a routine that had begun in my childhood. Even so, I always kept my faith in God.

"The hardest moment for me was when I had to go out and wander the streets before I had even turned ten. That change was harsher than the beatings I received. I still remember the silence of the streets I walked through, until suddenly I reached the noise of a busy avenue. At my age, all of it frightened me. The street demands that you stay alert to any opportunity, and I did not have that ability. When you are unprotected, without your parents, you feel that anyone can harm you, that you will not find work, that someone may abuse you at any moment. I felt clumsy, and everything scared me. I became insecure and distrustful.

"In those days, each morning was more confusing than the one before. As my only way out, I began cleaning windshields on a busy avenue in Santiago. It was a place of fights and tragedies. Almost every day, some kind of trouble would break out: one boy would hit another, or one group would hurt a rival group. One day, a fight broke out between two of them. Each one held a sharpened shard of glass bottle, trying to reach the other's throat. Finally, *el Macho* wounded *el Pití* near the neck, and in the midst of all that blood, *el Pití* slashed his face while no one dared to separate them.

"That is how violent the traffic-light corners are where boys clean windshields. They are places where anything can happen, dangerous from every side. If you made money, the older boys, the 'owners' of the spot, took it from you. And if you made nothing, you felt the disappointment of having gone through all that misery for nothing," Juan explained, rolling up the sleeves of his shirt.

"Passersby would say very hurtful things to me in a contemptuous tone: 'Get out of there, you good-for-nothing! Don't bother me with your begging! Don't come near me, you old punk!' And that made me feel deeply ashamed. But I have always been optimistic, and the next day I would get up again with my spirit lifted, still searching for a place in a better world.

"I remember going home very afraid, because I never knew what state I would find my father in, or what the next beating would be like. I would arrive exhausted and reeking of that dry smell of burnt gasoline that clings to those corners of God."

As he described that place to me, sadness rose into his face, as if he were stirring something painful that still remained in some crevice of the heart.

"I would leave there and many times go to Mass in any chapel that was open. I felt welcomed when I spoke with God, and I became an altar boy so I could be closer to Him. One day I walked into Mass at the Hospicio San Vicente de Paúl and met doña Natalia Díaz. I believe God brought me near her so I could receive her guidance and companionship during those very difficult moments in my life. I knew I could count on her whenever I needed her, and she even became my graduation godmother at Cenapec."

And there, at last, came the spark that allowed me to remember that past clearly. I recalled that frail boy, slow in speech, with kindness in his smile and love in his eyes, who bore no resemblance to the young man before me. I also saw him in memory operating a floor scrubber as an employee of a well-known company. I relived Cinthya's efforts from the Foundation and the follow-up offered by Yohanny, who always supported him. Also returning to my mind was the care given to him by the Dominican Sisters of the Presentation at the Hospicio San Vicente de Paúl, especially Sister María Belén.

The young man continued his story like someone emptying a heavy suitcase of worn-out memories, and he told me about the trauma he had endured washing windshields.

"One day, the driver of a public-route car said such ugly things to me that I stood there paralyzed. Out of sheer malice, he ran the two left tires of the car over my feet. For several days I was in so much pain I could barely walk, but there was also a wound in my soul from seeing how heartless people can be toward the boys who clean windshields. Along with the contempt we received came the fights and the drugs, two evils that were common at those spots.

"All the money I made from that work, I took home to help my parents. I even went hungry so I could hand over everything I had earned. I spent a long time sacrificing myself in search of my father's approval, but it was never enough.

"In the midst of so much hardship, it was there, in that very place, that I thought again about continuing my studies, thanks to a compassionate man who passed through the traffic light and spoke to me quickly about the importance of studying. Before the light turned green, he offered me a job washing cars near Calle Sabana Larga.

"I discussed the offer with Cinthya, from Acción Callejera, and after she inspected the place and approved it, I accepted the kind man's offer. At the same time that I began the new job, I enrolled at Santo Hermano Miguel School, run by La Salle, in El Ejido. I studied there only until my third year of high school, because the schedule conflicted with my work. But I was able to finish at Cenapec, in the Saturday program."

"Everything I earned from work, I continued to share with my family, even though I was still enduring my father's abuse and humiliation.

"After I finished high school, I began working at a cleaning company, putting in long hours for little money and carrying heavy responsibilities. Even so, I managed to study Hospitality Service and Housekeeping Supervision at Infotep, and I even attended a job fair for hotels.

"That was how I decided to take two important steps: to enroll at the Universidad Abierta para Adultos (UAPA) so I could study online, and to move to Punta Cana. I had applied for a position at a hotel in the East, and right away I qualified as a room attendant, making beds and arranging rooms.

"In 2021, I began my degree in Psychology through virtual classes. I work twenty-four days straight and then have a week off, which I use to travel to Santiago and take my in-person exams at the university.

"I study Psychology because I see it as a tool for understanding and managing emotions. I also know that, through this profession,

I can help others like me, people with serious difficulties who do not know how to face them.

"In July of that same year, 2023, my father died of a devastating cancer that left him bedridden. He spent only a short time in the hospital. In his final days, he asked me to forgive him, and I have to admit that I forgave him in words so he could leave in peace. But in my heart, too many questions remained unanswered. I still have not found the answers I need in order to heal the wounds left open during a crucial stage of my life," this young man finally said, his face undone.

The image of that fragile child who had once hidden from abuse and wandered dangerous streets was transformed before my eyes into the image of a strong man. I could see that the boy marked by physical and emotional scars had managed to find his way. His story is a living testimony to human strength, and to the way a wounded heart can heal and flourish when it finds a spark of hope, or a hand extended in genuine support.

I thanked him for sharing his story and for transforming pain into strength. I understood then that Juan no longer belongs only to the sorrowful memories of a broken childhood. He now walks firmly in the present, master of his own future.

The sunset was already yielding its soul to the night when Juan took the first sip of a tea that had gone cold on the table. We walked together and talked along those warm paths that lead to the sea, and in his gaze, melancholy as the dusk itself, I discovered the serene and courageous face of a young man whom the generous sea had placed in my path as a gift from the same God who had accompanied him.

Goodness, Juan, how blessed I have been to know you.

In God's Hands

When home is the worst prison, the greatest longing is to escape. But where does one go? What kind of freedom can the street offer? The author presents two sisters who flee that hell, and this is their story.
Patricia Solano

"I was born in Comedero Arriba de Cotuí, a country place near all those hills swollen with gold as far as the eye can reach. There are thirteen of us siblings. A number that, according to my grandfather, brings bad luck — and it seems he was right.

"We grew up hungry from birth and lived a very hard life, marked by the alcohol my father drank every day, whose consequences all of us paid for at a very high price. He worked in the mines of a foreign company for as long as I can remember, but almost everything he earned went on rum, *aguardiente*, or whatever drink could get him drunk.

"I still remember my grandmother, who used to tell us in a resigned voice: 'Forgive your father, it's just that drink turns him bad.' Then I would watch her walk slowly away, her bent figure on the donkey she used to carry water in *higüeros*. That scene and that plea repeated themselves for many years. For us, my grandmother was always a great support.

“Dad left very early in the morning and came back at sundown. As a child, that routine confused me. I wanted him to be at home so he could protect me from the danger that he himself caused, but when he came back drunk, I wished he would never come back, because he unloaded all his fury on me, on my siblings, and most especially on my mother.

“Dad was a good man, but very violent. For any little thing we did, as children will, he'd give us a lash. I remember how every night, when my mother served him his dinner, he would throw the plate through the air, staining the walls with grease and leaving scraps on the floor. He always wanted to find a special menu on the table, even though he never brought home the money for that to happen. Many times my mother put us to bed with sugar water, or some lemon juice, or sour orange from the patio, so she could save the best of our scant inventory for him.

“To remember my childhood is to see my mother gathering up the pieces of broken plates and cleaning the walls, always in silence.

“One day I tried to enroll in school along with my sister Belkis. That simple attempt was enough to unleash his fury. He gave us such a brutal beating that I still carry a mark on my ribs. I remember I had long hair then, and he wrapped my hair around his hand and slammed me against the wall.

“When I heard on the news about men who killed their whole families, I thought the same thing could happen in my house, because when Dad hit us he seemed to lose control of himself, as if a demon had gotten into him and wanted to finish us all off.

“For my father, women studying was a waste of time. The right thing, according to him, was for us to learn only household chores, while the men's role was to work in the fields. And that order had to be obeyed. Resting was also forbidden. Sitting down for a moment to ease our tiredness was a mortal sin in my father's eyes, because it meant we were lazy.

"My mother, like my grandmother, used to talk to us trying to convince us that we should forgive and understand Dad, but I never understood that compassion, especially when she was the one who suffered most.

"None of us went to school. Everything was hard work. We had to gather wild cacao, roast coffee, clean houses for some pay, gut cattle for *mondongo*, wash and iron other people's clothes in the river, and cook for wakes or for crews of farmhands. We also swept patios, sold boiled beans, carried water from the river, and sometimes even milked cows.

"Weekends were a nightmare with Dad in the house. One Sunday afternoon, he gave my mother such a cruel beating that he left the socket of one of her eyes permanently dry. To protect him, we declared at the hospital that she had fallen. My mother always made excuses for him out of fear, and over time, we ended up doing the same.

"On another occasion, I remember he hit my brother Alfredo, six years old, with such force that he tore the skin of his penis. When he saw the blood running down his little legs, the poor child went to take refuge in my mother's arms. That day she finally confronted him, and all of us were ready to back her up.

"Even so, the next day, Dad came home drunk once again and tried to do the same to my younger sister. This time we joined together to protect her. My father, feeling defeated, broke down crying. But no — that moment of supposed remorse lasted only a short while. Very soon, the blows, the insults, and the humiliations were once again normal in the house. I remember Dad had a rough belt with a big buckle that he used so the punishment would hurt us more. I hope God has forgiven him...

"Some time later, one morning the six sisters gathered in the *conuco*. We had to gather beans, lima beans, and pigeon peas to sell by the cup to the neighbors. While we worked, Belkis and I began to plan how to escape from that prison without visible walls. We decided to flee without saying anything, and one Good Friday at dawn, we caught a pickup truck down to the city, in God's hands. Then we took the bus that left at sunrise.

"We wanted to get to Santiago because we had a cousin there who knew about our suffering; but that cousin played dumb and never answered our calls. Meanwhile, Maritza, my older sister, was left in charge of calming Mom by telling her the truth.

"To make matters worse, we took the wrong bus, because fear paralyzed us and kept us from thinking clearly. We thought we were heading toward Santiago; but by the time we reached Villa Altagracia, we realized our destination was Santo Domingo. When we got to the capital, we noticed that the young man at the ticket window was looking at us with suspicion, and now I understand why: fear was clearly written on our faces. I remember we sat in a corner of the waiting room, holding a small bag as our only luggage to face life with.

"Then we spoke with a young woman from the bus company, who consulted our situation with someone else and, generously, decided to help us. That Samaritan young woman even got us a taxi to the bus, so we could finally make it to Santiago, and this time we bought the tickets making sure of the destination. Today, when I remember that episode, I feel that God was always with us, because that young woman gave us back more than twice the cost of the tickets, and that gesture turned out to be a real relief.

"Evening was falling when we reached Santiago. We were starving and completely defenseless. Fear shrank our hearts, because we had nowhere to spend the night. It was a painful moment — it's not the same to summon the devil as to see him arrive. With that fear weighing on us, we walked without direction until we caught sight of the tip of the Monumento a los Héroes. When we got there, the atmosphere did not feel right to me: drunk men, just like Dad; smiling little girls begging for money; loud music and many hungry children begging too. So we decided to move away. We went down Calle del Sol and then turned onto Avenida Francia. There, where Calle Restauración comes to an end, we found a dirty, foul-smelling cave; but no one was there, and I thought maybe we could rest. At least that's what I thought, because Belkis refused to stay in that hideout and would not stop crying.

"Once we were both lying on the ground, I held her and spoke to her gently until she calmed down. I put the bag of clothes under her neck as a pillow, and she fell asleep. I, on the other hand, was awake the whole night through that first night, watching over her sleep and praying to God, because in some way I felt responsible for both of us. It was a calm, quiet night, except for the parade of cockroaches and other crawling things that, like me, watched over my sister's sleep. In that cave we suffered more than the lining of a cot.

"That's where we spent the longest days of my life. We felt time was passing very slowly. Both of us were overwhelmed by a deep sadness as we wandered the streets, because that was a way of living completely unknown to us. One day doña Isabel Vargas, an educator from Acción Callejera, made contact with us. There they guided us, fed us, and we were able to clean ourselves with scented soap, which made us feel like people again. Doña Isabel welcomed us beautifully, and on top of that, she had the consideration of going to Cotuí to let our parents know that we were all right. From that visit we learned that my father had savagely beaten my mother the day we ran away and accused her of being irresponsible. That hit us hard, but we had to keep going.

"Living in the streets, I came to understand that those who are forced into that condition do not know when they will find a bathroom, much less where they will change their clothes or wash them. It is a very heavy burden for a child to carry. Besides, many men eye young girls with looks full of abuse and bad intentions.

"Acción Callejera arranged for us to be placed in a foundation that took in vulnerable children in safe homes. We spent a good while there, under the supervision and biweekly visits of the educators from Acción Callejera during the first six months. Then we enrolled in a regular school. Belkis went up to eighth grade, and I went up to seventh.

"After that we left and worked as domestic employees. Our only condition was that we work together and with lodging included. We worked that way in several family households, until we met a foreign couple, very kind-hearted, who took us in with affection and respect. Over time, the chance arose to help them care for their respective mothers in a very elegant section of Madrid, on Calle Alcalá, very near the Parque del Retiro, a magical place we never imagined we would come to know.

"In those days, there was a lot of talk about how young women were being taken to Europe through human trafficking. For that reason, Acción Callejera interviewed our employers and made them responsible for guaranteeing us the work for which we had been hired. That was how we were able to obtain the visa under the protection of this couple, to whom we are so grateful.

"The institution supervised the entire process of our trip, and every month we communicated with doña Isabel to keep her informed of our stay and our adjustment. We worked with the two grandmothers in this great city for fourteen years, an experience that left us with fond memories. They are our family here today, and they have taken us to see much of Europe accompanying the grandmothers, two beings of great worth.

"To migrate is not easy. Leaving your own people is very hard; living in the streets is terrible; living with an abusive father is a constant nightmare; seeing your mother battered all the time is a stab to the soul; and living in another country, with other customs and other ways of looking at you, is no easy bite to chew. Even so, we do not regret a thing.

"If we are capable of understanding that every process leaves a lesson, then we can recognize that living in the streets taught us to value every meal and every sincere embrace. Migrating opened new possibilities for us and let us discover the richness of human solidarity. That doesn't mean the road has been easy, but we are grateful for the angels we found along the way — like our employers, doña Isabel, and the other educators of Acción Callejera, who became our refuge when we needed it most. Today I understand that, in spite of the difficulties of our origins, it was precisely that experience that gave us the strength to face every obstacle.

"I am especially grateful to doña Isabel, who watched over our present and also over our future. And I am grateful to that God to whom we cried out so much. I live in gratitude for every experience we lived through and for that couple who opened the way for us, caring for our dignity and strengthening our self-worth.

"At present, the two of us live in Madrid. My sister works in a beauty salon, and I work three days a week at a fast-food restaurant. The rest of the week I live with doña Gracia, the mother of my employers — all of them now turned into our Spanish family.

"Belkis is married to a young Catalan man who respects her. I am still single, trying first to heal old scars. About my dad, I don't want to keep talking. He went to heaven five years ago, and I am still working on forgiveness. My sister and I share what we earn with our family in Cotuí. We've already bought the tickets to come back this Christmas, even if it's only for two weeks, to embrace our people and be filled by them again."

So she finished stringing together the events of her life, like a necklace, this woman with the soul of tempered steel.

She and her sister, two courageous women, wished to tell their story from a distance through a long telephone call. And in the words they let rise from their souls, I heard the voices of so many other women who have not been able to speak of those misfortunes that pass within their own homes, from generation to generation, like a life sentence that custom does not allow to be broken.

I feel an immense pride in writing about their example of struggle and hope. I knew them in their childhood, and when I spoke with them, they expressed to me their wish that I publish this story so that other girls might know that, although it demands great effort, there are always paths that lead toward a better life.

Trying to convey their feelings, when the sisters wanted to make themselves better understood, they reached for the colorful expressions of Dominican popular wisdom. It made me happy to know that, even after so many years away from here, they still keep the sayings learned in this land, along with the love for their family.

From their words I sense that they are no longer the girls who fled in fear, but women who have found their bearings and conquered their own space. That is why they come home often — to reconcile themselves with the girl each of them once was, to honor their mother, and to remind us all that, against every kind of obstacle, beginning again and finding one's way is always possible.

This story is a tribute to the educator Isabel Vargas, who walked alongside and guided these and so many other girls in conditions of high social risk. By the time of this book's publication, Isabel had already taken her eternal flight. May the light embrace her soul.

The Real Mambo Is Yet to Come

The author introduces us to Miguel, a young man whose childhood was marked by violence and deprivation. Guided by his mother's example, he finds in education and community service a path forward. His story is a testimony of resilience and hope, reminding us of the urgent need for many more Miguels: people capable of transforming their own lives and, with them, the life of an entire society.
Lina García de Blasco

"I was a working child, not a *tíguere* of the street."

With that statement, spoken solemnly as he looked me straight in the eyes, Miguel began our conversation. To meet him again after so many years is a great honor for me. In fact, speaking with this slender young man left me with a life lesson I treasure.

He was born in La Leonor de Toma, a rural community between Monción and Santiago Rodríguez. He was the eighth of twelve siblings: five girls and seven boys. There, in that remote corner of the country, he experienced violence in living flesh.

"My father beat my mother again and again, almost all the time," he said in a calm voice, though it was heavy with memories that still hammer at his life. "One day he beat her so badly he left her for dead. Another day he grabbed a machete with the intention of killing her, and she, defeated on the ground, waited for the end. But just then, a gust of wind rose into a whirlwind and swept into the yard, and my father was frightened. He took it as a sign from God, and because of that, he spared her life."

With a mixture of resignation and a breaking voice, he continued:

"When they got together, my father was fifty-three and my mother was barely eighteen. He had been one of Trujillo's guards, and he was also a farmer, carpenter, and merchant. He would lay into my mother with his fists in front of all of us, and in front of anyone else who happened to be there. His true trade seemed to be violence, and mistreating her was his favorite sport. Dad was not only violent at home; he was violent with relatives and friends too."

Miguel paused, like someone gathering the strength to go on.

"I remember once he fought with three men from the family. He told them, 'Go clear the patch where we're going to fight, because that is where I'm going to kill you.' And he did. He killed all three of them with a sharpened machete and then had to flee into the countryside."

His mother, by contrast, was another story.

"My mother was born and lived in a rural community in San Juan de la Maguana. She was the eldest in a large, extremely poor family. My grandfather handed her over to my father even though she was not in love with him, and out of the respect one was expected to show in those days, she did not dare disobey. That was how she accepted living with a man thirty years older than she was.

"The violence in my house kept escalating. Because the beatings were so frequent and so brutal, the day came when she fled to Santiago with all of us. We settled in Rafey, but trouble sticks to the sore finger: Hurricane Georges swept away all the little houses in the community, and we were left helpless in the middle of the world. On that occasion, the State gave us shelter in La Barranquita, and after a long wait of more than two years, we went to live in Villa Liberación, in La Otra Banda.

"The time we spent in La Barranquita was extremely difficult. Many displaced families were concentrated there: people from Bella Vista, from Rafey, from under the Mateo Pelón bridge, and from other neighborhoods the river had swept away. We were all thrown together, but some were tougher and more violent than others, and that was enough to measure strength in the daily fights.

"In the pavilions, we built little shelters with makeshift partitions of tarps, cardboard, and sticks from the brush. The desperate cries of children at midnight kept us all awake. We lived piled on top of one another, filled with unease, with no hygiene at all. When we needed to relieve ourselves, there was nowhere to go, so the surrounding grounds filled with excrement. The place looked like a human pigsty, with filth at its worst and infections and viruses everywhere. Many people died from disease, and others from fights among the refugees of that terrible hurricane.

"Every day, fights broke out with bare fists or with whatever happened to be within reach. Nothing makes people more violent than hunger.

"We waited anxiously for the *chao*, as we called the lunch that arrived punctually at eleven in the morning. Unfortunately, the food was a punishment in itself: soggy, clumped rice served in sticky lumps, with crumbled elbow macaroni on the side. Other times it was the same macaroni, clumped together and lifeless, tasting like anything but food. Since the ration the State gave us was so bad, we had no choice but to improvise a cooking spot on the ground or use charcoal stoves in order to survive.

"Still, in the midst of so many hardships, hope also found a way in. We organized baseball and softball games to release the tension, and in that way we turned that hell into a place of unity and relief. And even though we had trouble bathing afterward, after sweating so much, those games among the refugees managed to lift, if only for a moment, the weight of uncertainty.

"The Catholic Church also gave us invaluable support through the tireless work of Father Nino, bringing donations of basic necessities. Each mattress they handed out was more than an object; it was a promise of relief for the body and the soul. And so time passed, between struggle and hope, until the nightmare finally ended the day we were given a roof of our own. That was the dawn of a new stage.

"Despite all those adversities, my mother never gave up. Her memory and her strength sustain me. They truly do.

"Those were years of a hard, stubborn streak of bad luck, but Mom never gave up, and she raised us to be strong so we could face that difficult situation. She began making mops from the rejected polo shirts discarded by the free-zone factories. We cut them into strips, and with a small tube fitting, the whole family made mops. That was why they called us 'the mop makers.'

"But the money was not enough, so my seven-year-old sister and I, barely nine, picked up two humble little shoeshine boxes we had put together and went out looking for some extra income. All of us felt responsible for contributing to the household, except for the older good-for-nothings; they lived by making excuses.

"We began by shining shoes in the free-zone area, taking advantage of the constant coming and going of people. We worked near Plaza Ramos and around it. My sister had an advantage over me because customers noticed her incredible skill at shining shoes. If the price was two pesos and fifty cents, they would give her twenty pesos because she was a girl and so efficient. That helped lighten the burden a little, but it also kept me alert, making sure no one's generosity was really flirtation, because I protected her from everything.

"I remember going to the Hospedaje with a sack, looking for rejected root vegetables and produce to take home. I also remember the owners of little roadside stalls and produce stands who gave me hands of plantains, yuca, and anything else they could donate. I think perhaps they did it because they saw the hunger in my eyes. Dominicans stand with each other, ma'am, and I believe that is why more people do not die of hunger in this country.

"At home, all of us had a daily quota imposed by our older brothers, those big good-for-nothings who waited anxiously for whatever the younger ones managed to gather. They squandered the little coins on courting girls and drinking rum in the street, while they left us scrambling to survive. They never felt any responsibility to help at home or stand in solidarity with my mother. On the contrary, they were the first to push for us to get a beating if we came home with less than fifty pesos a day."

And so the days passed in that struggle, between shining shoes, selling mops in the streets, and looking after my little sister.

Miguel remembers when his life took a hopeful turn after he found Acción Callejera.

"It was while selling mops that we came to Acción Callejera, referred by a friend. That institution immediately welcomed my little sister and me. I will never forget my first day at the Foundation. The welcome was very warm. I remember some Americans who bought fifteen mops from us, and in that moment, it changed our lives. Raydiris Cruz was the director, and she received us kindly.

"There, I drew from all the services they offered. I began in the educational area, where I was trained to help others with reading and writing. Later, I moved into sports, specifically on the court in the courtyard.

"At Acción Callejera, I was encouraged to attend an educational program for adolescents offered at CONANI, and later I moved on to Telésforo Reynoso School. Because of my age, I was transferred to the night program at that same school. Encouraged by the educators at Acción Callejera, I continued forward and trained in the legal side of the birth-certificate program, a very important document, especially for children at social risk. Carmelo Mateo trained me in that work.

"Seeing how doors opened for people once they had identification made me fall in love with the law, because I understood the importance of having that document, and how hard life could be without it.

"I continued my formation at Acción Callejera, taking part in workshops on the use of harmful substances, leadership, masculinity, gender violence, sports leadership, and sociocultural activities. I also attended the programs *Deportes para la Vida* — Sports for Life — and *Chicos Brillantes* — Bright Boys — sponsored by USAID and designed for young people at social risk.

"I also joined the trainings and activities of the Movimiento de Vida sin Violencia (MOVIDA), a network of organizations in Santiago dedicated to fostering a culture of peace and eradicating violence against women.

"I take part in these activities with genuine interest and a firm civic commitment as a citizen. But I also do it because, deep down,

I feel that in doing so I honor my mother. It is a way of paying tribute to her by helping prevent other women from suffering what she suffered.

"Through those experiences and trainings, I felt prepared to volunteer with Fundación Niños con Esperanza, in the La Mosca sector of Cienfuegos.

"I also worked as an interim secretary during vacation at the Court for Children and Adolescents of Santiago, under Judge Antia Beato. I did volunteer work at Núcleo de Apoyo a la Mujer (NAM), where I have now served for fourteen years.

"For me, Acción Callejera means everything in my life. Even today, it remains the place that defined every step of my path.

"Three times a week, I work as a driver for the Vice Mayor's Office in Santiago. On the remaining days, I distribute sweets and snacks to colmados — *bolones*, mints, cookies, and chocolates.

"My life, in the end, is a mosaic of realities that, by the grace of God, I have exchanged for experience. Dad died some time ago, and later my mother formed a relationship with another man, also violent, which once again became a burden for everyone in the family. My mother's passing left all of us with a deep emptiness, a wound that has not fully closed. I pray her story of violence is never repeated.

"My brothers have made their way as best they could, each in his own manner. Some are taxi drivers; others are soldiers, *motoconcho* drivers, construction foremen, and even odd-job workers. The sister who was with me the most, however, took a different path. Raised by another family, she graduated as a psychologist from UTESA. Today she has her practice at the Hospital Metropolitano de Santiago (HOMS), where she works with excellence and professionalism.

"I'll close by telling you that I still have many plans for my life. I am married and have three children: one is seventeen and nearly finished with high school, another is eight, and the youngest is a ten-month-old baby. Together with my wife, they are my greatest blessing, and I fight for them every day.

"I am currently in my fifth term of Law at the Universidad de la Tercera Edad (UTE) in Santiago, and I swear to you that, by the grace of God, I will become a man of the Law with a strong sense of duty and social justice.

"So now, the real mambo is yet to come."

Miguel ended his story with a reflection:

"It is essential for me to practice love with my children within the family, setting an example of responsible fatherhood until the last day of my life."

As I said goodbye to Miguel, I remembered the boy who shined shoes with his little sister and the young man who had made his way through so many hardships. Time has passed, but his eyes still hold the same nobility.

Today he studies Law, works, and raises his family with pride. "Now the real mambo is yet to come," he says, with the assurance of someone who has learned not to give up.

And then I could not help wondering how many young men like him are still walking our streets today, unseen by anyone who might recognize the future they carry within.

The Colors of Love

While those of us with shelter fantasize about the freedom to leave, Ricky struggled to enter a home that had been denied him. Outside, his life was tragedy — sleeplessness, dust, cement, hunger, and a scorching sun. Inside, in that warm space, an old hope was sleeping: the one that reminded him that on some idle day on the calendar, the doors of that house would open to take him in... and the miracle happened.
José Luis Taveras

The celebration of Mother's Day holds a very special meaning for the children who wander the streets. In the midst of their hardships, the date takes on a singular weight, because it becomes an opportunity to express deep feelings through art — whether in a painting, a poem, a dance, or an improvised song.

In one of those celebrations I remember Ricky... or rather, Ricardo. He was just eight years old, with large eyes the color of old gold, eyes that seemed to hold a quiet sadness inside them. He was living through a painful conflict because his mother would not let him stay home. She said she was afraid he would fall into drugs, the same abyss from which she had not been able to escape herself. Each evening, as the sun went down, she would close the door on him. So Ricky spent his nights out in the open, looking for some corner where he could take shelter from fear.

That child lived for long years among the ruins of the historic center of Santiago, sleeping in abandoned old houses and surviving with other children in conditions of extreme abandonment. His story moved everyone, but no lasting solution was ever found. He faced that reality with the constant accompaniment of a team of educators and psychologists from Acción Callejera who, with affection, with listening, and with perseverance, held up the soul of that boy who was asking for help even in his silence.

The nights were endless, and Ricky learned to light fires with pieces of cardboard to chase off the cold, while his days filled up with running from hunger and from the dangers of the street. Even so, he kept a sweetness that had not been defeated. His smile came easily — a mixture of innocence and endurance. He had an overflowing imagination, and with his new friends he invented games with stones and branches, drew with borrowed chalk, and told stories of a secret world where everything was possible.

He dreamed of having a home, of arriving at night and not having the door closed in his face. But his mother, trapped in her own ghosts, would not give in. Ricky was an orphan of a father and, in some crueler way, of a mother too. He received institutional help, but the real longing — a home that would embrace him — went on unfulfilled.

I remember with particular clarity an activity in which the children painted something for their mothers. Some drew flowers; others, smiling little faces, fruit trees, or landscapes from their imagination. The educators wondered whether Ricky would even want to take part. But, against all expectations, he was the one who made the most beautiful drawing of all. He painted a small house with doors and windows wide open, surrounded by flowers under a radiant sun. In the only doorway, a woman with long hair and a red dress was waiting for him with her arms open and a handful of flowers in her hands.

When he had finished his masterpiece, he asked for help to frame his drawing, and with scraps of cardboard in bright colors, he made a frame with his own hands. At the center, his purest feelings were captured.

Full of hope, on that special day, Ricky knocked on the door of his dreams... and his mother opened it.

She let him in and served him lunch. The everyday miracle he had waited for so long became real. Ricky told it later with his voice broken by joy, and his face — the one that had learned to endure — was shining as never before.

"She served me at her table," he said, and his eyes grew even wider.

"She gave me a big *bolón* at the end of the meal," he added with that hooked grin that came from his soul, like someone who knows himself loved, at least for an instant.

In that shared lunch, Ricky tasted love, and perhaps his mother reconnected with that double heartbeat from when she carried in her belly the boy who was now reclaiming his place. Then he told us that his mother embraced him, and although the embrace did not last forever, he kept it like a sacred treasure.

Many years went by without a word of him.

On one of those first days of the new year, I visited a children's amusement park with my granddaughters. As I was making my way to the ticket booth, I heard someone calling me by my full name. I turned, and there was Ricky — with the same smile, but more peace in him now. We embraced like people who recognize each other in the folds of time. We remembered episodes from those years burning with hardship, and his presence felt like a gift from life itself.

He told me he had worked as a delivery boy at a colmado and later as a doorman at a school. In each job he had found dignity. He had learned to read his name, to write a few words, and to add up just enough so no one could cheat him. Today he watches over the children who climb onto the merry-go-round in the park; he settles them in with tenderness and collects the ticket with a smile that is still his signature.

"I have never harmed anyone," he told me, "I have never been to prison, I don't drink, I don't smoke, I'm afraid of drugs, and I'm not improper with women."

His gaze was transparent. He told me he takes his nephews to school, that he likes looking after children and seeing them smile.

"I'm happy with them," he said, "with my soul dressed in the same colors I painted that Mother's Day."

Proud, he showed me a worn portrait of his family — a relic he keeps in his wallet like a talisman. We embraced, and in that moment, he gave me one last smile, the kind of smile that belongs to someone who has learned to embrace life without bitterness.

Ricky has built his own refuge, without walls and with doors always open. Perhaps, in the laughter of the children he now helps onto the carousels at the fairs, he discovered the childhood he had constantly dreamed of. Or perhaps, in the joy of other children, he recognized the warmth of the home he had always carried in his heart.

NEIGHBORHOOD OF HOPE

Sometimes a single act, done with love and a sense of justice, can transform many lives.

These stories gather generous gestures that arrived in time and marked destinies forever.

Thank you for believing in them when they needed it most.

Thank you, wherever you may be.

Famous Waiters

> *"The future of children is always today. Tomorrow will be too late."*
> *— Gabriela Mistral*

The 1990s were difficult years for children who lived much of their lives in the streets of Santiago. Many working boys, girls, and adolescents from impoverished communities arrived at Acción Callejera's educational programs in the midst of severe hardship. There were still no specialized teams capable of responding to the complexity of their lives.

Those children had no real place in the city's imagination. Many people struggled to understand why they were in the streets, why they had a right to guidance and support, or what sense there was in an educational mission created with them in mind. The program was not always understood, nor was it always clear to others that their lives were worth investing in — lives already judged, in many eyes, by where they came from, how they survived, and an appearance others too often mistook for destiny.

That indifference made their needs even harder to see, while the Foundation struggled to raise the funds required to offer dignified, appropriate care to that army of children moving between asphalt and despair.

It was then that Acción Callejera placed this urgent need in the hands of Freddy Ginebra, a creative spirit capable of inventing hope even in the midst of scarcity. He orchestrated a celebration called *Mozos Famosos* — Famous Waiters — held at the Casa Club of the Centro Español in Santiago, where well-known figures from the city agreed to take part in a dance routine choreographed by Tuti Almonte.

The so-called *Mozos Famosos* served guests at the tables, and ticket sales helped support the Foundation's budget, turning those evenings into a true act of shared solidarity.

At the first celebration, the artist Marisel Fernández painted a cardboard barrel that was auctioned off and purchased by Mr. Osvaldo Brugal, opening the evening with a gesture that lit the first spark of generosity. From that moment on, every item placed at auction became a bridge of hope for vulnerable children.

The evening was dedicated to Mr. José A. León, who, visibly moved, invited the public to join the cause and said that, in supporting children who lived in the streets, he felt closer to God.

The *Mozos Famosos* evenings proved decisive. They kept Acción Callejera's doors open to hundreds of children living at high risk. For four consecutive years, the event returned with the same noble purpose: to offer a breath of dignity to those who lived beneath the open sky.

Those dances, those tables tended by hands of solidarity, and those auctions that set the night alight became a true act of faith in childhood. There, amid lights and applause, one certainty took shape: a child's life can change when someone chooses to bet on their future.

Today, when I remember *Mozos Famosos*, those nights return to me — nights when music, dance, and generosity intertwined to sustain the dreams of so many boys and girls.

The whole city seemed to understand then that a child's life can change when someone bets on their future. May God allow that commitment to endure.

A Heart Made of Good People

> *"Many of the things we need can wait. The child cannot."*
> *— Gabriela Mistral*

It was 2012, and those of us committed to defending the rights of Santiago's working children were knocking on every door we could in search of help. Our mission was to keep open a dignified space for these boys and girls, a place where they could receive education, food, and other basic necessities. But our resources barely stretched far enough to sustain the educational programs and cover only the essentials.

Truly, God lives and breathes in that altar of blessings which, by His grace, remains wide open even today. Many companies and people of solidarity extended a hand to help, showing that Santiago carries noble causes on its shoulders. Even so, until then, we had never received a visit from a businessman who, of his own accord, came forward with the desire to contribute spontaneously and generously.

"Tell me what you need, because I want to help these children," he said, with humility written across his face.

Right away, we laid out a long list of needs. As we spoke, he looked silently toward the dining area. The children were eating lunch in a deteriorated space, seated on improvised benches much like the ones they used when they worked as shoeshine boys.

Without hesitating, he committed himself to donating a proper dining room — tables and chairs where those children, who spent the whole day in the streets, could sit down to rest and to eat with dignity.

The next day, a generous cabinetmaker sent by the donor came to take measurements, and before a month had passed the dining room was already equipped with new furniture. The space was transformed completely, and the children, with the eagerness of someone breaking in something of their own, asked to have their pictures taken so they could share them with their families.

But the help did not end there. When he delivered the donation, that benefactor shared an intimate talk before his family and his grandchildren, recalling his own story. His words moved the children and young people, planting inspiration and hope in their hearts, and awakening in the adults a deep feeling of admiration.

At the end, he also promised to remodel the bathrooms, adding sinks, doors, and everything that was needed. And he kept his word. In a short time, the bathrooms too were renovated. In this way, with genuine devotion and without seeking recognition, he kept covering need after need, always accompanied by his generous wife, doña Camelia Rodríguez de Ureña.

I am speaking of a man of deep civic conscience, who did not wait to be called — he went out to meet those who most needed him. He loved children with deeds, not with speeches, and he stood firmly behind every noble cause on behalf of the most vulnerable.

May his legacy commit us, don Manuel Arsenio Ureña. Don Arsenio departed for eternity, leaving the working children seated at the table of a dining room that to this day still lets them rest their tired backs and eat with the dignity they have always deserved.

One More Legacy

> *"Example is not the main thing in influencing others; it is the only thing." — Albert Schweitzer*

"I'll send something for the children this afternoon!"

When don José spoke those words, the sun slipped into his voice. His promise restored hope for thousands of working children and changed the course of an institution whose work, even today, benefits children and adolescents who make their lives in the streets.

Those were complex times. Winds of social hardship were blowing across the country. Santiago was receiving hundreds of families from every corner of the nation, families who left the countryside or their small towns to settle, in deplorable conditions, in the northern and southern areas of the city, hoping to find better opportunities in life. The central streets filled with minors doing different kinds of work to support themselves and their families.

The traffic lights filled with girls who risked their dignity, while others worked as domestic servants in family homes. The boys, for the most part, sold flowers and newspapers, unloaded produce at the Hospedaje Yaque, begged for a coin, washed windshields, or helped drivers park their cars, among other basic and informal tasks. To gather a little money, they worked long hours, from before dawn until late at night. Because of their constant wandering, especially in crowded places, they were contemptuously labeled "the children of the street."

The State had no educational tools to serve them or understand their basic needs. Nor did it have the resources or proper spaces to address the problems facing this population. The business world, for its part, did not bet on their future. In the collective imagination, investing in them was not considered a priority; their presence was seen as nothing more than an uncomfortable, unwanted reminder.

Santiago seemed like a whirlpool in which children without anyone to mourn for them struggled to stay afloat. Lodged in the heart of the city, where many of these unsheltered children gathered, there stood a large old house that served almost as a rescue boat, offering educational programs created for them. But the Foundation, which had embraced the mission of forming them, was facing extreme financial hardship.

The teaching staff had gone nine months without pay. The messenger had been let go because there was nothing left to deliver and nothing left to seek. The children were getting by on bread and watery hot chocolate, some donated *moro con maíz*, or a thin *aguají*. Each day, less was offered, because each day there was less to give.

The institution's founders, doña Margarita Guzmán de Torres and don Manuel Ulises Bonnelly, had taken out bank loans in their own names, backed by personal guarantees. The horizon was closing in: too many children, too little income, urgent expenses, and mounting debts had become the perfect formula for collapse.

Before making the painful decision to close, we considered inviting a few business leaders who might understand the situation. We summoned six men of recognized influence in the business world. In the end, only one came. He was a good man, undoubtedly busy, but his eyes carried the full radiance of the solidarity that lived in his heart.

Don José León Asensio accepted the invitation, and on the day he visited us, he brought the morning in his eyes. It was a fortunate Wednesday seeing off an uncertain spring of 2014. The universe seemed to smile, held in God's right hand, as it sent us that man of light, with his clean smile, a sower of kindnesses.

With the quiet humility of a man who had no need to announce his nobility, he entered the Foundation, touched a shoeshine box that stood in the reception area, and examined its contents. Then he walked through every corner, pausing over each detail and asking questions about the daily work and the educational methods used to accompany that unsheltered avalanche of children.

As we ate breakfast in the same austere dining room used by the children, we explained the delicate situation to him. He listened the whole time with calm, wise attention. When he said goodbye, he left us with words of hope.

That very day, we received a check from him and his brothers — the León Asensio family — for an amount that remains considerable even now. In addition to that timely contribution, the family donated two thousand CDs from the collection *Canciones Dominicanas en Concierto*, whose quality helped them sell quickly.

These donations stirred consciences, placed the needs of these children at the center of the public conversation, and lifted the institution's name. They put the children in a visible place, obliging society to recognize their existence. That select musical compilation made the urgent needs of the children of the traffic lights known to the business world and to the citizenry.

And so, in grand fashion, walking on a carpet woven of generosity, the name of Acción Callejera appeared, together with its children, beneath the lights of the Casandra Awards, the highest artistic distinction of the time. That gesture brought into full view the needs of a childhood so often ignored.

Don José was behind countless good works, and God made him a bridge that allowed this institution to remain open to this day. On the day of his visit, the sky seemed to change color, and the breeze of solidarity dispersed the heaviness. The traffic lights still seem to celebrate him, because that long-awaited miracle became real as a gift that took deep root among children who had been forgotten.

Those funds brought salaries up to date, restored dignity to the Food Services department, honored the bank debts, revived prevention programs in vulnerable communities, and made that refuge of providence beat strongly once more — the same refuge that, even today, welcomes so many children living at a social disadvantage.

Once the funds had been used, we gave don José a report accounting for how they had been spent. He received it graciously and told us that, for him, there could be no better report than knowing the doors of hope had been opened wide again for unsheltered children.

Don José, with goodness sown into his soul, offered one of the most valuable offerings ever given to Dominican working children. Thanks to that gesture from the León Asensio family, doors that had been on the verge of closing opened again for thousands of children who, even today, still find there a place to learn and to be called by name.

This is where the stories end, and the commitment begins. Stories like this remind us that even in the hardest places, someone always steps forward to keep hope alive.

After walking so many streets and listening to so many voices, we are left with one indispensable task: to learn to name, with respect, those who live this reality.

Naming with Respect

It has been a privilege to walk these pages together — through streets and city blocks, past murals and traffic lights, alongside the children and adolescents who live at high social risk. Along the way, we have learned to listen to their stories and to understand, without judgment, the complexity of their circumstances.

This glossary is born from that shared learning. It gathers a few of the terms necessary for understanding the realities the book has allowed us to see up close. To name with care and respect is also an act of conscience. Words can wound, and words can dignify.

For that reason we have chosen to name with precision and with humanity, taking care that each term should help us understand without pointing fingers, and explain without turning a circumstance into a permanent identity.

Let us begin with something essential: avoiding phrases like *street child* or *child of the streets*. The street is a space of survival, not an identity. Those expressions reduce a person to a condition, and end up erasing their dignity.

Thank you for coming this far and sustaining this conversation with us. Only through open and honest dialogue can we continue walking together.

Glossary

Foundational Concepts

Children who make their lives in the streets

Children and adolescents who spend much of their day in public spaces — working, selling, or asking for help — but who do not live in the streets permanently. They keep some family bond, however fragile. The street is a space of survival for them, not an identity.

Children in street situations

Children and adolescents who live in the streets fully or partially, exposed to multiple risks. They develop survival strategies in conditions of high vulnerability.

Street child / child of the streets

A term that has fallen out of use because of its stigmatizing weight. It reduces the person to a condition and disregards their dignity. The preferred terms are *children in street situations* or *children who make their lives in the streets.*

Invisibilized children

Children excluded from statistics, public policies, and social protection. Their absence from official records perpetuates that exclusion.

Structural Conditions

School abandonment

The interruption of schooling because of child labor, poverty, discrimination, or lack of support. It limits both present and future opportunities.

Family abandonment

Family abandonment does not always mean physical absence. It can take the form of indifference, violence, or an inability to provide care, leaving children without emotional or social protection.

Migrant children

Children who cross borders in conditions of vulnerability, exposed to abuse, discrimination, and lack of protection. They require special protection from the State.

Children in conflict with the law

Children and adolescents who commit offenses in contexts of exclusion and poverty. They require protection and accompaniment, not stigmatization.

Informal fostering

(*dar en crianza*) A cultural practice in which a child is handed over to another family for care. Without legal and emotional safeguards, the practice can lead to exploitation and the rupture of family bonds.

Forms of Harm and Exploitation

Child labor

Economic or domestic activity that interferes with education, play, and the full development of a child.

The worst forms of child labor

Including trafficking, servitude, sexual exploitation, armed recruitment, and any work that gravely harms a child's health, safety, or dignity.

Child labor exploitation

Work that deprives children of their right to study, to play, and to develop fully. It involves risk, abuse, and the absence of protection.

Forced begging

Children compelled to ask for money in the streets or at traffic lights, generally under the control of adults or networks that profit from their vulnerability. It is a form of exploitation.

Commercial sexual exploitation of children

A grave crime in which children are used in sexual activities in exchange for money or benefits. It produces lasting physical, emotional, and social harm.

Trafficking and smuggling of persons
Crimes that involve the recruitment, transport, or holding of children for purposes of exploitation. They are grave violations of human rights.

Substance use
The use of glue, drugs, or alcohol as a false escape from hunger, abandonment, or pain. It produces dependence and worsens conditions of exclusion and risk.

A Decalogue of Children's Fundamental Rights

1. The right to life and to an inviolable dignity.
2. The right to a name, an identity, and a family that protects and accompanies them.
3. The right to an education that opens paths.
4. The right to health, to nourishment, and to timely care.
5. The right to play, to rest, and to the time that belongs to childhood.
6. The right to grow up free of violence, exploitation, and fear.
7. The right to equality and to be free from discrimination on any ground.
8. The right to be heard and to be taken into account.
9. The right to special protection in contexts of migration, conflict, or abandonment.
10. The right to dream, to imagine their future, and to live with hope.

Voices from the Street

This appendix offers the English-language reader a brief guide to the Spanish words, Dominican references, and institutions that appear throughout the book. It is meant to accompany rather than replace the text. Where a word's meaning is already clear from the story around it, the entry simply confirms; where the cultural background runs deeper, the entry offers a fuller note. The aim is to make the world of these stories more visible — never to explain it away.

Acción Callejera – Fundación Educativa, Inc. The educational foundation at the heart of this book, based in Santiago de los Caballeros at Calle del Sol No. 131. Founded in 1989 by Manuel Ulises Bonnelly Valverde, his cousin Margarita Guzmán de Torres, and Irenarco Ardila, the foundation was created in response to a wave of children who had begun working and sleeping in the streets of Santiago — shining shoes, selling newspapers, washing windshields at traffic lights, unloading trucks at the Hospedaje Yaque. Acción Callejera offers homework rooms, food and hygiene support, sports, music, emotional support, advocacy through the courts, and educational programs for children and adolescents at social risk, including Haitian-born and Haitian Dominican children. The foundation continues to operate today. In the body of the book, it is also referred to as Fundación Acción Callejera or simply "the Foundation."

ácido del diablo Literally "devil's acid." A homemade weapon used in some attacks: a corrosive mixture of sulfuric and muriatic acid (the commercial name for hydrochloric acid) combined with paint strippers and sometimes molasses, so that it clings to the skin.

It causes severe burns and lasting disfigurement. The book describes one such attack on Manuel.

a mano pelá Literally "with bare hands." Dominican slang for fighting or working with no tool, no weapon, and no cover — relying only on whatever the body itself can do. The phrase carries a quiet pride alongside its acknowledgment of having nothing else to bring.

aguají A thin Dominican sauce or broth, traditionally made with bitter orange, garlic, and chili. In the book it appears as part of meager refugee rations.

aguardiente A strong distilled spirit, typically made from sugarcane, common in rural communities throughout Latin America.

Aguilita, el The mascot of the Águilas Cibaeñas (see below). In the book, *el Aguilita* is also the nickname of Jochy Taveras, who appeared in the carnival comparsa formed by Acción Callejera shoeshine boys.

Águilas Cibaeñas A Dominican professional baseball team from Santiago, founded in 1933, and one of the most beloved franchises in the Caribbean Winter League. The team plays at Estadio Cibao and carries enormous symbolic weight in the city. *Ganaron las Águilas* — "the Águilas have won" — is the celebratory chant raised across Santiago whenever the team takes the championship. The shoeshine boys' comparsa performed a *Ganaron las Águilas* choreography after their carnival victory, fusing two of the city's points of pride.

AMET Autoridad Metropolitana de Transporte. The traffic authority responsible for managing traffic flow and issuing fines in Dominican cities. *El Peje* serves as an AMET officer in his adult life.

anafe A small portable stove or brazier, often fueled by charcoal, used for cooking in homes without a built-in kitchen.

bolón A lollipop. In the book, a *bolón* is given to a child as a small reward at the end of a meal.

cabaré Dominican rendering of "cabaret." In this book the word refers to roadside venues that operated as combined bars and brothels, particularly in the rural south. The English word "cabaret" does not carry the same meaning and is not used.

canillita A newspaper boy. The term once described boys who sold papers on busy street corners; several of the children in the book worked as *canillitas*, calling out tragic headlines, real or invented, to draw passersby in.

cédula The Dominican national identity card. Without it, a person cannot enroll in school, sign a work contract, open a bank account, or access most public services. Several of the children in the book reach adolescence or adulthood without one, a structural condition that compounds their vulnerability.

cemento Literally "cement." In the language of the streets, it refers to PVC glue used as an inhalant — cheap, accessible, and brain-damaging. The book describes its use as a way of dulling hunger and pain.

Cenapec Centros APEC de Educación a Distancia, Inc. A Dominican nonprofit educational institution founded in 1972 under the auspices of Acción Pro Educación y Cultura (APEC). CENAPEC offers distance-learning programs, especially for adults and students who need flexible pathways to complete their secondary education.

chao In the book, a local term for the lunch ration distributed at a refugee camp at eleven in the morning. The food was notoriously bad: soggy, clumped rice or lifeless macaroni.

Chicos Brillantes A project at Acción Callejera designed to strengthen the foundation's emotional support department, so that children, adolescents, and family members at social risk could access psychosocial care focused on building self-esteem and supporting their full development. No longer active.

chimichurri In the Dominican context, *chimichurri* (often called *chimi*) is a popular street-food sandwich: seasoned ground beef or pork on a soft bread roll, dressed with cabbage and a pink sauce. It is unrelated to the Argentine herb sauce of the same name. The carts that sell *chimis* often gather around the Monumento.

Cibao The fertile valley region of north-central Dominican Republic, of which Santiago de los Caballeros is the principal city. The word also serves as a regional and cultural identifier.

clerén A Haitian distilled spirit made from sugarcane, typically stronger and rougher than commercial rum. In the book, it appears at Vodou-related celebrations in the Haitian villages from which some children have migrated.

colmado The neighborhood corner store, central to Dominican daily life. It sells groceries, beer, phone cards, and the small items people need from one day to the next; it is also a social space where neighbors gather, music plays, and news is exchanged. *Colmados* recur throughout the book as both businesses and meeting places.

comadre A woman bound to another by godparenthood: the godmother of her child, or the mother of her godchild. In Dominican usage the word stretches further to mean a woman who is a close, trusted friend — a woman one can count on. The bond is recognized as something between family and friendship.

comparsa A costumed troupe that participates in carnival, performing as a coordinated group with shared theme, costumes, and choreography. The book describes the formation of *Los Limpiabotas de Acción Callejera*, a *comparsa* of shoeshine boys.

concho A shared public taxi that runs along fixed routes, picking up multiple passengers at a fixed fare. *Conchos* are a primary form of urban transport in Dominican cities.

conuco A small farm plot, typically worked by a family for subsistence and small-scale sale. The word carries a long history reaching back to Indigenous Taíno agricultural practice.

Court for Children and Adolescents (Tribunal de Niños, Niñas y Adolescentes) A specialized Dominican court system that handles cases involving minors, both as victims requiring protection and as adolescents accused of offenses.

cuero A derogatory Dominican term for a woman who works in prostitution. In the book the word is reproduced as it was used by the children speaking; the author makes plain that these are people, not insults.

de apaga y vámonos Literally "turn it off and let's go." A Dominican expression of high praise, especially for a party, celebration, or event: a *fiesta de apaga y vámonos* is one so good there is nothing left to wish for — turn out the lights, we can go home satisfied. The phrase carries the warmth of a night that delivered everything it promised.

Deportes para la Vida A dynamic program at Acción Callejera that taught young people about HIV/AIDS prevention and leadership skills through games, group activities, and sports. Led by Peace Corps volunteers. No longer active.

Día de la Raza October 12, the date traditionally observed in much of Latin America to commemorate Christopher Columbus's arrival in the Americas in 1492. Once celebrated as a marker of Hispanic heritage, the day has, in many places, been recast — or replaced — to honor Indigenous peoples and reckon with the violence of the colonial encounter. In the Dominican Republic the date retains its traditional name. The boy in this book born on October 12 carries that date in his name as part of a wider history.

don / doña Spanish honorifics of respect, attached to a person's first name. *Don Bojolo, doña Natalia, doña Juana.* The English equivalents "Mr." and "Mrs." carry a more formal and distant register; *don* and *doña* are warmer and signal both respect and personal recognition. Used in the book as in everyday Dominican speech.

El Nacional A Dominican daily newspaper, founded in 1966 in Santo Domingo. *Canillitas* in the book sell *El Nacional* and *Hoy* on city corners.

en olla Literally "in the pot." Dominican slang for being broke — flat broke, with not a peso to spare, in the kind of trouble that can only be cooked through.

Estadio Cibao Santiago's principal baseball stadium and home of the Águilas Cibaeñas, one of the oldest and most beloved teams in the Dominican professional league. The stadium recurs in the book as a place of pride and possibility for the children who later work or perform there as adults.

fogón A wood- or charcoal-fired hearth, either built into a kitchen wall or standing outdoors. *Tulia*, in the book, ages before her *fogón*, roasting coffee in a *paila* over its flame for decades.

Futuro con Ideales A formative program at Acción Callejera, developed in collaboration with Peace Corps volunteers, addressing rights, emotional management, gender, masculinity, and violence. The program's name was chosen by its participants. No longer active.

Ganaron las Águilas "The Águilas have won." The celebratory chant of Santiago whenever the Águilas Cibaeñas take the championship — and the title of the choreography performed by the Acción Callejera shoeshine boys' comparsa after their own victory in the carnival contest. See Águilas Cibaeñas.

guayacán The lignum vitae tree (*Guaiacum officinale*), native to the Caribbean. Hardy, slow-growing, with intensely dense wood and small blue flowers. In the book the *guayacanes* dot the parched landscape of the southern Dominican countryside.

guayo A metal grater. In the book it appears as an instrument of torture: a young child is forced to kneel on one as punishment.

guazábara A spiny shrub or small succulent of the dry Caribbean lowlands, often growing alongside cacti. In the book, *guazábaras* line the country roads of the deep south.

güira A Dominican percussion instrument: a cylindrical metal scraper, played by drawing a stiff metal pick across its grooved surface. Together with the *tambora*, the *güira* is one of the two essential instruments of merengue, supplying the bright, rhythmic top line that drives the dance.

habichuelas con dulce A traditional Dominican dessert of sweet creamed beans, prepared especially during Lent and Holy Week. Made with red kidney beans, coconut milk, sweet potato, raisins, and spices.

higüero The calabash tree (*Crescentia cujete*), and the hollowed gourd produced from its fruit. *Higüeros* are used as containers for water and other staples in rural Dominican households.

hijab A head covering worn by Muslim women and girls. Not a Dominican word; appears in a chapter that takes the reader briefly into the imagined experience of children in other parts of the world.

HOMS Hospital Metropolitano de Santiago. A leading private medical center in Santiago.

Hospedaje Yaque A wholesale-market and warehouse area in Santiago where trucks arriving in the early hours of the morning unloaded fruits, vegetables, and provisions from Constanza and other farming regions. Many of the boys in the book worked here from before dawn, carrying sacks for piecemeal pay; some also slept in its alcoves and on its cardboard pallets.

Hospicio San Vicente de Paúl A long-standing Dominican institution offering shelter and care for elderly people in need.

Hoy A Dominican daily newspaper, widely circulated. Sold by *canillitas* on city corners.

Hoyo de Elías A neighborhood on the southern edge of Santiago, settled largely by families who migrated from rural areas in the late 1980s.

Hoyo de Puchula Another southern Santiago neighborhood, founded by migrant families. The word *hoyo* — "hollow" — describes the ravine-cut topography of the area, where housing clings to slopes and floodwaters reach into homes whenever the rains fall hard. The book returns to this neighborhood in several chapters.

Infotep Instituto Nacional de Formación Técnico Profesional. The Dominican Republic's principal vocational and technical training institute. Several of the young men in the book trained at Infotep in trades that allowed them to leave the streets behind.

juntiña A small crowd or informal group of friends, typically used in Dominican slang for a tight-knit cluster of young people who move together.

La Molino Blanco A country house in Villa Altagracia, in the central Dominican Republic, surrounded by rivers and set near Loma Novillero. Acción Callejera held weekend retreats for the children here — three-day stays of games, lessons, and reflection that, for many of the boys, became among the brightest memories of their childhood.

La Yagüita de Pastor A neighborhood on Santiago's southern edge, settled by rural migrants in the late 1980s. The book traces several lives that began here.

"Lechón cuajao, amarillo y colorao, brinca en la calle de lao a lao" A Dominican folk verse, traditionally chanted at carnival or during street play. Roughly: "Roast pig, all yellow and red, jumps in the street from side to side." The rhyme is part of a long oral tradition of *coplas populares* — short, rhyming, often nonsensical verses passed from one generation to the next. The book reproduces the verse as it was sung.

limpiabotas Literally "boot-cleaner"; a shoeshiner. A boy or man who shines shoes for a living, typically working with a wooden shoeshine box of polishes and brushes — often built by the boy himself from scrap crates. Shoeshining was one of the most common forms of street labor for the boys in the book, often beginning at six or seven years old.

los tres golpes Literally "the three hits." The classic Dominican breakfast — *mangú* (mashed plantains), fried cheese, salami, and eggs. The name refers to the three savory accompaniments served alongside the *mangú*.

madrina Godmother, or, by extension, a sponsor who stands beside someone in a ceremony or transition. In the book, a girlfriend serves as *madrina* at her partner's high-school graduation.

maipiolo A handler or middleman in the sex trade, who arranges encounters between sex workers and clients and takes a share of the payment.

malecón A coastal boardwalk or seafront promenade. Dominican cities along the coast have *malecones*; in the book, one appears as the place where a young man works briefly cleaning a restaurant.

mangú Boiled and mashed green plantains, traditionally seasoned with sautéed red onion, oil, and vinegar. *Mangú* is the heart of the Dominican breakfast; together with fried cheese, salami, and eggs, it forms *los tres golpes*.

más pa' lante vive gente Literally "people live farther on down the road." A Dominican folk saying, used to console someone after a setback or loss: not everyone you meet has been good to you, but keep going — there are good people farther on. *Don Bojolo* repeats the phrase to Robenson in the book.

menéutica A Dominican slang formation, used here to mean the unwritten knowledge and codes of life on the streets — how to find food, where to sleep, whom to trust, how to survive. The word appears to be a colloquial deformation of *hermenéutica* (hermeneutics, the art of interpretation), used with humor and seriousness at once.

mondongo A traditional tripe-and-vegetable stew, eaten throughout the Hispanic Caribbean and Latin America.

Monumento a los Héroes de la Restauración Santiago's iconic monument, a tall marble structure built in honor of the Dominican Restoration War of 1863–1865. It stands at the heart of the city. For the children in this book, the *Monumento* is a fixed point — a place to work the late-night corners, sleep on its grass, sell flowers and phone chargers to passing cars, and find one another. The name is often shortened in the book to "el Monumento."

moro con maíz A Dominican rice dish, cooked with corn kernels and seasoning, typically served as part of a main meal.

motoconcho A motorcycle taxi. *Motoconchos* are a primary form of short-distance urban transport in the Dominican Republic; the drivers carry passengers seated behind them on the back of the bike.

mulata A woman of mixed African and European descent. The word carries a long and complicated history in the Spanish-speaking Caribbean — at times affectionate, at times charged. In the book it appears as everyday Dominican usage, descriptive rather than judgmental.

paila A wide, shallow, heavy-bottomed pan used for slow cooking and roasting. In the book, *Tulia* roasts coffee in a *paila* over an open *fogón.*

patrona The lady of the house. In the book the word carries the weight of an employment relationship: the *patrona* is the woman who has taken in a child to "raise" her — and to put her to work.

pecho apretao Literally "tight chest." A folk description of an asthma-like condition, marked by labored breathing and recurring attacks. The book describes a small child suffering from *pecho apretao* during the family's flight from Haiti.

piedra Literally "stone." A cheap form of crack cocaine, common in the streets where the children of this book lived and worked. The book describes its devastating sixty-second high and the addiction that follows.

pica pollo Dominican fried chicken, often sold from small storefronts and street stands. A staple of inexpensive eating in working-class neighborhoods.

pícher The fare-caller on a Dominican minibus, who rides standing in the open doorway, calls out the route to passersby, collects fares, and helps passengers on and off. The role is unsalaried; the *pícher* earns by filling certain seats and keeping the bus moving.

pilón A tall, hand-carved wooden mortar used for grinding coffee, plantains, garlic, and other staples. The work is done with a long pestle, with the *pilón* standing at the height of the cook's elbows.

Plan PREPARA A Dominican accelerated secondary-education program for adults and out-of-school youth, with classes typically held on weekends. Allows students to complete high school in two years.

pollera A poultry shop, where chickens are sold and often processed for buyers.

poté A guide who leads migrants across the border from Haiti into the Dominican Republic, navigating the brush, river crossings, and steep ravines of the route. The word, like the work, is informal and dangerous.

pringamosa A stinging nettle (*Tragia volubilis*), whose leaves cause an intense burning rash on contact. In the book the leaf appears as a vehicle for a curse, written upon in red and blue ink.

PUCMM Pontificia Universidad Católica Madre y Maestra. A major private Catholic university with its main campus in Santiago.

pulpería A small grocery store, similar to a *colmado* but generally simpler and more basic. The two words overlap considerably.

recaíto Caribbean cilantro, also called *culantro* (*Eryngium foetidum*). A long-leafed herb with a stronger, earthier flavor than common cilantro, central to Dominican and Puerto Rican cooking.

rédito Literally "yield" or "return." In the book, a slang term for the mandatory payment that working children at Parque Duarte handed over to the older boys who controlled the territory. A protection tax, in effect.

sambá Dominican slang for the one in a group who is repeatedly picked on, scapegoated, and made the butt of every joke or fight. To avoid becoming the *sambá* of the plaza was a daily concern for the boys at Parque Duarte.

samán The rain tree (*Albizia saman*), a large spreading tree with a wide canopy, common in the Dominican countryside. In the book, a *samán* watches in silence as a hungry child throws a shoe into its branches.

sin mancar Literally "without missing." Dominican slang for doing something without fail, without skipping, without letting up — every day, every time, no exceptions.

tambora A small two-headed Dominican drum, traditionally made from a hollowed log with goat-skin heads tightened over each end. The drummer plays it on the lap, striking one head with a stick and the other with the open hand. Along with the *güira*, the *tambora* is at the heart of merengue.

taqiyah A short, rounded cap worn by Muslim men and boys. Like *hijab*, it appears in a chapter that imagines children of other parts of the world.

tap-tap A Haitian shared transport vehicle: a brightly painted pickup truck or small bus that runs along set routes, with passengers riding in the open back. The word also describes the rhythm of the driver's hand tapping the cab to signal a stop.

tejamanil Wooden shingles, traditionally used as roofing or wall siding in rural Dominican homes. A *tejamanil* house is built of light wooden boards and palm thatch; it weeps in the rain and offers little shelter against weather, but it is what many families can afford.

tíguere A figure of Dominican street culture: the streetwise hustler, the survivor, the one who knows how to navigate by his wits. The *tíguere* is by turns admired and condemned — a folk hero of resourcefulness and a name for the young men who turn that resourcefulness toward harm. There is no precise English equivalent; the word is preserved throughout the book. The plural is *tígueres*. The cultural phenomenon itself is called *tigueraje*.

topató A practice the book describes in a chapter of the same name: a multi-day gathering of teenagers at a motel, involving group sex, drinking, and drug use, with no commitments and no set partners. The word may be of recent or local origin. Children in the affected neighborhoods spoke of going to a *topató* the way one might speak of a party.

tostada A pressed sandwich, made on a flat hot griddle. In the book, *tostadas* are sold by vendors at Parque Duarte alongside fresh juices.

triculí A Haitian distilled spirit, similar to *clerén*: rough, strong, made from sugarcane. Appears in the book at Vodou celebrations in the Haitian villages from which some of the children migrated.

UAPA Universidad Abierta para Adultos. A Dominican distance-learning university serving adult students.

UASD Universidad Autónoma de Santo Domingo. The oldest university in the Americas, founded in 1538, and the principal public university of the Dominican Republic.

UNEV Universidad Nacional Evangélica. A private Dominican university affiliated with the country's evangelical Protestant community.

UTESA Universidad Tecnológica de Santiago. A major private Dominican university with campuses across the country, including in Santiago.

via crucis Literally "the way of the cross." The Catholic devotional practice of meditating on the fourteen Stations of the Cross, retracing Christ's path to crucifixion. In everyday Spanish the phrase has also come to mean any prolonged ordeal — a long, painful passage one must walk through. In the book it carries both senses at once.

víveres Root vegetables and starchy staples — *yuca* (cassava), *yautía* (taro), green plantains, sweet potatoes, and others — that form the foundation of rural Dominican cooking.

yagua The fibrous palm sheath that wraps the trunk of the royal palm. *Yagua* is used in rural construction as roofing, walling, and for fashioning containers. Light, water-resistant, and traditionally Dominican.

Yaque del Norte (Yaque River) The longest river of the Dominican Republic, rising in the central highlands and flowing west through the Cibao valley. *El Peje* swam in its waters as a child, earning his nickname.

Zona franca Free trade zone. Industrial parks where goods are manufactured for export, often by Dominican workers — many of them young women — under labor conditions that vary widely.

About the Author

Milagros de Jesús de Féliz was born in San Francisco de Macorís and has put down roots in Santiago de los Caballeros, where she raised her family and completed her studies at the Pontificia Universidad Católica Madre y Maestra.

After more than three decades in the banking sector, she has served on the boards of major corporate, social, and academic institutions in the Dominican Republic.

As an activist, she has spent twenty-six years defending the rights of children at high social risk. She has also taken part in initiatives connected to the fight against leprosy and cancer, and to other causes that uphold human dignity and social justice.

Today she shares her passion for literature through stories and accounts published in international anthologies. She is a member of the *Movimiento Interiorista* of the Ateneo Insular, and the author of *Me gustaría contarte* (2024), a book that gathers experiences and traditions from childhood to adulthood.

This is her second book — *The Courage We Lack* — a portrait of complex realities and moving testimonies that affirms the dignity of working children and young people who make their lives in the streets.

www.ingramcontent.com/pod-product-compliance
Lightning Source LLC
LaVergne TN
LVHW041102080826
845145LV00007B/1662